Good Girls, Bad Girls of the New Testament

Their Enduring Lessons

T. J. Wray

ROWMAN & LITTLEFIELD
Lanham • Boulder • New York • London

Published by Rowman & Littlefield
A wholly owned subsidiary of The Rowman & Littlefield Publishing Group, Inc.
4501 Forbes Boulevard, Suite 200, Lanham, Maryland 20706
www.rowman.com

Unit A, Whitacre Mews, 26-34 Stannary Street, London SE11 4AB,
United Kingdom

Distributed by NATIONAL BOOK NETWORK

British Library Cataloguing in Publication Information Available

Library of Congress Cataloging-in-Publication Data

Wray, T. J.
  Good girls, bad girls of the New Testament : their enduring lessons / T.J. Wray.
    pages cm
  Includes bibliographical references and index.
  ISBN 978-1-4422-1937-3 (cloth : alk. paper) — ISBN 978-1-4422-1939-7
(electronic) 1. Women in the Bible. 2. Bible. New Testament—Biography.
I. Title.
  BS2445.W73 2015
  225.9'22082—dc23

                                                                2015029456

∞™ The paper used in this publication meets the minimum requirements of
American National Standard for Information Sciences—Permanence of Paper for
Printed Library Materials, ANSI/NISO Z39.48-1992.

Printed in the United States of America

With much love to my best friend, Anne McFadden—
a truly great woman and a "good girl" extraordinaire.

Contents

Acknowledgments   ix
Introduction   1
Life for Women during New Testament Times   9

Part I:
Sisters, Sinners, and Supporters

CHAPTER 1
Sister Friends: Martha and Mary of Bethany: Sisters   17

CHAPTER 2
Suspicious Sisters: Bernice and Drusilla, the Great-
Granddaughters of Herod the Great: Sisters   31

CHAPTER 3
Caught in the Act: The Adulterous Woman in John's Gospel:
Sinner   51

CHAPTER 4
Blood Guilt: The Woman with a Twelve-Year Hemorrhage:
Sinner   63

CHAPTER 5
A Woman of Substance: Mary Magdalene: Supporter   77

CHAPTER 6
Widow's Rising: Tabitha, A Loving Benefactor: Supporter   95

Part II:
Mothers, Murderers, and Missionaries

CHAPTER 7
Angelic Gift: Elizabeth, Mother of John the Baptist: Mother   111

CHAPTER 8
Jesus' Mom: Mary of Nazareth: Mother   123

CHAPTER 9
Off with His Head! Herodias and the Beheading of
John the Baptist: Mother and Murderer   143

CHAPTER 10
I Had a Dream: The Wife of Pontius Pilate: Murderer   161

CHAPTER 11
Spreading the Good News: Prisca, a Missionary of Paul:
Missionary   179

CHAPTER 12
A Conversation with Jesus: The Woman at the Well:
Missionary   195

CHAPTER 13
Concluding Thoughts   209

Resources   219
Index   225
About the Author   233

Acknowledgments

MANY THANKS to my wonderful husband Denis and my amazing children, Bob, Anne, and Jack, for their love and support. I am also immensely grateful for my inner circle of friends and family who grace my life with joy and encouragement. Special thanks to Walter Burr, the man who started it all, Adelaide Stout for her research assistance, and my excellent and very patient editor, Sarah Stanton, for their enthusiasm and dedication to this book. Finally, as always, I'd like to express my heartfelt gratitude to the faculty, staff, and especially the wonderful students at Salve Regina University, whose questions and eagerness to learn served as the inspiration behind this book.

Introduction

AS I WRITE this chapter a tiny, 8 × 4 cm scrap of primitive paper is receiving a lot of attention. Written on an ancient type of writing material known as *papyrus*, the text contains a tantalizing clue that may help to answer the centuries-old question of whether or not Jesus was married. The so-called Jesus Wife fragment has eight lines on the front and six lines on the back. Written in Coptic, the language of Egyptian Christians during early centuries of the Common Era (CE), the text is dated to the fourth century CE. An anonymous donor gave the text to Harvard Divinity professor Karen King, an undisputed expert in the area of early Christianity, who has not only authenticated the text but also been able to decipher it. So what is it that has the scholarly world and Christians of every stripe all a-twitter (and on Twitter)? According to King, line 4 on the front of the text reads, "Jesus said to them, 'My wife . . .'" followed by line 5, "She will be able to be my disciple," and then, two lines later, "I dwell with her."

These words, written so long ago, give rise to many questions, such as Is the Jesus mentioned in the text *the Jesus* of the New Testament or is the text referring to some other Jesus? ("Jesus" is a very common name in antiquity). Is Jesus speaking to his disciples "Jesus said to *them* [emphasis mine]" or to some other group? And perhaps the most burning question on the lips of everyone who has heard about this precious fragment from the past centers on the identity of the "wife" in the text. Who is she? The text does not say, but some insist that the mysterious wife is none other than Mary Magdalene.

These questions are nothing new in the world of biblical scholarship as inquiring minds throughout the ages have wondered if Jesus was married. In more recent times, books such as Dan Brown's *The Da Vinci Code* have given birth to all sorts of speculations (most of them fanciful) regarding Jesus' marital status. And, while it is awfully interesting to postulate and imagine how a married Jesus might change the way in which we think about Christianity, let me just state, before we go any further, that at this time, we have no definitive evidence, including this latest piece of papyrus, that either proves or disproves the idea that Jesus had a wife.

I mention the current discussion underfoot about the Jesus Wife fragment as a way to introduce you to the complex and intriguing world of the first century and the women who occupy their place and time in the orbit of Jesus and later, Paul, the founder of Christianity.

In the past, not much consideration is given to the stories about women in the Bible. The focus is on the male characters, like Abraham, Moses, and Jesus, while the women in their lives, Sarah, Zipporah, and Mary of Nazareth, are viewed as peripheral characters. This is somewhat understandable because the majority of the women in the Bible are unnamed: Noah's wife; the Shunammite woman; the woman caught in adultery; and the daughter of Jairus, just to name (or not name!) a few. In the New Testament, counting the actual number of named women is difficult. For example, some women are referred to by more than one name; Tabitha, in Acts of the Apostles, is also known as Dorcas; so do we count two names or only one, since both names refer to the same woman? Most scholars agree that despite the many references to women in the New Testament, only between thirty to fifty are actually named. Why does this matter? Well, for one, unnamed women are often more forgettable, particularly in the patriarchal culture that has for centuries dominated Jewish and Christian religious institutions. The stories that feature nameless women can therefore be overlooked, seldom read, and rarely used as the subjects of sermons, homilies, or in preaching. Further, there may be an underlying assumption by some that stories about mostly unnamed women are less important than the stories about men. Fortunately, within the last several decades, thanks to the rise in (mostly) female biblical scholars dedicated to recovering women's stories, we find that quite often, it is the story about a particular *woman* that offers the important lesson that the biblical author sought to impart. As you make your way through this book, try to focus on the stories from the woman's perspective to see if such a perspective changes the meaning of the story (sometimes it does and sometimes it does not).

As with my previous book *Good Girls, Bad Girls: The Enduring Lessons of Twelve Women of the Old Testament*, I have divided these twelve stories into two rather broad categories. Part I, "Sisters, Sinners, and Supporters," contains a variety of stories about women, some of who are somehow involved in Jesus' earthly mission (Martha and Mary, the adulterous woman in John's Gospel, the woman with a twelve-year hemorrhage, and Mary Magdalene) or in the post-resurrection movement that would someday become Christianity (Tabitha). The first two chapters feature "sister stories" beginning with two women who are friends and followers of Jesus: the busy Martha and the more pensive Mary, both from Bethany, a town that figures prominently in the Gospels. Chapter 2 introduces the reader to Bernice and Drusilla, great-granddaughters of Herod the Great and members of the powerful Herodian dynasty. History has not been kind to Bernice and Drusilla, depicting them largely as villainesses, but we will question whether or not this is a fair and accurate portrait of the sisters. The sister tales are followed by two "sinner" stories, including two unnamed women, the first of whom is accused of adultery, a "crime" punishable by death in ancient Israel (Deut 22:13–21). Jesus' enemies bring the woman to Jesus in an attempt to entrap him in a tangle of legalities, but he adroitly sidesteps them and instead turns the tables on the woman's accusers. Chapter 4 features the moving tale of an unnamed woman who suffers for twelve years with debilitating hemorrhages. In the world of first-century Judea, such maladies are considered the result of sin. In healing the woman, Jesus dispels this notion.

Chapters 5 and 6 present two women who support the movement inaugurated by Jesus. Mary Magdalene is one of the most popular women in the New Testament and she supports Jesus on many levels. For example, she, along with other wealthy women, helps to fund Jesus' mission; she is consistently presented as a trusted friend and companion; she remains with him during his crucifixion and is the first witness to the resurrection in John's Gospel. After Jesus' death, women continue to be at the forefront of the early Christian movement, serving as leaders in house churches and helping to spread the Gospel; Tabitha is one of those women (chapter 6). She is involved in a ministry of helping women, in particular, the local widows. When she dies, the Apostle Peter raises her from the dead.

Part II, "Mothers, Murderers, and Missionaries," opens with two well-known mothers: Elizabeth, the mother of John the Baptist (chapter 7), and Jesus' mother, Mary of Nazareth (chapter 8). Elizabeth, Mary's elderly and formerly childless relative, teaches us, among other things, to remain faithful and open to the mysteries of God's plan. We will examine Mary of Nazareth both in her starring role as Jesus' mother and as a powerful and courageous woman in her own right. In chapters 7 and 8, I introduce Elizabeth and Mary of Nazareth as the mothers of two very powerful sons, John the Baptist and Jesus, respectively; in the chapters that immediately follow, the reader meets the two women associated in some way with the brutal deaths of both John and Jesus. Chapter 9 features another woman from the family of Herod the Great: Herodias, Bernice and Drusilla's aunt and the incestuous wife of Herod Antipas. She is remembered as the mastermind behind the beheading of John the Baptist, whom she despises. In chapter 10, questions are raised about the role of Pilate's wife, who has for centuries been portrayed as a "Jesus sympathizer." Is she a secret follower of Jesus, or is she as evil as her husband, the detestable Pontius Pilate? These dovetailing chapters (chapter 7 with chapter 9 and chapter 8 with chapter 10) form an interesting literary unit that highlights the power of both good and evil, which is a crucial New Testament theme.

Part II concludes with two very different types of female missionaries. Featured mostly in Acts of the Apostles, Prisca (or Priscilla) typifies many of Paul's early missionary associates as she works tirelessly alongside her husband, Aquila, to spread the Good News to the Gentile world. By way of contrast, the Gospel of John presents us with a rather unconventional missionary, the Samaritan woman who has a chance encounter with Jesus at her town's well. Following her life-changing conversation with Jesus, she brings others to faith in Christ as she shares her story with her neighbors. I decided to conclude the stories of New Testament women with the story of the woman at the well because it is such a positive and uplifting tale of transformation and hope. As a teacher, I consider the Samaritan woman to be a model student; she has her own ideas and notions about things, but she is receptive to Jesus' lessons. Because of her innate willingness to question and to learn, her life is forever changed. The final chapter of this book offers the reader some concluding thoughts, including the manner in which we might integrate the women profiled in this slim volume into the Bible as a whole.

The categories found in each section (Sisters, Sinners, Supporters, Mothers, Missionaries, and Murderers) alert the reader to the kinds of stories I discuss. This is not to say that all New Testament women fall under these six categories (for there are many others, including women as victims, prophets, and widows) but that the women I have selected seem to fit these particular designations. When I decided to write this book, I spent a great deal of time reviewing the stories that feature women in the New Testament, trying to decide which stories to tell. I wanted a mixture of well-known women, like Mary of Nazareth and Mary Magdalene, but I also wanted to highlight the tales of those less-popular women, such as Tabitha and the sisters Bernice and Drusilla, whose stories are largely unknown among most Christians.

You might be wondering why I chose these particular twelve stories— and why *twelve* stories—why not ten or thirteen? The main reason I decided to tell twelve stories is because the number 12 is biblically symbolic (e.g., the twelve tribes of Israel and Jesus' Twelve Apostles). Even as this book examines *twelve stories*, there are actually more than twelve women profiled in this book because in many cases, the story of one biblical woman is connected to another woman (or women). For example, the story of Herodias (chapter 9), the woman who instigates the beheading of John the Baptist, cannot be told without also telling the story of her dancing daughter, Salome. Likewise, the story of the unnamed woman with a twelve-year hemorrhage (chapter 4) is "paired" with the story of the dying daughter of Jairus, a Temple official. Jesus heals both the hemorrhaging woman and Jairus's twelve-year-old daughter (notice the number 12 cropping up in both of these stories?).

Each chapter is divided into two sections. The first section essentially tells the story from the author's perspective. In some chapters, I rely on sources outside the Bible to help us to better know and understand a particular woman. We are fortunate, in New Testament Studies, to have scores of extra-biblical texts that can help to shed light on material in the New Testament. The Roman period produces many historians and others who pen their version of events. For example, Titus Flavius Josephus, a Jewish defector to Rome, provides the backstories for some of the women in this book. Josephus's *Wars of the Jews* and *Antiquities of the Jews* are of particular import, and I refer to them often in several chapters. We must use caution in citing these outside sources as some accounts are more reliable then others. In the case of Josephus, we must remember that Josephus is born a Jew and initially fights against Rome; but then he joins the other side, so to speak. With the Roman censors reviewing his work, many scholars insist that his "history," at least on occasion, is biased.

The second section found in each chapter goes beyond the story of a particular woman and challenges the reader to explore the enduring lessons the ancient writer sought to impart. That is, what can we learn from the women whose lives seem so different, yet are in some ways quite similar to our own? There are dozens of lessons, but I tend to focus on two or three. If you are using this book as part of a class or in the context of Bible study, I encourage you to explore what the story means to you, personally, and come up with your own enduring lessons.

What that in mind, I highly recommend reading the actual story as it appears in the Bible along with this book. While I do not promote one translation of the Bible over another (currently, there are scores of English translations available, from the King James Version to the New English Bible), I have most often chosen to use the *New Oxford Annotated Bible* (the New Revised Standard Version, or NRSV), edited by Michael D.

Coogan and published by Oxford University Press; all citations, unless otherwise noted, come from this Bible.

It seems prudent at this early juncture, to offer some general information about the Bible itself, especially the New Testament. The Bible is divided into two main sections. The first section (the larger of the two) is the Hebrew Bible (commonly called the "Old Testament" by Christians). The second section (much smaller) is called the "New Testament" or the "Christian Testament." There are twenty-seven books in the New Testament and either thirty-nine (in the Jewish and Protestant versions) or forty-six (in Catholic editions) books in the Hebrew Bible. The New Testament includes the four Gospels, Acts of the Apostles, an apocalypse (the book of Revelation) and twenty-one letters (attributed to Paul, Peter, John, and others).

The New Testament is written in an ancient form of Greek (*Koine*). The first Christian writings come in the form of letters written by Paul during the years 49–63 CE, which makes Paul the earliest Christian writer. Before I go any further, let me emphatically state that the dates for nearly every biblical book are presently debated and contested by scholars. What I present here, and indeed throughout this book, represents the majority of scholarly opinions; there are some who argue earlier or later dating of the material in the New Testament, and, to be perfectly honest, I have, over the years, vacillated in my own opinion regarding the dates of composition of some texts in the New Testament. The dates and authorship presented in this book are not meant to be the final word on such matters, but rather, reflective of the current "best guess estimate" of most reputable commentators. Speaking of dates, in keeping with the conventions of modern historical and biblical scholarship, I will use BCE (before the Common Era) instead of BC (before Christ) and CE (Common Era) rather than AD (*Anno Domini*, Latin for "In the year of our Lord") when indicating specific dates. There is absolutely nothing wrong with using BC and AD, but the use of BCE and CE represents my professional preferences.

As you read the various chapters in this book, I will offer commentary on the texts under consideration as they pertain to a particular woman or women. In the interest of avoiding redundancy, what follows is a very brief and general synopsis of Paul's letters and the Gospels. Since most of the women we will explore in this book appear in the Gospels and/or Paul's letters, I will focus my remarks on these New Testament texts.

We must first begin with Paul, formally Saul of Tarsus, whose letters predate the Gospels by roughly two decades. There are thirteen letters typically attributed to Paul, but most scholars agree that only seven letters constitute the so-called authentic Pauline epistles: 1 Thessalonians, 1 and

2 Corinthians, Galatians, Romans, Philippians, and Philemon. The other six are written a generation or two after Paul's death by some of his followers, but in Paul's name, which is a common practice in antiquity. In general, Paul's letters are addressed to Christian communities founded by Paul during his various missionary journeys. In his letters, Paul is answering concerns, offering comfort, clarifying issues, and sometimes defending himself against detractors. What is most interesting about Paul's letters is that he does not have much to say about the events in Jesus' life; for that, we must turn to the Gospels.

There are four Gospels that appear in the following canonical order in the New Testament: Matthew, Mark, Luke, and John. For reasons that are not totally clear, the Gospels are not arranged chronologically. The dates (which, again, are debated) for the Gospels are as follows: Mark, 70 CE; Luke–Acts of the Apostles, 85 CE; Matthew, 90 CE; and John, 95 CE. Many commentators agree that Matthew, particularly treasured by the early Church, is placed first in the New Testament canon as a way to recognize and honor it. Whether or not this is the case, we do know for certain that it is not the first Gospel written; that honor goes to Mark. The author of Luke also writes Acts of the Apostles, a text about the first crop of Christians in the days, months, and years following the death and resurrection of Jesus. Luke, then, embarked on a two-volume work, the Gospel of Luke and Acts of the Apostles. I will have more to say about Acts of the Apostles in subsequent chapters.

Several *general* statements can be made about the Gospels: The word "Gospel" means "Good News," and sharing the Gospels means sharing the Good News of Jesus Christ. All of the Gospels are anonymous; that is, we do not know who wrote them. There are many theories and ideas, and there are some who insist there really are four men named Matthew, Mark, Luke, and John who write the accounts of Jesus' life, death and resurrection, but the simple truth is, at this time, we cannot definitively state who wrote them. The Gospels can best be described as theological stories about Jesus' life, with a focus on his ministry, which lasts between one to three years. All of the Gospels describe Jesus as a Galilean who travels from place to place with the Twelve Apostles and various other disciples that includes both men and women. He is a worker of miracles. Finally, all of the Gospels agree that Jesus is arrested on trumped-up charges, is crucified, dies, and resurrects from the dead.

The first three Gospels, Matthew, Mark, and Luke, are called the "Synoptic Gospels" because they express similar themes and recall similar events in the life of Jesus. The word "synoptic" comes from the Greek meaning "like view," and it is a word I will use often throughout this book.

The Gospel of John differs greatly from the Synoptics, both in the way in which Jesus is presented and in its theology. The Fourth Gospel is highly symbolic and literary. Though it is beautifully written and though I try to cultivate an appreciation for all of the Gospels, my students generally prefer the straightforward narrative style of the Synoptics.

Whether you are reading this book as part of a class, a religious education program, Bible study, or simply for leisure, I ask that you remain open to a variety of interpretations. My central focus when working with the Bible is to remain faithful to the author's thoughts, ideas, and intentions (as well as I may discern them). This does not mean that my interpretations always represent the only way to read a particular story, and your own interpretations may not be definitive either. Indeed, there are many ways to interpret each story, and there remain dozens of un-mined, enduring lessons far beyond those I have presented in this book. It is always my hope that my books will inspire lively discussion, debate, and reflection. With this very brief introduction to *Good Girls, Bad Girls of the New Testament*, it is my hope that you will enjoy reading this book as much as I have enjoyed writing it.

Life for Women during New Testament Times

THE DAILY LIFE of a typical woman in Roman-occupied Judea is filled with many chores and responsibilities. Roughly 90 percent of women live in rural towns and villages and so their day-to-day existence is remarkably similar. Women are in charge of keeping the house tidy, cooking, lighting the fires for the day, gathering water (a backbreaking chore that usually involves walking a mile or more to the town well and then lugging back enough water for her family and any livestock they might own), baking bread, and caring for the children. A woman's most important role is that of mother. She is expected to have children, and most women very much want to become mothers. Children are considered to be precious gifts from God and a sign of God's favor; but what about those women who are unable to have children? Childless, or "barren," women are often ostracized and shunned; their barrenness is viewed as a form of Divine punishment. The Hebrew Bible and New Testament feature many stories about barren women, most of whom experience miraculous conceptions and give birth to powerful sons. For example, in chapter 7, Elizabeth is an elderly, barren woman who, through Divine intervention, conceives and delivers a healthy son later known as John the Baptist. Elizabeth's story reminds us of Sarah (Gen 21:1–7) and Samson's mother in Judges 13; both women are old and childless until God removes their barrenness. Such stories emphasize the central role motherhood plays in the lives of women during biblical antiquity.

9

Living under the shadow of the Roman Empire, women are naturally concerned for the safety of their families, especially their children. While women who live in rural settings may have less contact with their Roman oppressors, the small percentage of women who live in cites, especially in Jerusalem, are likely to interact with Romans on a daily basis. They are surely accustomed to seeing Roman soldiers, many of whom are stationed in Jerusalem to maintain order, particularly during the inevitable influx of pilgrims who come to worship at the Temple during the various Jewish feast days, like Passover. Initially the Roman rulers are fairly tolerant when it comes to Jewish religious practice: they allow Jews to worship at the Temple, offer sacrifices, and practice other tenets of their faith. The yoke of occupation, however, grows heavy over time, and there are many instances when Jews and Romans clash—some of these clashes can be categorized as minor skirmishes, while others result in all-out wars. I have included some of these instances in this book, particularly in chapter 10 (the chapter dealing with the wife of Pilate). Women must therefore raise their children in rather precarious and at times dangerous circumstances. Under the thumb of Roman imperialism, men and women begin to imagine a world free of tyranny and oppression; they cast their eyes to the heavens in hopeful expectancy, ever on the lookout for the long-awaited Messiah. According to the Gospels, these hopes are realized in the coming of Jesus.

Since the Roman Empire serves as the "setting" for stories about women in the New Testament, it is important to try to understand a bit about what it is like to live under Roman occupation. Israel (called *Judea* by the Romans) is part of the Roman Empire that also includes portions of Europe, Asia, and Africa. Conquered by Pompey and his soldiers in 63 BCE, Judea remains part of the Roman Empire for 130 years. Jesus, Paul, and all of the women mentioned in this book live and die under Roman imperial rule. The empire is controlled by a stable of powerful men: the emperor, the senate, various appointed local leaders, and a professional military. The Roman emperor is the supreme authority and even enjoys *divine status* as implied in the common honorific *Augustus* ("He who is to be worshipped and revered"). Though all good citizens are required to publicly worship the emperor, emperor worship is viewed more as a citizen's civic responsibility, and it is doubtful that many Romans take it very seriously. They prefer instead to worship their own household deities, which include not only select members of the Roman pantheon, such as Juno, the goddess protector of women, and Mars, the god of war, but also imported gods and goddesses from other lands, such as the Egyptian goddess Isis and the Persian god Mithras. Worship of the Roman emperor is generally not a problem until a small group of people known as *Christians* begins to emerge in the second half of the first century. Apparently, some in this group refuse to worship the emperor, thus arousing suspicion and the active persecution of Christians that lasts for the better part of the next 250 years. But, we are getting ahead of ourselves.

The Romans designate a conquered nation as either a "province" or a "client kingdom." Judea is technically a client kingdom, ostensibly run by a local "puppet king" appointed by the Romans, the first of whom is Herod the Great, who rules from 37 BCE until 4 CE. Herod the Great is mentioned many times throughout this book. He is a complicated character and a genius builder who also happens to be brutal, paranoid, and prone to murder off the competition, including his own children. Following the death of Herod the Great, the Romans carve up Herod's kingdom and divide it among his three sons, Archelaus, Antipas, and Philip. Those who are inclined to favor the policies of the Herodian dynasty form a sort of sect, aptly called the Herodians, and they are mentioned in rather unfavorable terms in the Synoptic Gospels. In this book, I will make a distinction between the Herodian dynasty—the progeny of Herod the Great—and the Herodians, a political party.

With cookie-cutter-like precision, the Romans are experts in exporting their way of life: witness the many Roman baths, aqueducts, and amphitheaters that have been excavated in even the remotest parts of the empire. But perhaps the most important Roman export is found in their finely engineered road system that connects all corners of its vast domain, thus making travel to and from various corners of the empire quite easy. The Roman web of highways is a key factor in the spread of Christianity. Paul, who is considered to be the founder of Christianity, uses this road system to his advantage as he and his missionaries, who include many women, work to spread his version of the Gospel of Christ throughout the far reaches of the empire.

Though Paul is a Roman citizen, just because a particular country or territory is conquered and occupied by the Romans does not mean that the conquered people automatically become Roman citizens. Roman citizenship is based largely on wealth and social status, which necessarily makes it an elite and exclusionary privilege. Roman citizens can vote, hold public office, own property, and enjoy many other perks that non-citizens might envy. Unlike their male counterparts, women who hold Roman citizenship may not vote or hold public office, but they do have many other rights, including the right to conduct business, own property, and divorce.

Like the Romans, the Jews in Judea operate under a patriarchal system, which means that men dominate all areas of life. Men create laws and maintain order; they make all decisions concerning the family; and they are at the center of religious life and Temple worship. It is important to understand patriarchy as a cultural condition. In other words, the Bible did not invent patriarchy; rather, it is the social umbrella under which the Bible is written. The patriarchal system, however, is not as restrictive as we might think; many of the women profiled in this book are able to navigate the system, or in some cases circumvent it, and actually assume roles comparable to men. Some notable examples include Mary Magdalene, who, along with several other women, helps to finance the Jesus Movement (Luke 8:1–3; see also chapter 5), and Herodias, the evil wife of Herod Antipas, who manipulates events to arrange the execution of her nemesis, John the Baptist (chapter 9).

After Jesus' death, women become central figures in the post-resurrection community. Acts of Apostles relates, in a rather fanciful fashion, the communal life of Jesus' followers in the immediate aftermath of his death (Acts 2:42–47). His followers regroup in Jerusalem and thousands more join the movement; they are known as followers of the *Way* (Acts 9:2), or less often, as *Nazarenes* (Acts 24:5), and eventually, they are called *Christians* (Acts 26:28). They form what we might today call an *egalitarian utopia*: everyone sells their possessions and everything is distributed equally among men and women.

Over time, small "house churches" begin to emerge and (mostly) wealthy women preside over them, as Christians meet, break bread, pray, and remember Jesus (1 Cor 1:11; Acts 12:12, 16:14–15, 40). The names of some of these early church leaders are preserved for us in the New Testament, including that of Mary, the mother of John Mark, who leads services in her home in Jerusalem (Acts 12:12–17); Nympha in Laodicea (Col 4:15); Apphia, in Colossae (Philemon 2); and a woman named Phoebe, whose house church is in Cenchreae (Rom 16:1). In addition to their work in presiding over house churches, women work alongside men as missionaries. Like Prisca (chapter 11) and her husband, Aquila, women and men work side by side, filling the seats in house churches from Judea to the territories of Asia Minor and Greece with new converts (Rom 16:1, 3, 7).

The era of the house church and the egalitarian nature of early Christianity are short lived, however. The small, intimate house churches are soon replaced with larger, more ornate buildings, complemented with a hierarchal system of male clergy. By the dawn of the second century, the fair and equal treatment of women that so characterizes Jesus' ministry begins to gradually dissolve as women are nudged to the sidelines. Certainly by the mid-second century, the egalitarian utopia described in Acts 2:42–47 is replaced with a form of exclusionary sexism where women are no longer active missionaries and presiders but instead are expected to sit down and be quiet (Eph 5:22–24; 1 Tim 2:11–15).

In this book, however, we will focus on that exciting time when Jesus walks the earth, discovering those women who walk beside him, and who, in one way or another, serve as helpmates in his ministry. We will also meet the women who continue Jesus' work, the female followers of the Way who help to spread the Good News of Jesus Christ as they excitedly await the arrival of the Kingdom.

Sisters, Sinners, and Supporters

Martha and Mary of Bethany

Bernice and Drusilla

The Adulterous Woman in John's Gospel

The Woman with a Twelve-Year Hemorrhage

Mary Magdalene

Tabitha

Keep alert, stand firm in your faith,
be courageous, be strong.
(1 Cor 16:13)

Martha and Mary of Bethany: Sisters

Sister Friends

Luke 10:38–42; John 11; 12:1–8

Now as they went on their way, he entered a certain village, where a woman named Martha welcomed him into her home. She had a sister named Mary, who sat at the Lord's feet and listened to what he was saying. But Martha was distracted by her many tasks; so she came to him and asked, "Lord, do you not care that my sister has left me to do all the work by myself? Tell her then to help me." But the Lord answered her, "Martha, Martha, you are worried and distracted by many things; there is need of only one thing. Mary has chosen the better part, which will not be taken away from her." (Luke 10:38–42)

W E BEGIN our exploration of New Testament women with the sisters Martha and Mary, who are part of Jesus' inner circle of friends and supporters. Martha and Mary appear only in the Gospels of Luke and John in three different "visitation" stories, the first of which is found in Luke 10:38–42. I refer to these three episodes as "visitation" stories because in each instance, Jesus visits the sisters in their hometown of Bethany. The first visit is sandwiched between Jesus' well-known Parable of the Good Samaritan (Luke 10:25–37) and the Lord's Prayer (Luke 11:1–4). Most scholars agree that Luke's thoughtful placement of the story indicates its importance. The visit begins as Martha welcomes Jesus and his disciples into her home: "Now as they went on their way, he entered a certain village, where a woman named Martha welcomed him into her home" (Luke 10:38). It is unclear if "her home" means that the house belongs to Martha alone, or if it is a family homestead, shared with her sister Mary and perhaps other relatives, such as their brother Lazarus. It is possible that in referring to the residence as belonging to Martha, the author is alerting the reader to the fact that Martha is acting as the head of the household in officially welcoming Jesus, something that would be highly unusual in the patriarchal world of first-century Judea. Although the location of the home is not specifically mentioned, we know from other sources, including the Gospel of John (John 11:1, 18; 12:1) that what Luke calls "a certain village" is indeed Bethany (Luke 10:38). Martha and Mary are inexorably linked to the village of Bethany, thus it is fitting to say a few words about the village that is the setting for all of the stories about the sisters.

Bethany is located less than two miles from Jerusalem and is frequently mentioned in the Gospels as several important events take place there, including the anointing of Jesus (Matt 26:6–13; Mark 14:3–9; John 12:1–8) and the raising of Lazarus (John 11:1–44). Archaeological evidence suggests that Bethany is a small, bustling agricultural village and not the one-camel, dusty desert town modern readers of the New Testament often imagine. Jesus and his disciples frequently visit Bethany, and because of its proximity to Jerusalem and Jesus' close friendship with Martha, Mary, and Lazarus, he chooses to stay there during the final week of his life, commuting, as it were, back and forth from the home of his friends to the Holy City. Following his resurrection, Jesus meets and then leads some of his followers on the road to Bethany before his ascension to Heaven (Luke 24:50–53). It is noteworthy that in addition to the trio of siblings who reside in Bethany—Martha, Mary, and Lazarus—is another well-known biblical character, Simon the Leper. Scholars have debated the identity of Simon the Leper, some arguing that he is a Pharisee while others assume that he is the father of Martha, Mary, and Lazarus or perhaps even the husband of one of the sisters. The Gospels are lacking in the details we need to make a definitive statement about Simon the Leper's true identity, but what we do know for certain is that he is a resident of Bethany and that Jesus visits him there.

In returning to our first important story of Martha and Mary, Luke narrates that when Jesus and his disciples arrive at the home of Martha, she welcomes them with typical Middle Eastern hospitality, occupying herself to the point of distraction with the many chores involved in making visitors feel comfortable in one's home. Martha's actions reflect a customary role of women during the first century in that it is typically the woman of the house who assumes most of the household duties. This traditional role is in sharp contrast to her sister, Mary, who does not busy herself with such things as cooking and cleaning. Instead, Mary finds a comfortable place at Jesus' feet, ready to listen to what he has to say. Mary's position is typical of a student or disciple. During this time period, rabbis (teachers) do not take on female students, but Jesus seems to ignore this practice. Martha, too, is a disciple, but the demands of her duties as hostess seem to take precedence on this particular occasion. Perhaps Martha would rather sit beside her sister and the other disciples, but there are too many chores that must be done. Martha seems irritated with Mary and feels that her sister should help her with the "many tasks" at hand (Luke 10:39–40). Martha's annoyance at her sister's perceived laziness is conveyed in no uncertain terms to Jesus: "Lord, do you not care that my sister has left me to do all the work by myself? Tell her then to help me" (Luke 10:40). There are several notable details in Martha's question and request. Martha's use of the honorific "Lord" (comparable to the English word "sir") indicates respect, but she is not deferential. On the contrary, the tone of her question and request is almost familial, indicating that Martha and Jesus are close friends. Her words are direct and do not mask her frustration at having to do all the work while Mary does nothing. Martha asks Jesus, in an almost sarcastic way, if he cares about the inequality of the workload between the sisters and then she essentially demands that he tell Mary himself to get up and do her share.

Jesus' response is curious and has resulted in a variety of scholarly debates as to its "true" meaning: "Martha, Martha, you are worried and distracted by many things; there is need of only one thing. Mary has chosen the better part, which will not be taken away from her" (Luke 10:41–42). Some commentators assert that Jesus' response is meant to castigate Martha for complaining while promoting the silent, sitting Mary as a model disciple. Jesus challenges Martha to shift her focus away from the mundane tasks of hospitality—something she does not *need* to do—to the "one thing" that she *does* need. What is it that Martha needs? Quite simply, she needs to listen to Jesus. Those who hold this view feel that Martha's chores distract her from the "better part" exemplified by Mary.

Others argue that this story, written by the anonymous author we call Luke in about 85 CE, reflects the nascent Christian faith and its conflicting views regarding the role of women. Though Luke–Acts features women in prominent roles, change is in the air during the final decades of the first century. Whereas Paul, writing between 49 and 63 CE, makes it clear that women may assume leadership and ministerial positions within the Church (such as Prisca in 1 Cor 16:19 and Phoebe in Rom 16:1–2; see also chapter 11), later Christian writers indicate a more subservient role for women (1 Tim 2:11–15). Some scholars point to Luke's story of Martha and Mary as an example of the vertiginous push and pull regarding the place of women in the emerging Christian Church and how they might best serve. That is, should they serve through "traditional" roles, like Martha, or should they assume the role of disciple, like Mary? Similar questions surface in the second story about Martha and Mary in the Gospel of John, to which we now turn.

In Luke, Martha is mentioned first as the sister of Mary (Luke 10:38–39), but in John, the order is initially reversed: Mary is mentioned first and then Martha (John 11:1). Mary also receives a special designation as "the one who anointed the Lord with perfume and wiped his feet with her hair" (John 11:2). Interestingly, this action does not take place until later in John (John 12:3), making the mention of it here premature. Most scholars assume that in John's community the anointing story is well known and inextricably linked to Mary. I will have more to say about the anointing story later.

In John 11:5, Martha's name appears first, followed by her unnamed sister, presumably Mary. Some observe that the accent seems to fall on Jesus' preference for Martha. Commentators often make much of name placement in the Gospels, noting that in general, when there are several names, the more important figure in the narrative is named first. The stories about Martha and Mary are no exception and have resulted in fevered discussions regarding which sister is most important. Since there is no real consistency regarding the name placement of the sisters and since Jesus seems not to favor one sister over the other, we will proceed from the premise that both sisters are equally important, even as their words and actions may represent different ideas or theological messages, however subtle or direct.

In John's Gospel, we encounter circumstances so dire that the conflict between the sisters in Luke 10:38–42 seems almost like child's play. The sisters occupy an important role in a pivotal story in John, one that foreshadows Jesus' death and resurrection. John situates the events with a brief backstory: Jesus' friend Lazarus is ill and his sisters send a message to an out-of-town Jesus: "Lord, he whom you love is ill" (John 11:3). Of course, Lazarus is not the only one whom Jesus loves: "Jesus loved Martha and her sister and Lazarus" (John 11:5). But if Jesus loves the siblings from Bethany, why does he continue on his journey, rather than hurrying to the side of his sick friend? The simple answer is that Jesus does not feel that Lazarus will die but that the situation will be an occasion to reveal the glory of God (John 11:4). Does Jesus know that it is the actual death of Lazarus that will provide that occasion? The text is unclear; we know only that Jesus continues his travel plans for two more days, during which time Lazarus dies.

After a brief discussion with his disciples, Jesus seems to know that Lazarus has died (John 11:11–14) and then he finally travels to Bethany. When she finds out that Jesus is coming, Martha goes out to meet him while Mary remains at home, and as usual she is *sitting*. This time, however, she is observing *Shiva*, surrounded by others (in John, "the Jews") who have come out to console the sisters. From the Hebrew word for the number 7, *Shiva* refers to the Jewish custom of a weeklong mourning period for close relatives, in this case, a sibling. This custom is still observed by most Jews today. Quite often, mourners sit on low stools or even on the floor, indicating their low mood. All the mirrors in the house are covered and friends, neighbors, and extended family members bring food and words of consolation to the bereaved. The roots of sitting *Shiva* can be traced to the book of Job. In a single day, poor Job loses his livelihood, all of his wealth, and all ten of his children in a freak storm, and then he falls ill. Three of his friends come to console him and sit beside him for seven days, "and no one spoke a word to him, for they saw that his suffering was very great" (Job 2:13).

In the midst of her sorrow, Martha confronts Jesus, using the same frank language she uses when she confronts him about her sister's refusal to help with the chores in Luke 10:40. Without any sort of preamble or welcome, she says to Jesus, "Lord, if you had been here, my brother would not have died" (John 11:21). If this accusation is left alone, it is a stark, direct statement that places the responsibility of Lazarus's death on Jesus' shoulders; however, Martha has much more to say. What follows mitigates her initial statement with a powerful confession of faith in which she affirms Jesus as the "Messiah, the Son of God, the one coming into the world" (John 11:27). Martha then abruptly returns to her sister and tells her, "The Teacher is here and is calling for you" (John 11:28).

Though John does not narrate a summons from Jesus, we must assume that Martha is telling the truth. Martha refers to Jesus as "the Teacher" when she speaks to Mary, and we are immediately reminded of the image of Mary in Luke 10:39, seated at the feet of her rabbi. Mary leaves the house, followed by many of the Jews who are mourning with her "because they thought that she was going to the tomb to weep there" (John 11:31). Mary meets Jesus, who, as it turns out, is still standing in the same place where he met Martha (John 11:29–30). Overcome with grief, Mary kneels before Jesus and repeats her sister's accusation, word for word: "Lord, if you had been here, my brother would not have died" (John 11:32). Unlike Martha, however, Mary's statement is not followed with a confession of faith. In one of the most moving scenes in John, Jesus surveys the crowd, looking first at Mary, his friend and student, and then at the other weeping mourners. Jesus is "greatly disturbed in spirit and deeply moved" (John 11:33). Feeling the full magnitude of their grief and, no doubt, experiencing his own profound sense of loss, Jesus, too, begins to weep (John 11:35).

It is in the midst of all this misery that Jesus approaches the tomb of Lazarus and asks that the stone in front of it be removed. Martha suddenly reappears (or perhaps she is with Mary and the crowd of mourners all along—the text is unclear) and objects: "Lord, already there is a stench because he has been dead four days" (John 11:39).

We must pause here and say a few words about Jewish burial customs during the first century. Jewish law dictates that the dead are to be buried within twenty-four hours and that all burials take place outside the city. The body is washed, perfumed, and wrapped in linen. During the time of Jesus, the deceased is either buried in a shallow grave or, as in the case of Lazarus, placed in a rock-hewn tomb. Most tombs are quite small, but some are large and even ornate, depending upon the wealth and social status of their occupants. Many of these tombs are family tombs, and it is common practice to have essentially *two* burials. In the first burial, the deceased is laid to rest on a stone slab (*arcosolium*) where the body will remain for about a year, after which time, the second burial takes place. Family members reenter the tomb, collect the skeletal remains of the departed, and deposit them in a small bone box, called an *ossuary*, that is made of limestone and roughly the size of an orange crate. The name of the dead man or woman is usually etched on the outside of the ossuary, and then the ossuary is placed in a burial shaft (*kokh*) within the crypt. Often there is more than one set of bones in a particular ossuary. Thousands of these ossuaries have been excavated in Israel—some are in museums and others are stacked and stored in special facilities after the bones have been reburied. The tomb of Lazarus is today a pilgrimage site for the faithful, located in the West Bank town of al-Eizariya ("Place of Lazarus" in Arabic), believed to be the site of Martha and Mary's Bethany. Unfortunately, little if any of the original tomb remains.

Let's return to our story. Martha initially tries to prevent Jesus from opening her brother's tomb. She mentions the stench of a rotting corpse, driving home the point that Lazarus is not in a coma or in a state of unconsciousness but is truly dead. Throughout history, including recent history, there are stories about people who are pronounced dead but who are actually still alive. As I write this chapter, a story appears in the news about a man from Mississippi who is presumed dead, but he wakes up at the funeral home just before he is about to be embalmed! Such stories have given rise to countless horror tales about zombies, vampires, and ghouls, but Martha's graphic language helps to clear up any misconceptions—then and now—about Lazarus's condition. What sort of miracle is it, after all, if Lazarus is merely unconscious? Jesus reminds Martha of his promise: "Did I not tell you that if you believed, you would see the glory of God?" (John 11:40), and then Martha fades from the narrative as Jesus steps forward to perform a miracle. After he prays to the Father, "for the sake of the crowd standing here, so that they may believe that you sent me," Jesus commands Lazarus to come out of the tomb (John 11:41–44). John describes the eerie scene: "The dead man came out, his hands and feet bound with strips of cloth, and his face wrapped in a cloth" (John 11:44). Lazarus is clad in the traditional burial garments of his day that include linen wraps and a separate piece of fabric for the face.

John does not record Martha and Mary's reaction to this miracle, but one can imagine that they are both shocked and overjoyed. There are many in the crowd of astonished onlookers who are not so happy, however, and these include the malignant group of Jesus' enemies who plot against him throughout much of John's Gospel. Jesus knows that he is now a wanted man—that his beautiful miracle of raising Lazarus from the dead is considered too much of a threat for his enemies (John 11:53)—so Jesus keeps a low profile, at least for a while.

We meet up with the sisters one final time in Bethany at the home of Lazarus, though it is unclear if this is only Lazarus's home or if it is the home Luke mentions as specifically belonging to Martha. In any case, it is the festive time when Jews gather from far and near to celebrate the Passover. Six days before the feast, Jesus and his disciples turn up in Bethany and, as I mention earlier, Jesus will use Bethany as his base of operations during the final week of his life, moving between Bethany and Jerusalem and eliciting the ire of those among the Temple elite who feel so threatened by him. But for now, this is a joyous occasion as John narrates a celebratory dinner among friends (John 12:1–8), including Martha, Mary, and Lazarus. Once again, we see the sisters taking on different, but important roles. Martha, mentioned first, offers hospitality and serves the meal, reminiscent of her role in Luke 10:38–42. Mary too offers hospitality, but in a unique way. For the third time, she is again at Jesus' feet, but this time, she is not a student or bereaved sister. Her role in this scene is that of a loving and devoted friend. She anoints Jesus' feet with expensive perfume and then wipes his feet with her hair (John 12:3). When the indignant Judas complains, "Why was this perfume not sold for three hundred denarii and the money given to the poor?" (John 12:5), Jesus defends Mary. He knows that Judas will betray him, and John warns the reader that Judas's objection is not sincere: he is a thief and does not actually care for the poor at all (John 12:6). According to Jesus, Mary's actions are rooted in kindness and are symbolic of Jesus' death. We might also view her actions as a gesture of gratitude for Jesus' raising of Lazarus.

The anointing story is one that appears in each of the Gospels, but it is told somewhat differently. In Luke, Jesus is dining at the home of Simon the Pharisee when an unnamed woman, labeled only as "a sinner," barges in on the meal. The intruder anoints Jesus' feet with tears, kisses, and ointment, and then she dries them with her long hair (Luke 7:37–50). Her actions, though bizarre, are meant to demonstrate her deep respect for Jesus. When Simon rebukes her, Jesus defends her. Jesus goes even further: he forgives her sins and affirms her faith (Luke 7:48–50).

The anointing stories in Mark (14:3–9) and Matthew (26:6–13) differ from the stories in Luke and John. In Mark and Matthew, Jesus is having dinner at the home of Simon the Leper, who, as you will recall, lives in Bethany. It is easy to see how questions about the identity of Simon can surface. In Luke, Jesus dines at the home of Simon the Pharisee at an undisclosed location; in Mark and Matthew, the dinner host lives in Bethany and is also named Simon. Questions also arise concerning the identity of the woman who does the anointing. In John, the woman is Mary, Jesus' friend and disciple; in Luke, the woman is a nameless sinner.

In Mark and Matthew, however, the woman is an unnamed woman from Bethany who does not anoint Jesus' feet (as in Luke and John) but his head. In Mark, Matthew, and John, there are complaints about the cost of the perfume, mention of the poor, and a direct connection between the anointing and Jesus' burial. Of these anointing stories, only John specifically names Mary, and thus the "anointing women" are often confused. For instance, the nameless sinner in Luke's version is sometimes confused with Mary of Bethany, leading to the erroneous conclusion that Mary is a sinner. Of course, this is a complete misreading of the story, and I mention the four anointing stories for this and two other reasons: First, John clearly identifies Mary as the one who does the anointing. Given that she and her sister, Martha, are the subject of this chapter, her anointing story provides us with a fuller appreciation of her complex character. Second, most scholars agree that historically, the stories appear to be cherished traditions among all four Evangelists, even though each has a slightly different version of the events. The preservation of this story helps us to better understand the emerging Christian Church as it sorts out the theological and social growing pains regarding the role of women. Jesus' attitude toward women puts him clearly outside the first-century mainstream model of Mediterranean patriarchy that considers women to be second-class citizens. Indeed, the "anointing stories" make it clear how Jesus feels about women in general—how he defends them, respects them, and treats them with the dignity they deserve as daughters of God.

Martha and Mary's Enduring Lessons

Among the hundreds of stories that can be told of Jesus' life—a fraction of which are preserved in the Gospels—Luke and John prominently feature stories about the sisters from Bethany, Martha and Mary. As we read their stories, Martha and Mary offer us, individually and together as sisters, three enduring lessons which have to do with the nature of true friendship, the meaning of service, and the challenges of faith.

As we explore the nature of true friendship, we must first recognize that Martha and Mary are part of a select group of trusted friends, beloved family members, and loyal disciples who represent the roots of the Jesus Movement. The stories that feature Martha and Mary offer us a unique insight into the personal life of Jesus. We no longer see the sober, solitary, itinerant preacher from the Galilee, as he is so often portrayed; instead, we see a passionate teacher with an extraordinary message, surrounded by ordinary people who live ordinary lives. In the context of Jesus' inner circle, alongside the miracles and parables, we are able to glimpse a rare side of Jesus, one that is underemphasized in a traditional reading of the Gospels. Martha and Mary help to illuminate this broader image of Jesus. In the narratives that include the sisters, we see Jesus visiting his friends, mediating a squabble between the sisters, weeping over the loss of his friend Lazarus, and later, enjoying himself at a dinner party in his honor.

At the center of every true friendship is acceptance and love. When Martha complains about Mary, Jesus accepts her complaint and gently urges her to make another choice. Notice too the frank and honest way the sisters and Jesus communicate with each other without fear of judgment or criticism. True friendship allows us to speak our minds, even when we do not agree, without fear of offense or loss of the relationship. This type of friendship is only possible when it is firmly grounded in love. Jesus' love for the sisters and their brother is plainly stated and is manifest in his actions, particularly in the raising of Lazarus. Later, in the Gospel of John, Jesus asserts, "No one has greater love than this, to lay down one's life for one's friends" (John 15:13). This sort of friendship is indeed rare, but like kindness, we recognize it when it touches our lives, and we cherish it. As the ancient writer of the apocryphal book of Sirach writes,

> Faithful friends are a sturdy shelter:
> whoever finds one has found a treasure.
> Faithful friends are beyond price;
> no amount can balance their worth.
> Faithful friends are life-saving medicine. (Sir 6:14–16)

Just as Martha and Mary help to expand our understanding of friendship, they also challenge us to consider the meaning of service. In Luke 10:38–42, we are presented with what appears to be a conundrum regarding the best way to serve. One image features the bustling Martha, who is concerned with the many tasks of hospitality; the other is of the studious Mary, who assumes the role of student. Commentators continue to parse and dissect the meaning of Luke 10:38–42, offering many thoughtful and practical interpretations, some of which I have already mentioned. One of the most popular ideas is the notion that Martha and Mary represent concerns of the growing Church during the final decades of the first century, the time period when Luke pens his Gospel, rather than concerns from Jesus' actual lifetime. These concerns center largely on the manner in which women may serve within the Church.

In Luke, the busy sister Martha is often portrayed as complaining while Mary chooses "the better part." This type of analysis divides the sisters and seems to favor one type of service over the other. Mary, at least in this story, appears to be the preferred model, representing a type of silent devotion. In fact, her actions are often connected with contemplative orders and the contemplative life in general. Martha's actions, on the other hand, reflect a type of service in which women roll up their sleeves and serve. Her service is, in a sense, utilitarian: there are guests in her home who must be welcomed, made comfortable, and fed.

I can imagine that many women—then and now—relate more to Martha, who is expected to do all of the work with little or no help from those whom she serves. We can almost hear the collective groan of all the Marthas throughout the ages who have felt overworked, underappreciated, and taken for granted. Busy Martha alerts us to the fact that sometimes, when we work behind the scenes, creating, say, a memorable holiday meal for our families, we might miss out on much of the fun and the joy that others experience. While Martha may indeed bear the brunt of the chores, she does it almost grudgingly. She forthrightly asserts that Mary should do her part, but Jesus seems to disagree. We note that despite the fact that Luke has Jesus declare Mary as the one who chooses the "better part," maybe the "better part" is determined more by circumstance and less by choice. Does Martha really have a choice in this circumstance? After all, *someone* has to do the cooking and wash the dishes. Jesus seems to think that she *does* have a choice: Martha should take off her apron and pay attention to what Jesus has to say.

I am certain that there are many people, most of whom I am guessing are women, whose experiences resonate with Martha's resentment at having to do all of the work while others sit back and reap the benefits of their labor. Of course, those "Marthas" may wonder how anything will get done if they simply take off their aprons and sit down! If your life seems filled with obligations and expectations, whether from others or self-imposed, then Jesus' message to Martha might be aimed at you. When Jesus credits Mary with having chosen the "better part," perhaps he is telling Martha, and by extension, the rest of us, that we should not allow the busywork of life to consume us and that sometimes it is better to simply sit down and listen. When we do this—when we take off our metaphorical aprons—perhaps others will rise to the occasion with helpful hands and assist us in attending to the practical matters of life. We may need to ask for support, and we may need to learn to accept offers of help when proffered, but finding a balance between Busy Martha and Sitting Mary is really the key.

Finally, if we read this story with an eye to Luke's careful placement of it between the Parable of the Good Samaritan (Luke 10:25–37) and the Lord's Prayer (Luke 11:1–4), a triptych of sorts emerges. Jesus answers a lawyer's question "Who is my neighbor?" (Luke 10:29) by launching into the Parable of the Good Samaritan. The powerful lesson of this memorable parable is the imperative to treat others with mercy and compassion (Luke 10:36–37). In Luke 11:1–4, Jesus teaches his disciples how to pray. In the Lord's Prayer, or the Our Father, the only prayer Jesus gives to us,

Jesus emphasizes the centrality of forgiveness. We are to forgive as God forgives: completely and unconditionally—something that is often quite difficult for most of us. Inserted between the tandem lessons of compassion and forgiveness is a call to discipleship. In the Martha and Mary stories, perhaps Luke, whom scholars agree is very mindful of the way in which his material is arranged, seeks to emphasize the way of discipleship in Christ, the heart of which is mercy, compassion, and forgiveness.

In the Gospel of John, Martha and Mary resurface as bereaved sisters whose faith is sorely tested. The story begins as the sisters send a note to Jesus telling him that their beloved brother Lazarus is ill. Jesus receives the message but delays his visit to Bethany because he does not feel that Lazarus will die from his illness (John 11:4). We can only imagine the sisters' suffering as they watch their brother succumb to illness and can almost see them watching from the window in hopes that Jesus will heed their urgent message and show up in time to heal their brother. But Martha and Mary's hopes are dashed when Lazarus dies, and they have four long days of mourning before Jesus resurfaces.

When Jesus finally makes his way to Bethany, the sisters confront him about his absence and connect his failure to come to the aid of their brother with Lazarus's death. Their accusations of Jesus upon his arrival to Bethany are identical ("Lord, if you had been here, my brother would not have died" [John 11:21, 32]), so one can only imagine what sort of conversation transpires between the sisters during the initial shock and grief that follows their brother's death. Perhaps it is something like this:

> Martha: I cannot believe Jesus did not come when we sent the message to him about Lazarus.
> Mary: I know! He is such a close friend! I wonder why he didn't come?
> Martha: I'm thinking that if he had been here, our brother would not have died.
> Mary: You know, I am thinking the same thing. If Jesus had been here, our brother would not have died.

It is clear that both Martha and Mary are women of great faith, yet in the turmoil and tragedy of their brother's death, we see a struggle that mirrors our own. In the throes of despair and grief, how can we make sense of such suffering and sorrow? We lament over things that we did or did not do, and it is common to assign blame, which seems to be an element in the story of Lazarus's demise. The sisters assert that it is Jesus' absence during Lazarus's illness that is responsible for their brother's death. In sorting all of this out, the character of Martha is enormously helpful. Recall that when Martha goes out to meet Jesus, the first thing she says to him is "Lord, if you had been here my brother would not have died," which is immediately followed with an affirmation of faith: "But even now I know that God will give you whatever you ask of him" (John 11:21–22). Jesus consoles her and reminds her that her brother will rise again, and Martha agrees that Lazarus will "rise again in the resurrection on the last day" (John 11:24).

Jesus then speaks to Martha, reminding her of what it is—exactly—that she believes: "Jesus said to her, 'I am the resurrection and the life. Those who believe in me, even though they die, will live, and everyone who lives and believes in me will never die'" (John 11:25–26). He then pointedly asks her, "Do you believe this?" and Martha responds with a firm confession of faith (John 11:26–27). Yet when she stands at her brother's tomb, that firm faith seems to waver in the face of the physical reality of Lazarus's death. When Jesus asks that the stone be removed from the entrance of the tomb, Martha objects because "already there is a stench because he has been dead four days" (John 11:39). Jesus must once again remind her to maintain her faith, even when everything around her points to another reality: "Did I not tell you that if you believed, you would see the glory of God?" (John 11:40). John does not provide us with Martha's reaction to Jesus' question for it is unnecessary. We already know that Martha is a believer. Like Martha, when we are faced with a profound loss—and there is no greater loss than the death of someone we love—it is sometimes difficult to maintain our faith. We question, we waver, and like a boat that comes untethered from its mooring, we may need the love and support of friends and family to gently guide us back, reminding us of the faith that sustains us.

The sisters from Bethany invite us into their village, into their home, and into an inner circle of loving friends that includes Jesus. As we come to know them, we can relate to them in that their lives are richer and sometimes more complicated through the companionship of friends and family. On a daily basis, they must discern "the better part"—which means finding that delicate balance of service to others without loss of self in the giving. And, finally, Martha and Mary must face life's most difficult challenge when the mettle of their faith is tested through the profound loss of their brother. We gain strength and courage as we witness the same from the sisters who place their trust in their friend, Jesus.

2

Drusilla and Bernice: Sisters

Suspicious Sisters

Acts 24:24–27; 26:30–32

Some days later when Felix came with his wife Drusilla, who was Jewish, he sent for Paul and heard him speak concerning faith in Christ Jesus. And as he discussed justice, self-control, and the coming judgment, Felix became frightened and said, "Go away for the present; when I have an opportunity, I will send for you." At the same time he hoped that money would be given to him by Paul, and for that reason he used to send for him very often and converse with him. After two years had passed, Felix was succeeded by Porcius Festus; and since he wanted to grant the Jews a favor, Felix left Paul in prison. (Acts 24:24–27)

Then the king got up, and with him the governor and Bernice and those who had been seated with them; and as they were leaving, they said to one another, "This man is doing nothing to deserve death or imprisonment." Agrippa said to Festus, "This man could have been set free if he had not appealed to the emperor." (Acts 26:30–32)

IN THIS CHAPTER, we will explore the sisters Bernice and Drusilla, who make brief appearances only in Acts of the Apostles, the second volume of a two-volume work attributed to the anonymous author of Luke's Gospel. Acts details the life of the post-resurrection community and the trials and tribulations of the emerging Christian faith. Though often neglected by Christians in favor of the Gospels, Acts is a glorious read that offers us a brief look into the world of the first generation of Christians.

Though very little information about Bernice and Drusilla is available to us from the actual pages of Acts, there is much more written about the pair in sources outside of the New Testament, particularly in Josephus in his *Wars of the Jews* and *Antiquities of the Jews*. Despite this dearth of information about Bernice and Drusilla in the New Testament, the sisters are important in our overall exploration of women in the New Testament for several reasons: First, as members of the Herodian dynasty, Bernice and Drusilla offer us a unique view into that powerful yet highly toxic family. The Herod family figures prominently in the overall story of Jesus in the Gospels, and certain family members, including Drusilla and Bernice, also appear in the life of Paul. In fact, we find Herod family members popping up in all sorts of places, beginning with the story of the massacre of the infants in Matthew when Herod the Great, in a vain attempt to destroy Jesus, the infant Messiah and future King of the Jews, orders the execution of all baby boys under the age of two (Matt 2:1–16). Fortunately, an angel appears to Joseph in a dream and tells him to flee.

"Get up, take the child and his mother, and flee to Egypt, and remain there until I tell you; for Herod is about to search for the child, to destroy him." Then Joseph got up, took the child and his mother by night, and went to Egypt, and remained there until the death of Herod. (Matt 2:13–15)

When Herod the Great dies, his son Herod Archelaus inherits half of his father's territory, including areas in and around Jerusalem. Archelaus is a murderous brute like his father, hence Joseph decides not to return to Bethlehem after their sojourn in Egypt and instead brings Jesus and Mary to Nazareth, a territory out of Archelaus's murderous grasp (Matt 2:19–23). Another of Herod the Great's sons, Herod Antipas, imprisons John the Baptist and orders his execution (Mark 6:17–28). Herod Antipas is every bit as sly and manipulative as his father, and even Jesus refers to him as "that fox" (Luke 13:32). One of Herod the Great's grandsons, Herod Agrippa I, the father of Bernice and Drusilla, executes the Apostle James and briefly imprisons the Apostle Peter (Acts 12:1–11). Agrippa

I's son Agrippa II is an important Herod in our particular story as he is mentioned in Acts and he is Bernice and Drusilla's only surviving brother. The second reason why Bernice and Drusilla are important to us is because they are present during Paul's imprisonment and trial in Caesarea, which affords us the opportunity to discuss the actions that lead to Paul's arrest and eventual deportation to Rome. Finally, the way in which Luke presents Bernice and Drusilla in Acts 24–26 gives us cause to consider the larger reason for their inclusion in the narrative at all; namely, are the sisters merely "ornamental," as some scholars assume, or does their mention underscore some sort of political motive on the part of the author that speaks to a particular situation during the second half of the first century CE?

The best way to start is by setting the stage, so to speak, first by introducing the cast of characters followed by a discussion of the situation; that is, what does Paul do to land himself in jail in the first place and what if any part do the sisters play in all of this? We will begin broadly, first discussing the Herod family in a general way, and then we'll narrow our focus to Bernice and Drusilla before finally turning to the events in Acts 24–26.

I offer a brief introduction to the Herod family in chapter 9, but much of what I say there is in the context of the subject of chapter 9, the infamous Herodias. Although this book need not be read sequentially, I suspect that most readers will read it that way. I will try not to repeat much of what I say in chapter 9, but it is important to provide the necessary background for understanding Bernice and Drusilla, and that includes a brief discussion of the Herods. The complicated family tree of the Herodian dynasty begins with Herod the Great. A master builder and political genius with a penchant for cruelty, Herod the Great rules over Roman-dominated Judea from 37 BCE until roughly 4 CE. During his long reign, Herod the Great rebuilds the Temple in Jerusalem and constructs three impressive fortresses: Masada, located in the Judean desert and overlooking the Dead Sea; the Antonia fortress in Jerusalem; and the Herodium, located about seven and one-half miles south of Jerusalem. The Herodium was first positively identified by Edward Robinson in 1838, and many wonder if Herod the Great is entombed there. A tomb was uncovered during excavations at the Herodium in 2007 led by Hebrew University archaeologist Ehud Netzer, who spent nearly four decades searching for Herod's tomb. Netzer was convinced that the tomb discovered in 2007 belonged to Herod the Great. Sadly, in 2010 Netzer died from injuries suffered during a fall onsite at the Herodium. Today, some question whether the mausoleum and sarcophagus believed by Netzer to be that of Herod the Great is really the king's resting place. Only time and further testing will (hopefully) reveal the answer.

In any case, Herod the Great also constructs the magnificent port city of Caesarea Maritima, which serves as the administrative center for the Roman government in Judea. Herod the Great is gifted with many talents, but in a famous quote credited to Emperor Julius Caesar Augustus, Caesar observes that "it is better to be Herod's pig than son" (the implication is that as a Jew, Herod will not consume pork, hence the pig is safer than one of his sons). Susceptible to rumors and ever fearful of disloyalty and rebellion, Herod executes one of his wives, Miriamne I, in a fit of jealous rage, believing that she has taken a lover. By all accounts, Herod truly loves Miriamne and regrets his actions. Herod grieves deeply, but he apparently does not learn to ignore idle gossip. In 7 BCE, Herod murders two of his sons by Miriamne I, Alexander and Aristobulus, when he hears (and believes) rumors of their impending betrayal, and later, in 4 BCE, he has his son Antipater, by wife Doris, executed for similar reasons. Drusilla and Bernice are the granddaughters of the executed Aristobulus. Their father, Herod Agrippa I, is one of three children born to Aristobulus, including a brother, Herod of Chalcis, and a sister, Herodias, the aforementioned villainess who arranges the murder of John the Baptist.

Drusilla and Bernice also have a brother, Herod Agrippa II, and another sister, Miriamne. By now, your head is probably spinning, not only because of the level of dysfunction among the Herod family, but also because of their tendency to keep certain names—like Herod, Miriamne, and Agrippa—in the family generation after generation, which only adds to the confusion of who is who in this powerful and ruthless clan. For our purposes, we will remain focused on the individuals only as they relate to the stories of Bernice and Drusilla.

Since much more is known about Bernice (sometimes spelled *Berenice*), we will begin with her. Though there is some disagreement among scholars, according to Josephus, Bernice and Agrippa II are twins who are sixteen years old when their father, Agrippa I, dies. According to Acts, Agrippa is eaten alive by worms! (Acts 12:23). Before his untimely and gruesome death, Agrippa I arranges Bernice's marriage to Marcus Julius Alexander, a nephew of the great philosopher Philo of Alexandria. Though there is some disagreement as to whether she is actually married or merely engaged to Marcus, most commentators assume Marcus to be Bernice's first husband. There is also considerable debate surrounding Bernice's actual age at the time of her marriage; some contend that she is between the ages of thirteen and fifteen, while others insist that Bernice is sixteen when she weds Marcus. If this is the case, that Bernice is sixteen when she enters into a politically arranged marriage with Marcus Julius Alexander, then Bernice marries and is widowed within the same year! After Marcus's death, Aggripa I quickly arranges a second marriage for his widowed daughter, this time to his brother, Bernice's own uncle, Herod, King of Chalcis, and Bernice becomes a queen alongside her middle-aged husband. Needless to say, it is a busy year for young Bernice. She has two sons with husband number two and is again widowed when Herod Chalcis dies around the year 50 CE. Bernice, now a single mother, is around twenty-two years old.

Bernice does not immediately remarry, nor does she shrink from public life into the dismal world of widowhood. It is during this time that Bernice is often mentioned in the frequent company of her brother Agrippa II, and together they rule as king and queen, which leads to rumors of incest, both by Josephus (*Antiquities* 20.7.3) and by the Roman satirist Juvenal:

> And finally a diamond of great renown, made precious by the finger of Berenice. It was given as a present long ago by the barbarian Agrippa to his incestuous sister, in that country where kings celebrate festal sabbaths with bare feet. (*Satire* 6, "The Ways of Women," trans. G. G. Ramsay)

According to Josephus, in an effort to thwart the rumors of incest that have apparently already found an audience in Rome, as Juvenal so blatantly proclaims, Bernice marries once again. This time, she weds Polemo, King of Cilicia, who converts to Judaism, which means, of course, that he must be circumcised. Rumors assert that Polemo marries Bernice for her riches, but for a grown man to submit to circumcision, we must question the veracity of such rumors. On the outside, it appears to be true love, but the marriage does not last very long. Bernice leaves Polemo, her heart filled "with impure intentions" (*Antiquities* 20.7.3), and she returns to the safety and comfort of her brother.

We have no way of knowing, of course, whether the rumors of incest between Bernice and Agrippa II are true, but we do have ample evidence to support the fact that the pair spend a great deal of time together. For example, certain letters are addressed to *both* Bernice and Agrippa II, a convention normally reserved for husband and wife, and, archaeologically speaking, their names appear together on certain inscriptions as "Queen" Bernice and "King" Agrippa II, again, evocative more of a husband-and-wife relationship rather than a sibling one. History tells us that Agrippa II is more reserved than his sister and that he never marries, something that is virtually unheard of among aristocratic Jewish men (and women). A strong argument can be made, however, against the incest allegations when we consider the notion that perhaps Bernice merely accompanies her brother in an official capacity, which certainly appears to be the case when they agree to hear Paul's defense in Acts of the Apostles (25:13–27; 26).

Bernice seems to be the adventurous type and she is not content to remain in Judea, cavorting with her brother from one boring function to the next and fending off rumors of incest. Instead, Bernice begins to set her sights on a more exciting prize. Indeed, several Roman sources, including Tacitus and Suetonius, indicate that Bernice has a love affair with a much younger Roman general, Titus. Perhaps best known for his brutal siege of Jerusalem in the year 70 CE and the arch that still stands today in the Roman Forum commemorating that terrible event, Titus is a powerful general who becomes emperor in 79 CE. Bernice and Titus have an on-again off-again love affair that spans nearly a decade, but apparently the good citizens of Rome do not feel that the much older, thrice-married Jewess accused of incest with her brother is a good enough match for *their* emperor. Bowing to public opinion, Titus ultimately rejects Bernice, and she seems to retire from public life and from the pages of history.

As I read her story, I find myself wondering if the historians have anything good to say about Bernice. Ironically, at least one historian, who is also her biggest detractor, Josephus, does have a few good words to say about Bernice. In the midst of the Jewish revolt against Rome (66–70 CE), Bernice courageously appeals to the then procurator, Gessius Florus, for restraint. Apparently Florus is slaughtering innocent Jews by the thousands, and Bernice is in Jerusalem at the time performing some sort of religious vow, possibly the *nazirite vow*. When one takes the nazirite vow (*nazirite* is from the Hebrew word meaning "consecrated"), he or she is prohibited from drinking alcohol, consuming ritually unclean food, touching dead bodies, and cutting their hair. Nazirites are sacred volunteers, dedicated to serve the LORD, and although the nazirite vow (Num 6:1–21) is normally taken for a brief period of time, there are a few, like the judge Samson and the prophet Samuel (both of whom appear in the Hebrew Bible), and, in the New Testament, John the Baptist, who take this vow for life. We do not know if Bernice has taken the nazirite vow, but if this is the case, she is the only woman recorded in the Bible to have done so.

Bernice appears before Florus barefoot (we are at once reminded of Juvenal's satire in which he portrays Bernice as barefoot). Her petitions on behalf of her people fall on deaf ears, however, and the slaughter continues (*Wars* 2.15.1). This portrait of Bernice—as a religious, pacifying noblewoman—is in sharp contrast to the lurid image of a woman who has a sexual relationship with her brother and who is a "cougar" lusting after Titus, some thirteen years her junior. Who is the real Bernice? This is a question we will ponder a bit later in the Enduring Lessons section of this chapter. But for now, we must turn to Bernice's sister, Drusilla, a beautiful woman who is ten years younger than Bernice.

In his *Antiquities*, Josephus tells us that before his death, Drusilla's father, Agrippa I, arranges a marriage for his then six-year-old daughter to a non-Jew, Epiphanes, son of Antiochus IV. Our questions about the possibility of child marriage can be put aside for the moment (it is likely that Drusilla would not have married at age six but would instead remain engaged until age thirteen or fourteen) for this marriage never takes place. Drusilla's betrothed backs out of the engagement, refusing to convert to Judaism and the rite of circumcision (no true love there!). Drusilla's brother, Agrippa II, as the head of the family following his father's death, arranges for her at age fourteen to marry King Azizus of Emesa (in Syria). Unlike his predecessor, Epiphanes, Azizus submits to the Jewish rite of circumcision. Despite his show of devotion, their marriage is doomed, thanks to a man named Antonius Felix, the Greek-born and then Roman procurator of Judea. Captivated by her beauty, "for she did indeed exceed all others in beauty" (*Antiquities* 20.7.2), Felix falls madly in love with Drusilla. His unbridled passion for Drusilla inspires him to concoct a rather novel means to lure her away from her current husband. According to Josephus, Felix arranges for his Jewish buddy, a man named Simon, to masquerade as a magician, and somehow (unfortunately, Josephus does not detail the means) Simon convinces Drusilla to marry Felix. This leaves us wondering just how Simon accomplishes this. Does Simon give Drusilla some sort of love potion? Does he hypnotize her? And just who is this Simon character? Is he the same Simon who appears in Acts 8:9–13?

> Now a certain man named Simon had previously practiced magic in the city and amazed the people of Samaria, saying that he was someone great. All of them, from the least to the greatest, listened to him eagerly, saying, "This man is the power of God that is called Great." And they listened eagerly to him because for a long time he had amazed them with his magic. But when they believed Philip, who was proclaiming the good news about the kingdom of God and the name of Jesus Christ, they were baptized, both men and women. Even Simon himself believed. After being baptized, he stayed constantly with Philip and was amazed when he saw the signs and great miracles that took place.

On the surface, the Simon in Acts does not seem to be Felix's friend; *that* Simon seems to be a bit of a rogue, but it is still worthy of consideration. If we are talking about the same man, perhaps Simon works his magic on Drusilla before he converts to the Way?

We can't help but observe that Drusilla is either very superstitious or impossibly naive. It is unclear if Drusilla actually divorces Azizus or merely abandons him, but Josephus notes that Drusilla is quite unhappy with her own actions for two reasons: First, she suffers some sort of religious guilt, an indication that perhaps she does not legally divorce her first husband before marrying Felix, which is likely the case. Second, her misery is somehow tied to Bernice's jealousy of her. It is unclear why Josephus links Drusilla's marriage-guilt with Bernice's envy of her, but this is what he has to say about it:

> Accordingly, she [Drusilla] acted ill, and because she was desirous to avoid her sister Bernice's envy, for she was very ill-treated by her on account of her beauty, was prevailed upon to transgress the laws of her forefathers and to marry Felix. (*Antiquities* 20.7.2)

Josephus leaves us scratching our heads as we attempt to reconcile two very disparate problems facing Drusilla: her neglect of Jewish law regarding divorce and remarriage, and Bernice's jealousy. We can only suppose that Drusilla fears that her sister's jealousy might be inflamed should she learn of Felix's passionate love for the beautiful Drusilla. It is interesting to note that all three of Agrippa I's daughters ignore Jewish regulations when they leave their husbands. Josephus tells us that Miriamne, Drusilla's older sister by about four years, leaves her husband Archelaus for another man, Demetrius. Here the motivation seems to be greed, for Demetrius comes from a wealthy family (*Antiquities* 20.7.3).

Before turning to the situation in Acts that brings the sisters into the world of Paul, I feel compelled to insert an interesting aside connected to Drusilla. The events leading up to and the actual eruption of Italy's Mt. Vesuvius in 79 CE have long been a topic of fascination for me. I have visited Pompeii and Herculaneum, cities destroyed by the eruption, many times, and I even brought my students there several years ago as part of a study-abroad program through my university. In conducting research for this book, I was surprised to learn that there is a connection between that terrible event on August 24, 79 CE, and Drusilla. According to Josephus, Felix and Drusilla had a son together, Agrippa (not to be confused with her father and brother who share the same name!). Sadly, Drusilla and her son die during the eruption of Vesuvius (*Antiquities* 20.7.2). Some sources erroneously assert that it is Agrippa and his wife who die in the catastrophe, but it is the child, Agrippa, and his mother who perish.

And when he [Felix] had had a son by her, he named him Agrippa. But after what manner that young man, with his wife [Drusilla], perished at the conflagration of the mountain Vesuvius, in the days of Titus Caesar . . . (*Antiquities* 20.7.2)

Having thus introduced the sisters, Bernice and Drusilla, let us now turn to the situation in which they are mentioned in Acts. At the center of it all is the Apostle Paul. Returning to Jerusalem after his third missionary journey through Asia Minor and Greece, Paul is confronted by some detractors, described only as "Jews from Asia" (Acts 21:27), who attack Paul verbally and physically. Who are these "Jews from Asia" and why do they have it in for Paul? I mention Paul's adversaries in chapter 11, but it seems pertinent to say a few words about them here as they are essentially responsible for Paul's imprisonment. When I discuss the missionary efforts of Paul in my college classroom, students are often surprised to learn that Paul's life in Christ is not an easy one. Not everyone was interested in what he had to say, and he had his share of enemies. In chapter 11, I note that Paul's detractors are usually referred to as "Judaizers," a group of Jewish Christians who believe that circumcision and the observance of Mosaic Law should be obligatory requirements for Gentile converts. Not all of his detractors are referred to as Judaizers, but for simplicity's sake here, I will use this as a catchall term for Paul's enemies. Paul is largely responsible for waiving the circumcision requirement, thus allowing Gentiles to convert to the Christian faith with relative ease.

There are many who openly and quite vociferously disagree with Paul on this issue, and they actively seek to undermine his missionary efforts, insisting that all converts to the Way must first become Jews. Large and small groups of detractors follow Paul from place to place, keeping their distance. Once Paul moves on to new regions in search of fresh converts, however, his enemies backtrack and infiltrate the often fragile new Christian communities founded by Paul, casting aspersions against him and sowing seeds of doubt among the newly converted. We can imagine how frustrating this must be for Paul and his missionaries, and he mentions his detractors with a great deal of consternation in some of his letters (Gal 2:4; 2 Cor 11). The Judaizers also appear to be the "Jews from Asia" who turn up in Acts 21 and accuse Paul of blasphemy and of profaning the Temple by bringing non-Jews into that holy sanctuary.

> The Jews from Asia, who had seen him in the temple, stirred up the
> whole crowd. They seized him, shouting, "Fellow-Israelites, help! This
> is the man who is teaching everyone everywhere against our people,
> our law, and this place; more than that, he has actually brought Greeks
> into the temple and has defiled this holy place." (Acts 21:27–28)

Things quickly escalate and a riot ensues. Paul is dragged out of the Temple as a furious crowd, whipped up by his enemies, attempts to kill him; indeed, all of Jerusalem is "in an uproar" (Acts 21:31). Paul is taken into protective custody and imprisoned at Caesarea Maritima. The procurator (or governor) at the time is Antonius Felix, the besotted husband of Drusilla. Josephus seems to have a rather low opinion of Felix, whom he derides in both *The Jewish Wars* and *The Antiquities of the Jews*. Felix appears to be a highly ineffective ruler, known mostly for his mismanagement and ruthlessness. Felix keeps poor Paul imprisoned for two years without official charges, hoping to perhaps shake him down for the customary bribe (Acts 24:26). During Paul's early imprisonment, Felix visits Paul and brings Drusilla with him.

> Some days later when Felix came with his wife Drusilla, who was Jewish, he sent for Paul and heard him speak concerning faith in Christ Jesus. And as he discussed justice, self-control, and the coming judgment, Felix became frightened and said, "Go away for the present; when I have an opportunity, I will send for you." At the same time he hoped that money would be given to him by Paul, and for that reason he used to send for him very often and converse with him. (Acts 24:24–26)

There are several noteworthy verses in this passage. First, Luke specifically mentions that Felix has a wife who happens to be Jewish. From this, we can surmise that the two are married, but Luke does not allude to the illegality of their union. He also does not mention the fact that Drusilla leaves her first husband because she is charmed by Felix's pseudo-magician friend, Simon. When Paul begins to speak to the pair about faith in Christ, Paul focuses on "justice, self-control, and the coming judgment" (Acts 24:25). This sort of talk frightens Felix and prompts him to send Paul away. Given the unsavory and religiously illicit manner in which Felix (a pagan) and Drusilla (a Jew) wed, perhaps Paul touches a nerve. Let us probe this possibility more closely.

Paul speaks of three important aspects espoused by the followers of the Way: justice, self-control, and the coming judgment. How does Felix measure up to these aspects of "Christian" life? First we must ask, Is Felix

a just man? Felix wrestes Drusilla away from her first husband in a duplic-
itous way—through the use of lies and sorcery—both of which are forbidden in Jewish law (Lev 19:31; 20:6, 27). So the answer to our first question
is a resounding no! Felix is not a man of justice. Turning to question number two, we ask, Is Felix a man who is able to exert self-control? All good
and decent men should look the other way when they are attracted to a
married woman, but Felix does not. He gives in to his lust, and instead of
looking the other way he contrives a plan to destroy a legal marriage. Felix
is attracted to Drusilla's beauty, and all of his machinations are rooted in
a sort of perverse superficiality. Felix, then, obviously lacks self-control.
Our final question concerns judgment. Does Felix understand what Paul
means when he speaks of the "coming judgment"? Luke tells us that Felix
is "rather well informed about the Way" (Acts 24:22). Does he fear that
God will judge his "crimes" when the Kingdom comes, an event that the
followers of the Way feel is imminent? If Felix does indeed believe in the
coming of the Kingdom, is it any wonder that he hurriedly sends Paul
away? But what about Drusilla—is she at all ruffled by Paul's speech?
Luke does not tell us; Drusilla merely appears in the scene alongside Felix.
Interestingly, despite her legendary beauty, the only notable attribute Luke
mentions is her Jewishness.

As Paul languishes in prison without charges for two years, Felix is
recalled to Rome and is replaced by a new procurator, a man named Porcius Festus (Acts 24:27). This change in the guard signals new hope for
Paul, and he appeals to Festus, asserting his right as a Roman citizen to
have his case presented to the emperor (Acts 25:10). Festus agrees with
Paul, and arrangements are made to send Paul to Rome. Luke narrates
that King Agrippa and Bernice go to Caesarea to welcome Festus (Acts
25:13), and they remain in Caesarea to hear Paul's long-winded defense
(Acts 25:23–27; 26). Bernice does not speak, but her name is specifically
mentioned three times (Acts 25:13, 23; 26:30). Despite the fact that she
appears in the company of her brother, Agrippa II, Luke does not address
the rumors of incest, nor does he mention Bernice's envy of Drusilla or
her multiple marriages. Bernice is simply a member of the assembly who
arrives at Caesarea to listen to Paul's defense. Significantly, she agrees with
the other members of the retinue who profess Paul's innocence.

> Then the king got up, and with him the governor and Bernice and
> those who had been seated with them; and as they were leaving, they
> said to one another, "This man is doing nothing to deserve death or
> imprisonment." Agrippa said to Festus, "This man could have been
> set free if he had not appealed to the emperor." (Acts 26:30–32)

In the introduction to this chapter, I asked the reader to consider the way in which Luke presents Bernice and Drusilla in Acts 24–26. If we read the text just as it is written, we might miss the mention of Bernice and Drusilla altogether. In the narrative that spans Acts 24–26, the sisters do not speak; they appear as one-dimensional characters and seem to be merely ornamental. Why then does Luke decide to include them at all? It is clear from the extra-biblical sources explored in this chapter (and there are other sources I have not included that make mention of the sisters, including Tacitus, Suetonius, and Dio Cassius) that the pair is fairly well known in antiquity. Surely Luke's audience is familiar with the Herod family and the gossip that seems to envelop them like a cloud. Luke's inclusion of the sisters—specifically mentioning them by name—might actually speak volumes, as we shall see in the Enduring Lessons section below.

Bernice and Drusilla's Enduring Lessons

The first time I encountered Bernice and Drusilla was as a graduate student many years ago. I was taking a course on Paul that concentrated mostly on Paul's letters, but an important aspect of the course was to look at certain key events in Paul's life (for example, Paul's conversion) as described by the Apostle himself in one or more of his letters, and then to compare what Paul wrote with Luke's version of the same event in Acts. In general, Acts presents a fanciful version of events and often includes characters and stories that are absent in Paul's letters. In any case, it was during one of these sleuthing assignments that I first came across Bernice and Drusilla. I was intrigued by Luke's mention of the sisters and I wanted to learn more about them. Since I practically had the university library to myself on that sunny Saturday afternoon, I picked up dozens of books and commentaries from the stacks and began sifting through their pages. I recall feeling disappointed because there was so little information written about the sisters and what information I managed to unearth was quite negative: incest, envy, greed, and insanity. Consequently, in the past I assumed a negative opinion about Bernice and Drusilla, lumping them together with the rest of the mostly evil, self-serving Herods, and when I teach my course on Women in the Bible, I frankly do not spend much time discussing the sisters.

As I began research for this book, specifically, my second chapter having to do with sisters in the New Testament, my initial thought was to include Bernice and Drusilla largely because they are complete opposites to Martha and Mary, the other pair of sisters profiled in chapter 1. I thought the contrast between the "good sisters" (Martha and Mary) and the "bad sisters" (Bernice and Drusilla) would be interesting and entertaining for the reader. But as I reread their stories, and took a closer look at what the ancient, mostly Roman (and all male) historians have to say about Bernice and Drusilla, I found myself drawing some very different conclusions. Indeed, I think it is time to take a fresh look at Bernice and Drusilla as we explore the enduring lessons they impart to us. Chief among these enduring lessons is the destructive nature of rumors. The second enduring lesson has to do with toxic families: how much does the accident of birth and birth order affect the trajectories of Bernice's and Drusilla's lives? For us today, how can we recognize, navigate, and recover from toxicity in our own families and in other relationships?

We begin by examining the rumors about the sisters, largely perpetrated by Josephus. Before we address these rumors, however, it is important to understand that gossip, the means by which rumors are generally spread, is rampant in the ancient world. There are dozens of injunctions against such behavior, in both the Hebrew Bible and the New Testament, thus attesting to the fact that it is a common problem. Jesus' condemnation is nothing short of riveting.

Either make the tree good, and its fruit good; or make the tree bad, and its fruit bad; for the tree is known by its fruit. You brood of vipers! How can you speak good things, when you are evil? For out of the abundance of the heart the mouth speaks. The good person brings good things out of a good treasure, and the evil person brings evil things out of an evil treasure. I tell you, on the day of judgment you will have to give an account for every careless word you utter; for by your words you will be justified, and by your words you will be condemned. (Matt 12:33–37)

People in the ancient world are not that dissimilar to us today with regard to gossip. Some might argue that gossip is one of the ways through which information is disseminated, particularly in the world of biblical antiquity where illiteracy abounds. This is true, at least to some degree, but one of the problems with gossip it that sometimes, we get it all wrong.

Years ago, I worked as a high school teacher. One of the courses I taught was a class on Christian morality. During a class discussion about the destructive nature of gossip and rumors, we would play a game called Telephone. This is a wonderful way to teach students some of the harmful effects of gossip—in this case, the human tendency to miss facts, embellish or distort information, and then pass on untruths about someone or something to someone else. If you are unfamiliar with this game, it begins when someone, in this case, it would be me, the teacher, whispers a specific message into the ear of someone else, in this case, a student. That first student then turns to the person beside him or her and whispers the same message, and the process is repeated until everyone has heard the message. Once the message has circulated around the entire classroom, usually some twenty-five students have heard it. The last student to receive the message then stands up and says it out loud, and then the original message is read to the entire class. Inevitably, the final message does not remotely resemble the original. Everyone is laughing and talking about what they heard or did not hear, but when the exercise is over and all of the giggling subsides, the discussion that follows is a somber one. That silly little game teaches us that even in the course of a few minutes, an original message often becomes so distorted in the retelling of it so as to become a different message entirely.

By far the most harmful accusation leveled against Bernice is that of incest with her brother Agrippa II, something that is forbidden in Jewish law (Lev 18:6–18; 20:11–12, 17, 19–21). Josephus also accuses Bernice of an almost pathological envy of her younger sister Drusilla, and Bernice's jealousy is somehow connected to Drusilla's marriage to Felix, though the connection is unclear. In any case, I must restate that the use of Josephus, a Jewish defector to Rome, as a primary source must be weighed with equal amounts of credulity and suspicion. Generally speaking, if Josephus's claims can be corroborated elsewhere, then I am usually more comfortable in trusting the legitimacy of his history. In the case of Bernice, the Roman satirist Juvenal also accuses Bernice and Agrippa II of incest and even alludes to Bernice's impassioned and barefoot appeal to the bloodthirsty Gessius Florus for restraint in slaughtering innocent Jews during the Jewish revolt against Rome.

For some, the combination of Josephus's and Juvenal's testimonies confirms Bernice and Agrippa II's guilt. According to Josephus, Bernice's short-lived marriage to Polemo, King of Cilicia, is just a desperate move to deflect the incest rumors, but she soon abandons Polemo, presumably to return to her beloved brother Agrippa II. To add another blemish to her sexual history, which so far includes three marriages, one of which is to her uncle, and rumors of incest with her twin brother, Bernice then embarks on a hopeless love affair with the enemy, a Roman general who would be emperor, Titus. If Josephus is to be believed, we can now add the term "traitor" to the list of Bernice's debaucheries.

The portrait of Bernice in Acts is at odds with the negative image Josephus and Juvenal promulgate. In Acts, Bernice is mentioned in the company of her brother and other notables as one of those who come to

Caesarea Maritima to hear Paul's defense. She, like the others who listen to Paul's impassioned pleas for justice, is convinced that Paul is innocent. Luke presents her in the best possible light, but why? It is well known that Luke harbors a great dislike for the Herod family, so we must wonder why, if Bernice has such a checkered past, does Luke not mention it? There are many possibilities, but two appear most plausible. The first is that perhaps the author of Acts ignores the rumors about Bernice because in his estimation, they are unfounded and not to be believed. Maybe Luke understands that when someone comes from a famous family, rumors are bound to surface. It is much the same in our modern world. Standing in line at the supermarket on any given day, we are barraged by tabloids and magazines filled with all sorts of rumors about celebrities. The popularity of reality television, with shows like *Keeping Up With the Kardashians* and *The Real Housewives of* [insert any city] speaks to our obsession with the rich and famous, people who live very different lives than most of us. With a few exceptions, I believe that most celebrities have just as many problems and hang-ups as the rest of us, and I can't help but think that they are hurt and scandalized by the lies told about them and their families in the tabloids. Is it possible, then, that the rumors about Bernice and, to a lesser extent, Drusilla are just fabrications? In Bernice's case, maybe the real story is that she has a close relationship with her brother and simply enjoys his company. There is absolutely nothing wrong with that, but it takes only one person to create something sinful out of something that may be actually quite innocent.

As I mentioned earlier, we have no way of knowing what sort of relationship Bernice has with her brother, but why does the scandalous and salacious version always seem to prevail? Could it be because we are talking about a woman? There are other instances that lead us to ponder the possible sexism that may lie at the heart of the negative portrait bequeathed to us of Bernice. For example, in chapter 5, I discuss the erroneous portrait of Mary Magdalene, who for centuries has been branded as a prostitute. How did this happen to a woman who is Jesus' close friend and confidant and who is never described as a sinner of any kind in the Gospels? The short answer is that in the sixth century, Pope Gregory the Great delivers a public sermon in which he confuses the stories of three completely unrelated biblical figures: Mary Magdalene; Mary, the sister of Martha; and an unnamed female sinner from Luke's Gospel (Luke 7:37–50). Because of Pope Gregory's massive mistake—and because the people who hear his sermon are too biblically illiterate to catch his error—a perfectly fine and decent woman, a woman filled with faith and love, is branded a repentant prostitute. While this negative image of Mary Magdalene may have begun with Pope Gregory's blunder, it was fueled through the ages by a pervasive patriarchal sexism that failed to recall Jesus' egalitarian treatment of women. (For more on Mary Magdalene, see chapter 5). I am not saying that Bernice and Drusilla are victims of character assassination, only that we need to consider the possibility that perhaps there is more to their stories and that Luke, who does not mention any of the questionable accusations leveled against the sisters, offers us some clues that may be closer to the truth.

With this, we turn to the other plausible explanation for why Luke chooses to present the sisters in a positive light. Perhaps Luke, who certainly has no great affection for the Herod family, chooses not to take aim at Bernice and Drusilla for fear of reprisal. Luke composes his Gospel and Acts under the watchful gaze of the Roman censors—something to keep in mind when we read anything in the Bible from this time period—and it would be a considerable risk for Luke to attack Bernice, who is a powerful queen from a prominent family and a known Roman sympathizer, or Drusilla, who is married to Felix, a Roman official known for his brutality. Moreover, some scholars assert that Luke himself is pro-Roman, or at the very least, interested in pacifying the Romans. We need only take a brief look at Luke's version of Jesus' arrest and crucifixion in the Gospel of Luke for verification. For example, in Luke, Pilate, who by all other accounts is a ruthless sociopath (see chapter 10), is presented as someone who sympathizes with Jesus and seeks to have him released (Luke 23:1–16)!

Luke includes Bernice in the group present at Paul's defense, and she professes Paul's innocence. During a time when Christianity is still an illegal religion, getting essentially a nod of approval from Bernice might go a long way in helping to legitimate the faith. Drusilla's silent presence alongside her husband, Felix, during Paul's early imprisonment accomplishes a similar objective: she offers a tacit approval of Paul and the followers of the Way (Acts 24:24–26). Recall that Luke does not air Drusilla's dirty laundry: her nasty feud with her sister, and her association with a sorcerer and illegal marriage to Felix, two infractions that are expressly forbidden in Jewish law (Deut 18:10; 24:1–2). Instead, the appearance of both sisters in an understated but dignified manner presents them as royal women who approve of the new "Christian" religion.

We cannot know for certain Luke's motives, but we must not depart from our first enduring lesson without saying a few more words about the detrimental effects of rumors. Words, then and now, have power. They can destroy relationships and end careers. How many times have you said cruel and unkind things in the midst of an argument with someone you love? How often have you wished that you could take back the hurtful things you have uttered in the heat of the moment? Spreading rumors is a lot like that. Sometimes we slip and say or do things in a spate of anger or just to fit in. We feel special to be included in the gossip about someone else, and sharing what we have heard with others can increase a feeling of belonging because they exclude others but include us. Ironically, gossip and rumors have the opposite effect. Our words, in the end, alienate us, and as I often say to my students, if you think you are immune to gossip and rumors because you have been embraced by the group that generates them, you are wrong; the moment you step away, the group will turn on you and you will be the subject of their newest round of nattering.

Perhaps the worst thing about gossip and rumors is the fact that they destroy trust. People whom you once believed to be your friends instead end up betraying you. This sort of thing can happen even within families, as alliances form and certain family members are either "in" or "out." Rumors in the workplace can affect one's career, can cause suspicion, and can erode collegiality. Finally, if you find yourself in the midst of a gossip fest but do not participate in it yourself, you are still guilty. As in the case of Drusilla, silence is usually perceived as tacit approval. There is really only one way to peacefully avoid getting caught in the net of gossip and that is to simply walk away.

If Bernice's and Drusilla's stories warn us of the dangers of spreading gossip and believing in rumors, their second enduring lesson may help to explain why the sisters are the subjects of rumors to begin with. Being born into a wealthy and powerful family has its advantages and disadvantages. One of the disadvantages is that other people often scrutinize and criticize famous or wealthy people with impunity. My brief description of the Herod family in the opening of this chapter makes it clear that, *in general*, we are dealing with a highly dysfunctional and toxic family. Historically, we know that brutality, murder, betrayal, manipulation, greed, and malice are the hallmarks of this large and powerful dynasty. But we also know that in large families, there is great diversity and we cannot assume that all of the Herods behave like Herod the Great!

In light of this, we must return to the question posed at the opening of this section: How much does the accident of birth and birth order affect the trajectories of Bernice's and Drusilla's lives? We can use as an example Josephus's assertion that Bernice mistreats Drusilla. If we believe his assertion, can we assume that Bernice's appalling behavior is rooted in her upbringing? That is, perhaps Bernice is exposed to cruelty at an early age and such behavior is acceptable in her family. After all, children live what they learn—at least some of the time. We might even go so far as to allege that nastiness is part of her DNA. All of this, of course, hinges on whether or not we accept what Josephus says about Bernice's jealousy of Drusilla. Another way to look at this toxic family is through the lens of the historical time period in which Bernice and Drusilla live. They are rich Jewish women living in Roman-occupied Judea during the first century. Their family has a history of collaboration with the Romans, and they are likely despised by the majority of their countrymen and women. Moreover, Bernice's and Drusilla's fates are in the hands of their father, Agrippa I, who basically uses them as political pawns, marrying them off to certain men not for love but in order to create political alliances. This sort of thing is commonplace among the rich and powerful, yet, sadly, it reveals the fact that neither sister has the power to control her own destiny, at least not initially. Once their father dies and their brother takes over, the sisters seem to have more freedom. I have already noted that all three sisters—Bernice, Drusilla, and Miriamne—leave their husbands for other men in an apparent disregard for Jewish divorce customs. I offer these stark realities not as a means to excuse anyone's behavior, but only as an alternative way to look at their lives and the legacies they leave behind.

Bernice and Drusilla eventually take control of their own lives, and though they continue to make mistakes (for instance, Bernice's doomed love affair with Titus), they nonetheless transcend the social restrictions that govern their early lives and begin to make their own choices. Bernice's courage in facing the murderous Gessius Florus in hopes of saving her people from slaughter is a good example. These sisters, as imperfect as they are, inspire us to face and deal with toxicity in our own families and in other relationships. We learn that we are not simply the products of the families into which we are born but individuals who are not defined by the past or expectant roles. We also learn that there is more than one way to read a story and more than one way to tell a story, including our own life story. The Herodian family is a complicated family and Bernice and Drusilla are complicated characters. We cannot assume that their inclusion in Acts is unintentional or an afterthought. As I mentioned earlier, some scholars, particularly those who tend to date Luke–Acts to the early part of the second century and well after the disastrous (and failed) Jewish revolt against Rome (66–70 CE), feel that Luke presents the sisters in a positive light at the imprisonment and trial of Paul so that Christianity might be viewed as a legitimate religion within the empire.

Perhaps Luke has another motive: to challenge us to look beyond the obvious and to shake off the shackles of judging others based on hearsay and rumor. Perhaps Luke is telling us that the earliest followers of Jesus, just like Bernice and Drusilla, are subjected to rumors and judgment;

they are mistreated and misunderstood, largely based on suspicion and mistruths. In the same way, the first "family" of Christians are scrutinized and criticized simply because people do not understand them and make false assumptions based on rumors. This reality is much more apparent to the first generation of Christians, who are far better able to read between the lines than we are. They understand that ignorance, malice, and distrust often obscure the truth, but that in the end, faith guides, faith endures, and faith prevails.

3

The Adulterous Woman in John's Gospel: Sinner

Caught in the Act

John 7:53–8:11

[[Then each of them went home, while Jesus went to the Mount of Olives. Early in the morning he came again to the temple. All the people came to him and he sat down and began to teach them. The scribes and the Pharisees brought a woman who had been caught in adultery; and making her stand before all of them, they said to him, "Teacher, this woman was caught in the very act of committing adultery. Now in the law Moses commanded us to stone such women. Now what do you say?" They said this to test him, so that they might have some charge to bring against him. Jesus bent down and wrote with his finger on the ground. When they kept on questioning him, he straightened up and said to them, "Let anyone among you who is without sin be the first to throw a stone at her." And once again he bent down and wrote on the ground. When they heard it, they went away, one by one, beginning with the elders; and Jesus was left alone with the woman standing before him. Jesus straightened up and said to her, "Woman, where are they? Has no one condemned you?" She said, "No one, sir." And Jesus said, "Neither do I condemn you. Go your way, and from now on do not sin again."]] (John 7:53–8:11)

THE WELL-KNOWN STORY of the adulterous woman in John's Gospel has for centuries been viewed as a tale that warns us of the dangers of judging others, but it is actually much more. Ancient and contemporary readers alike see a bit of themselves in the plight of the nameless woman accused of being a sinner by a group of men who are themselves equally sinful. As we begin to unpack this story, I should point out that the actual text of John 7:53–8:11 is a bit of an enigma; readers are alerted to this fact by the use of brackets in the New Revised Standard Version (NRSV), which I have preserved in my quote on the previous page. Most scholars believe that the text, which is not found in the earliest manuscripts of the Gospel of John, may possibly originate in the Gospel of Luke, as it is sometimes positioned after Luke 21:38 in older manuscripts; others contend that the story of the adulterous woman is an independent tale, inserted into John's Gospel possibly around the fifth century. If this is the case, then we cannot really examine it within the overall context of John's Gospel, which, at least from a scholarly point of view, is problematic. There is no clear consensus concerning the authorship of this passage, but most commentators agree that is does not come from the hand of the Fourth Evangelist and that the style of the story is more in keeping with the Synoptics.

The insertion of the story as it presently stands is linked to John 8:15 and Jesus' statement regarding judgment: "You judge by human standards; I judge no one." Whatever its origin, we know that the story holds great meaning for early Christians (and later ones too) because it exemplifies so many of the teachings of Jesus, which we shall presently explore. Since I am in agreement with most scholars in that the story is an interpolation, that is, not original to John but grafted into it by an unknown ancient editor, I will treat it as such and not attempt to reconcile it with John's Gospel as a whole but will instead examine it as an independent unit. With these preliminary issues of authorship and text in mind, let us now turn to the story that has for centuries challenged readers to consider alternative views and new perspectives regarding what is right and just.

The story begins with Jesus arriving early at the Temple, prepared to teach the large crowd who has gathered there to listen to him. It is unlikely that Jesus teaches *inside* the Temple, but more than likely in one of the many spaces surrounding the huge Temple complex. During this time period, it is not at all unusual for rabbis, sages, and philosophers to attract followers and to instruct them in the open air. Some of these teachers travel from place to place, like Jesus, but most set up shop, so to speak, in open areas with more or less regular hours so that students, both old and new, know where to find them. Jesus' ministry, therefore, is not as unique as some might imagine, though his teachings do have a profound and lasting impact, unlike those of most of his ancient colleagues, who are largely nameless and their teachings lost to us in the sands of time.

The author narrates that Jesus "came *again* to the temple" (John 8:2; emphasis mine) indicating that perhaps it is his custom to hold early morning classes before the heat of the day. John 8:2 is often overlooked in the exegesis of this story in favor of rushing ahead to the more titillating aspects of the tale, but John 8:2 is important for several reasons. First, it establishes Jesus as an authoritative teacher with many disciples: "*All the people* came to him and he sat down and began to teach them" (John 8:2; emphasis mine). We are reminded of the story of Martha and Mary in Luke 10:38–42 (see also chapter 1) and the manner in which Mary assumes the position of a student alongside Jesus' other disciples. It is clear from the Gospels that Jesus has many disciples, not only in his native Galilee, but apparently also in Jerusalem. The second reason why John 8:2 is important will not be missed by seasoned teachers familiar with the concept of *experiential learning*. Jesus' students (or disciples) will not have a sermon or lecture as they might expect this morning; instead they will have an *experience*. They will watch as their teacher puts his lessons into action, dealing compassionately with the woman while at the same time, skillfully subverting the malfeasance of his enemies. Finally, John 8:2 presents us with the assembled crowd who act as silent witnesses and then become actors in the drama as it unfolds.

Like his students, the scribes and the Pharisees know just where and when to find Jesus; unlike his students, however, the scribes and Pharisees keep track of Jesus' movements throughout the city because they view him as a threat and they are forever plotting against him. Jesus, of course, is aware of their machinations and is not surprised when they interrupt his lesson, appearing *en masse* with the central figure of the story, a woman accused of adultery. The unknown author sketches a powerful tableau: Under the shadow of the Jerusalem Temple, Judaism's most sacred site, the accused woman is forced to stand before Jesus and the startled crowd of disciples as her menacing accusers surround her. Because of the early hour, some scholars suggest that the woman's arrest takes place the day before and that she has already been tried and condemned. If this is the case, she is undoubtedly exhausted, humiliated, terrified, and *confused*. Why are her tormentors bringing her to Jesus if she has already been tried and condemned? The obvious answer is that she is being used as pawn in a scheme to entrap Jesus.

Before we forge ahead, let's first address a question that is often raised in my college classroom when we read this story. My justice-minded

students are quick to ask, "What about the man? Where is he? Why isn't
he punished?" These are all good questions. The penalty for adultery,
death by stoning, is severe, and it does not take much imagination to envision the brutality involved in being pummeled to death. It is important
to note, however, that in cases of adultery, the Law stipulates equal punishment for both convicted parties (after all, it takes two!).

> If a man is caught lying with the wife of another man, both of them
> shall die, the man who lay with the woman as well as the woman.
> So you shall purge the evil from Israel. (Deut 22:22; cf. Lev 20:10)

In this particular story, the male adulterer is absent. There have been all
sorts of speculations about the identity and the whereabouts of the male
adulterer, ranging from the supposition that he escapes the trial by running
away or by paying off his accusers to the notion that perhaps he is tried
separately, either before or after the woman. But we are just guessing here
as the male partner is never mentioned directly nor is he part of the ruse
to entrap Jesus.

Returning to the scene, we note that it resembles a modern courtroom
proceeding, with the scribes and Pharisees in the role of prosecutors, the
woman, of course, as the defendant, and Jesus, who assumes two roles,
acting as both her defense attorney and the judge in the case. Jesus' students (or disciples), morph from happenstance witnesses into a sort of
mute jury. The woman's crime—adultery—is undeniable as she is apparently "caught in the very act" by at least two witnesses, presumably part of
the assembly of accusers who present the case to Jesus. Jewish law requires
that a crime must have two or more reliable witnesses in order for the case
to be a valid one.

> A single witness shall not suffice to convict a person of any crime or
> wrongdoing in connection with any offence that may be committed.
> Only on the evidence of two or three witnesses shall a charge be sus-
> tained. (Deut 19:15; cf. Deut 17:6)

In cases of adultery, one can't help but wonder how such a crime could
produce a single witness, let alone the required "two or three." With the
threat of capital punishment hanging over adulterers' heads along with
the paltry methods of birth control available during the first century, we
can assume that discretion and the timing of illicit affairs is of paramount
importance. Of course, when people are caught up in the allure of passion,
coupled with the human tendency toward stupidity when the brain is con-

sumed with carnal desire, mistakes are made. In the case of the adulterous woman, at least two individuals witness her having intercourse with her paramour. We at once feel her sense of embarrassment and humiliation at the thought of being seen engaged in such an intimate act. But we must next question the exact circumstances. Are the lovers caught in an open field, behind a shed, or in one of the many caves found on the outskirts of the city? Does the aggrieved husband (or wife) walk in on the adulterers, and then run off to find another witness? Unfortunately, the text does not provide us with any answers to these and other questions, leaving us instead to our own imaginings.

Jesus is asked to judge what appears to be a clear-cut case (John 8:4–5). The scribes and Pharisees remind Jesus that the penalty for adultery is death by stoning (Lev 20:10; Deut 22:22–24), but all of this is really just more trickery, part of a larger effort to ensnare Jesus "so that they might have some charge to bring against him" (John 8:6). Jesus' foes often use this sort of ploy in the Synoptics, and this is one of the reasons why many scholars assume that John 7:53–8:11 comes from the Synoptic tradition. For example, in Matt 19:3 (see also Mark 10:2ff), some Pharisees ask Jesus a question about the legality of divorce: "Some Pharisees came to him, and to test him they asked, 'Is it lawful for a man to divorce his wife for any cause?'" Their query is not really genuine at all, but merely a feeble attempt to bring some sort of legal charge against Jesus, should he interpret the Law differently. Interestingly, Jesus' enemies always fail to trip him up, and in the story of the adulterous woman, they will not succeed either.

Though we tend to focus on the action between Jesus, the woman, and Jesus' foes, we must be ever mindful of the crowd assembled in the background, watching the way in which their rabbi handles a situation that may have deadly consequences. As we continue to probe this story, I invite you, the faithful reader, to imagine yourself as part of the "silent jury" of onlookers. To do this, you must, for the moment, lay aside any feelings you have about the case and approach it with an open mind. Allow yourself to visualize the scene: the accused woman and her tormentors; Jesus, who will defend her, and your fellow jurors who, like you, have unwittingly been drawn into this drama.

The scribes and Pharisees present the accused woman to Jesus, expecting a quick verdict: "Teacher, this woman was caught in the very act of committing adultery. Now in the law Moses commanded us to stone such women. Now what do you say?" (John 8:4–5). To their surprise, Jesus says nothing. Instead, he bends down and begins to write with his finger on the dusty ground. This curious action, which Jesus repeats in John 8:8, has elicited two key questions from anyone who has ever read this passage: *Why* does Jesus choose this moment to bend down and write in the dirt, and *what* does he write? Many possible explanations have been put forth, but as to the question of *why*, there are two popular motives. The first is that Jesus is attempting distance himself from the accusers by ignoring them. This supports the notion that the woman's trial and sentence has probably already taken place and Jesus' action is basically a nonverbal way of indicating that he is fully aware of his enemies' ruse. The second possible reason why Jesus steps away and nonchalantly begins drawing on the ground is a more practical one: he is essentially buying time. In other words, ruse or not, Jesus must gather his thoughts in order to circumvent his enemies. He wisely takes a few extra moments to consider his options before responding, a lesson we would all do well to remember. I must confess that the latter option appeals most to me. I often teach my students that not every question requires an immediate response. Just because you receive a text message or e-mail from someone does not mean that you must immediately respond; in fact, sometimes deciding *not* to answer is, in fact, an answer.

As to the question of *what* Jesus writes, among the many creative and interesting answers suggested by commentators, the two most popular are that Jesus writes absolutely nothing; he is merely "doodling" as a means to either ignore the scribes and Pharisees or to buy some time, as suggested above. The other answer, often a favorite among scholars who point out that this instance is the only example in the New Testament of Jesus writing *anything*, feel that perhaps Jesus is writing a verse from the prophet, Jeremiah, best preserved in the King James Version:

> O LORD, the hope of Israel, all that forsake thee shall be ashamed, and they that depart from me shall be written in the earth, because they have forsaken the LORD, the fountain of living waters. (Jer 17:13)

The connection to this passage in Jeremiah is obvious a few verses later when all of the woman's accusers, one by one, depart in shame (John 8:9). All of this is totally speculative as the text does not provide us with any definitive answers to the questions of *why* or *what*, if anything, Jesus writes in the dust.

We can, however, almost feel the tension as Jesus' enemies, with their net cast, wait for an answer. The woman, whose life depends upon Jesus' ability to somehow rescue her from a death sentence, remains silent. We can imagine that the woman is consumed with fear, for she knows what happens to convicted adulteresses. As I mentioned earlier, the usual form of execution is death by stoning (Lev 20:10; Deut 22:22–24), or somewhat later in Jewish law, strangulation, but in this particular instance, the sentence seems to be the former. I draw your attention to this detail once more because some commentators assert that the question posed to Jesus is not about the woman's guilt at all, for she is "caught in the very act of committing adultery" (John 8:4), but instead concerns the *manner of execution*. While this is certainly one way to interpret the text, the rest of the story does not seem to support this hypothesis.

There are also some questions as to whether or not the Sanhedrin (the ancient Jewish court) even holds the power to impose capital punishment on the woman, as this power appears to have been revoked at some point by the Romans. A passage in John, part of the Passion Narrative, seems to affirm this: "Pilate said to them, 'Take him yourselves and judge him according to your law.' The Jews replied, 'We are not permitted to put anyone to death'" (John 18:31). If this is correct, that the Sanhedrin has lost its power to impose the death penalty, then in the snare set up by the accusers (presumably themselves members of the Sanhedrin), Jesus will find himself caught between the dictates of Mosaic Law and the iron-fisted Roman imperial law. Given this scenario, Jesus is in an impossible situation. If he upholds the penalty and orders the woman to be stoned, in keeping with Jewish Law, he will likely find himself in hot water with the Romans; if he ignores the Mosaic injunction that clearly stipulates that the adulterous woman must be stoned to death, then he is in violation of Jewish law.

On the surface, however, it looks as if Jesus is asked to make a ruling as to whether or not the woman should be stoned to death for committing adultery, but as we can see, the case may be more complicated. Whatever the nature of the trap set by the woman's accusers, Jesus manages to find a way around it. As the woman's accusers continue to pester him for an answer, Jesus stands up and addresses them: "Let anyone among you who is without sin be the first to throw a stone at her" (John 8:7). He then returns to whatever he is writing in the dust. Notice that Jesus sidesteps the thorny issues of Jewish Law concerning the punishment for adultery—which is clear and known to everyone present—and brilliantly turns the tables on the woman's accusers. Stunned into a bit of self-reflection, the woman's accusers and, presumably, the silent jury of onlookers, one by one, walk away, leaving the woman alone with Jesus (John 8:9). With no witnesses, the condemned woman's sentence is now commuted. In Jewish Law, witnesses to the crime—in this case, adultery—cast the first stones, and then "the hands of all the people" participate in the execution (Deut 17:7). Perhaps the woman has witnessed this grim, barbaric practice in the past and is at the moment greatly relieved to have escaped such a fate. Does she watch in amazement as all of the would-be stone throwers skulk away, mindful of their own sins, many of which may be graver than her own? Or does she close her eyes in prayer, and upon opening them, find that she is alone with the rabbi from the Galilee? Unfortunately, such details are missing from the narrative.

Following this climactic scene, the accused woman emerges as more than simply a pawn, used by her accusers to trick Jesus. To them, she is merely an object, a means to a disreputable end; but to Jesus, she is a human being who has sinned but is nonetheless deserving of mercy. The way in which Jesus treats the woman contrasts sharply with the manner in which her accusers treat her. Jesus stands up from drawing on the ground and speaks directly to the woman. In the world of biblical antiquity, social intercourse between men and women is limited to immediate family and friends. In the Gospels, however, Jesus consistently rejects such conventions and treats women with respect and a measure of equality that is largely unprecedented in the patriarchal society in which he lives. When Jesus speaks to the adulterous woman, he addresses her only as "woman." Some may find this manner of address a bit offensive, particularly when Jesus addresses his own mother as "woman" at the wedding feast at Cana at the beginning of John's Gospel, and then again, as he hangs from the cross at the end of John's Gospel. As you might recall, at the wedding feast at Cana, Jesus' mother goes to him when she learns that the wedding hosts have run out of wine (John 2:3). Jesus' response, to our modern ears anyway, seems disrespectful and almost flippant: "Woman, what concern is that to you and to me?" (John 2:4). In the same way, from the cross, as Jesus commends the care of his mother to the beloved disciple, he says to Mary, "Woman, here is your son" (John 19:26). In all of these instances, including his interaction with the adulterous woman, Jesus' use of the term "woman" is actually a polite form of address common during biblical times, much like the modern use of "Madam."

We can almost hear the accused woman's sigh of relief and see the gratitude in her eyes as Jesus rises to speak with her: "Woman, where are they? Has no one condemned you?" (John 8:10). The woman does not defend her actions or plead for mercy; she merely answers Jesus' second question in an honest and forthright manner: "No one, sir" (John 8:11). In yet another contrast to her complainants, Jesus does not convict her; he instead liberates her, sending her on her way. It is a mistake, however, to assume that Jesus condones her behavior, for as she departs, he enjoins her not to sin again. "And Jesus said, 'Neither do I condemn you. Go your way, and from now on do not sin again'" (John 8:11). Jesus does not condemn the woman; rather, he offers her mercy. He does not ignore her sin but instead forgives it. These tandem lessons of mercy and forgiveness are the hallmarks of Jesus' ministry and are the central themes in the story of the adulterous woman.

The Enduring Lessons of the Woman Caught in Adultery

The story of the woman caught in adultery is often called a "homeless" text because it is an interpolation grafted into the Gospel of John; its real roots, including authorship, origin, and date of composition, remain a mystery. Despite the technical issues such a text presents for scholars, most people who read the story of the adulterous woman do not ponder such technicalities; rather, they are moved to consider the meaning of the story and the ways in which it might enrich their lives. In this section, we will explore the enduring lessons of the woman caught in adultery with a focus on judging others, mercy, and forgiveness.

Recall that the story opens with a gathering of disciples (or students) who have come to the Temple precincts so that Jesus may teach them. Certain scribes and Pharisees arrive with a nameless woman accused of adultery and interrupt Jesus' lesson. Jesus' attention does not shift away from his disciples to the woman, as we might expect, or even to the scribes and Pharisees, but instead, he remains focused on all of the characters involved in the story. This is an important detail, for when Jesus makes the statement "Let anyone among you who is without sin be the first to throw a stone at her" (John 8:7), Jesus is not directing his remarks to the accusers alone but to everyone present at the scene, and even to us, who read this story over 2,000 years later. With this single directive, the accusers, the crowd of students, the adulteress, and readers are in a way suddenly indistinct from one another, as all are placed onto equal footing and called to consider their own sins, failings, and shortcomings before venturing forward to judge another. Jesus' challenge is meant to unwrap us from the haughty insulation that may make us feel superior to the woman, whose guilt is unequivocal, and we find ourselves standing beside her and all of the characters in the story, as they, as we, represent the complex nature of humanity and our ever-changing roles based on circumstance, choice, and chance. Stated in the most basic way, this means that sometimes we are the saint, other times, the sinner, or, more often, someplace in between.

If we learn to think of ourselves as part of the greater circle of the human family, our tendency to judge the woman, or anyone else, including ourselves, is mitigated by the innate longing of every soul to be heard and treated fairly. Jesus' challenge to turn inward before casting a stone at another seems to be a central aspect of his teachings. It is important to note that when Jesus speaks to the woman, he asks, "Has no one *condemned* you?" (John 8:10; emphasis mine), and when she replies, "No one, sir," he tells her, "Neither do I *condemn* you" (John 8:11; emphasis mine). Jesus' use of the word "condemn" captures this concept of judging others, rather than acting as a sort of legal pronouncement. This sort of non-judgment is perhaps best immortalized in the following.

> "Why do you see the speck in your neighbor's eye, but do not notice the log in your own eye? Or how can you say to your neighbor, 'Let me take the speck out of your eye,' while the log is in your own eye? You hypocrite, first take the log out of your own eye, and then you will see clearly to take the speck out of your neighbor's eye." (Matt 7:3–5)

Jesus' hyperbolic imperative is so memorable because we have all, at one time or another, judged someone or felt the sting of indignation as others pass judgment on us. The problem with judging others—and try as we may, we all do it—is that too often we make assumptions based on appearance, gender, race, age, and dozens of other external factors. With very little information, we jump to judgment when in truth, in most cases, we do not know the first thing about the person we are judging! When Jesus advises us to remove the giant log from our own eye before pointing out the speck in our neighbor's eye, he is warning us how wrong and destructive judging others can be. Judging another, however, is different in the case of those who break the law and harm others.

In ancient Israel, the Law is in place to uphold justice and to punish the guilty. Israel's legal system is grounded in her unique connection to God; when the people of Israel "follow the Law," they are demonstrating their love of God and their adherence to the covenant. The religious and moral overtones found in much of Israel's laws illustrate the fact that we are talking about a *relationship* between God and his people as implied in the covenant. Jesus, a Torah-abiding Jew, views the Law as an authoritative source, but he denounces the hypocrisy of certain religious leaders who pervert the Law and use it for their own personal gain (Matt 23:1–36), which seems to be at least part of the problem in the story of the adulterous woman.

Many scholars believe that it is Jesus' respect for the Law that is being tested in the case of the adulterous woman. Whether this is accurate or not, there is something deeper, richer, and more meaningful in the manner in which Jesus treats the woman. We feel it when we read the story, and our Christian foremothers and forefathers felt it too. There is something that draws us into her predicament. Of course, it may be the human tendency to identify with the sinner. Or perhaps it is with some chagrin that we identify more with the accusers. For most of us, it is the fact that Jesus calls us to examine our own conscience before judging others. Yes, these are certainly powerful lessons in the story, but I think that most of us are moved by the way in which Jesus treats the woman with *mercy*. He does not condemn her—nor does he condone her sin, for he warns her not to do it again (John 8:11)—but through those who encircle her, judge her, and then one by one, walk away from her, we see mercy in action. If, as you read the previous pages, you accepted my invitation to imagine yourself as part of the "silent jury," how did you feel when Jesus said, "Let anyone among you who is without sin be the first to throw a stone at her" (John 8:7)? Most of us, I think, hope that if we were part of that crowd, we too would walk away, dropping the stone in our fist to the ground as we contemplatively exit the scene.

The Hebrew word *hesed* ("mercy") is usually translated in English as "loving kindness," and it is part of God's distinctive nature. The concept of mercy reverberates throughout the Hebrew Bible and New Testament and is an integral part of God's covenant with his people. God extends his mercy to us even when we are undeserving, and it is expected that in return, we should be merciful to one another. At the heart of mercy is forgiveness, the liberating gift of freedom from distress, anxiety, and shame that we give to others and ourselves. In the Bible, *hesed* functions in much the same way as the Law. When we treat others with mercy, we are acting as God acts in the world; when we treat others with justice, we uphold the covenant, forged with love, between God and God's people.

Modern psychology has latched onto this very biblical concept, and much research has been done on the emotional, physical, and spiritual benefits of forgiveness. In any discussion about forgiveness, we must begin by talking about what forgiveness is not. Forgiveness does not mean that reconciliation has occurred (though this is certainly possible); forgiveness is not forgetting, ignoring reality, pretending that an offense never happened, or excusing an injury. Instead, it is a decision to let go of the past, embrace the present, and look with hope to the future. Anyone who has ever been hurt by another knows that forgiveness is difficult, but the process of forgiveness restores peace of mind and frees us from anger, resentment, and thoughts of retaliation.

Each time I read the story of the woman caught in adultery, I understand why this "homeless" text has found residence in the hearts of countless Christians throughout the ages. The adulterous woman stands as a symbol of the folly and pettiness of judging others and invites us into the hallowed halls of our own introspection. When Jesus treats the adulterous woman with mercy and forgiveness, he does not deny her guilt but instead calls her to a new life. He thus offers her the promise of transformation from a life of sin to one in accord with the Covenant. While the struggle to avoid the lure of sin is just as difficult today (if not more so!) as it is during biblical times, the story of the adulterous woman teaches us that our mistakes do not define us and that change is possible. Her story carries us from the brink of despair and certain death to a reformed life filled with possibilities. Through the practice of mercy and forgiveness in our own lives, we free ourselves from egocentric obsessions and the many empty promises of this world as we embrace a more gentle way of living. Unfettered by the chains of sanctimonious judgment, hard-heartedness, and festering grievances, we treat our brothers and sisters with *hesed* and look forward to a life filled with the healing light of hope and love.

4

The Woman with a Twelve-Year Hemorrhage: Sinner
Blood Guilt

Mark 5:25–34; Luke 8:43–48; Matt 9:20–22

A nd a large crowd followed him and pressed in on him. Now there was a woman who had been suffering from hemorrhages for twelve years. She had endured much under many physicians, and had spent all that she had; and she was no better, but rather grew worse. She had heard about Jesus, and came up behind him in the crowd and touched his cloak, for she said, "If I but touch his clothes, I will be made well." Immediately her hemorrhage stopped; and she felt in her body that she was healed of her disease. Immediately aware that power had gone forth from him, Jesus turned about in the crowd and said, "Who touched my clothes?" And his disciples said to him, "You see the crowd pressing in on you; how can you say, 'Who touched me?'" He looked all round to see who had done it. But the woman, knowing what had happened to her, came in fear and trembling, fell down before him, and told him the whole truth. He said to her, "Daughter, your faith has made you well; go in peace, and be healed of your disease." (Mark 5:25–34)

THE STORY of the unnamed woman with a twelve-year hemorrhage is found in the Synoptic Gospels (Mark 5:25–34; Luke 8:43–48; Matt 9:20–22) but is absent in the Gospel of John. Normally, when a particular story is included in all three of the Synoptic Gospels, we can assume that the story is well known and treasured among early Christians. Mark offers us the most detailed version of the story, hence, we will rely on Mark's account of the events rather than the more pared-down versions found in Luke and Matthew. The story of the woman with an issue of blood is a powerful one that moves the reader from desperation to hope to the power of faith.

I am always somewhat surprised when I teach this story in my college classroom—surprised that most of my students already know something about this story, for it is a rather obscure one for most modern readers. I am equally surprised at the way in which their initial uneasiness in discussing such a story (something I anticipate and very much understand) changes as they begin to unpack and sympathize with the woman's plight and her subsequent healing. Their reticence at the beginning stems from the nature of the woman's illness, which conjures up all sorts of images that many of my college-age students find unsettling; I sense this immediately as my normally chatty classroom falls silent as we open the Bible and turn first to Mark 5:25–34.

My students listen in silence, jotting down notes, as I offer my usual introduction to the story, and then, when together we begin to explore the text in more depth, they very slowly lay aside their initial discomfort and direct their focus on the story. For many, this particular healing miracle is very meaningful to them and it often becomes their favorite "miracle story" in the New Testament. You might be asking yourself why anyone would have any qualms about talking openly about this story, simply because the woman in question is bleeding vaginally (this seems to be at the heart of the squeamishness). My response to this question is that while I have no reservations whatsoever when it comes to talking about this story in minute detail, which I shall do presently, I am nonetheless sensitive to my audience, both in the classroom and beyond. The fact remains that for some folks, talk of such things as menstruation or uterine bleeding of any sort is considered to be a very personal matter. My many years of teaching this story have taught me that this is certainly true. The only reason I mention the possibility of discomfiture when reading the tale of the hemorrhaging woman is that this book will likely be used in classrooms and in Bible Study groups. Those leading the discussion should be mindful of others who may not approach the material with the same openness and ease as their teachers, ministers, priests, or group leaders.

In contrast to my sometimes blushing, squirming students who find conversations about things such as sex and bodily functions uncomfortable, people in the world of biblical antiquity are actually more open and relaxed when it comes to these things. This may seem a bit of a contradiction in light of the Bible's restrictive rules and regulations that govern every aspect of life, including ritual purity and sexual behavior. We must remember, however, that during biblical times, most of the population lives in rural towns and villages and that Israelite society is largely an agrarian one. Growing up in the company of livestock, even young children are exposed to animals mating and giving birth. We also know from archaeological excavations that most families live in small, modest homes called *pillared houses*, or *four-room houses*. These homes have two levels, with the upper level reserved mostly for sleeping. Families sleep together in the same cramped room on pallets, which are normally rolled up and stowed in a corner during the day. In such tight living spaces, it is unavoidable for children to hear and perhaps even see their parents making love; but these children understand that sexual activity is a normal and natural part of marriage. So while some moderns might blush when topics such as sex or uterine bleeding are discussed, our ancient ancestors are less likely to feel embarrassed or shocked by such conversations; their primary concern will center on the religious implications associated with the discharge of blood. In the case of the woman who has suffered hemorrhages for twelve years, worries about the "polluting" nature of her illness will be foremost in the minds of our ancient audience. In order to better understand the story of the hemorrhaging woman, it is important to first examine what the Bible has to say about who is "clean" and who is "unclean."

Because the woman in our story is suffering from an issue of blood, she is considered to be ritually unclean. This means that everyone and everything she comes into contact with is also considered to be unclean. If, for example, the bleeding woman sits on a chair, then the *chair* is unclean; if you happen to then sit on that chair, then *you* are unclean. If you, in your sudden state of uncleanliness, touch another person, then *that person* is rendered unclean, and on and on it goes. Found in the book of Leviticus, the laws regarding the polluting nature of vaginal bleeding and any other type of discharge are quite explicit.

> If a woman has a discharge of blood for many days, not at the time of her impurity, or if she has a discharge beyond the time of her impurity, for all the days of the discharge she shall continue in uncleanness; as in the days of her impurity, she shall be unclean. Every bed on which she lies during all the days of her discharge shall be treated

as the bed of her impurity; and everything on which she sits shall be unclean, as in the uncleanness of her impurity. Whoever touches these things shall be unclean, and shall wash his clothes, and bathe in water, and be unclean until the evening. If she is cleansed of her discharge, she shall count seven days, and after that she shall be clean. On the eighth day she shall take two turtle-doves or two pigeons and bring them to the priest at the entrance of the tent of meeting. The priest shall offer one for a sin-offering and the other for a burnt-offering; and the priest shall make atonement on her behalf before the LORD for her unclean discharge. (Lev 15:25–30)

As Lev 15:25–30 implies, religious purity laws are taken very seriously. If this particular regulation is not proof enough, we need only look at the laws regarding uncleanliness following childbirth.

According to Lev 12:2–5, women remain unclean for a specific number of days after giving birth. This is due to the normal flow of postpartum blood, called *lochia*, which continues for about two to four weeks after a baby is born. It is interesting to note that the period of time during which a woman remains unclean differs, depending on the sex of her infant. After the birth of a male child, a woman remains unclean for forty days; but if the baby is a girl, then the mother remains unclean for twice as long— eighty days. Why such a discrepancy? Traditionally, scholars assume that because women, and by extension, baby girls, are considered inferior to males, then the purification process is longer. I disagree with this common assumption and have my own theory. I should qualify this theory by saying that I worked for many years as a certified childbirth educator and had the privilege to teach and help hundreds of expectant couples of all ages prepare for childbirth and occasionally offered my services as a labor coach. In any case, when babies are born, they have maternal hormones coursing through their tiny bodies for several weeks. This accounts for some temporary conditions that are commonplace in newborns, including breast swelling (and even the secretion of a small amount of fluid from the baby's nipples, usually called "witch's milk"), infant acne, and genital enlargement in both male and female neonates.

In female newborns, there is usually a slight vaginal discharge, called *physiologic leucorrhea*. Often there is a slight tinge of blood, alarming to some new mothers, but nonetheless perfectly normal in newborn baby girls. This very common and transient condition is called *pseudo menses*, and it is reasonable to assume that mothers in the ancient world are aware of this condition, even though they may not have a particular name for it.

The mother of a baby girl is considered unclean because of her own flow of blood following the birth of her daughter, but it is likely that she is considered "doubly unclean" because of her infant daughter's vaginal discharge; this, more than gender preferences, might account for the mother's prolonged state of uncleanliness. It is important to note that the birth of a child in ancient Israel, regardless of gender, is a time of great joy and all children are considered cherished gifts from God. While there might be a slight preference for boys, largely due to an agrarian culture in which strapping sons might be more helpful to their fathers in the field, girls are also precious; after all, one's Jewishness is traced through the mother, rather than the father. My students often ask why one's Jewishness comes from the maternal side instead of the paternal and the simple answer is this: In the ancient world, you always know who your mother is; male paternity is never quite as certain.

Armed with the necessary background regarding ritual purity, let us now explore the story of the woman who suffers from uterine bleeding for twelve years. The story of the hemorrhaging woman interrupts the story of Jairus's daughter and can be classified as a "pairing story." Sometimes, particularly in Luke–Acts, pairing stories involve Jesus' healing of a man and then a woman, as in the case of the healing of a paralytic man named Aeneas, followed by the raising of Tabitha in Acts 9:32–42. In Mark 5:22–43, Mark pairs the story of the dying daughter of Jairus, a Temple official, with the woman suffering from hemorrhages. The number 12 appears in both stories, linking the pair: The sick child, on the brink of womanhood, is twelve years of age, and the hemorrhaging woman has suffered for twelve years with her affliction (Mark 5:42; 25). As I mention in the introduction, 12 is an important number in both the Hebrew Bible and New Testament for it marks the number of tribes in ancient Israel and the number of Apostles in Jesus' ministry.

Jairus implores Jesus to heal his daughter (Mark 5:22–23), and Jesus agrees to help the girl, but she apparently dies as Jesus makes his way through a large crowd to Jairus's house (Mark 5:35). When Jesus finally arrives, he finds the locals grieving and wailing loudly. Jesus says to them, "Why do you make a commotion and weep? The child is not dead but sleeping" (Mark 5:39). The mourners laugh at Jesus and he puts them outside and promptly raises the child from the dead (Mark 5:40–42).

Among the crowd of onlookers who press in on Jesus and delay his arrival at the home of Jairus is a nameless woman who is hoping for a miracle of her own. She is in physical pain, suffering the debilitating effects of a persistent uterine hemorrhage, which likely makes her weak and anemic. She is also in psychological pain, feeling the sting of religious impurity that makes her a social pariah. We can only imagine her sense of loneliness and isolation. In the small towns and villages that dot the landscape of ancient Israel, everyone knows your business and it is likely that the woman's condition is no secret. Shunned by the townsfolk who fear contamination, she remains sequestered in her home for many years.

Mark informs the reader that the woman "had endured much under many physicians, and had spent all that she had; and she was no better, but rather grew worse" (Mark 5:26). Many modern readers can relate to this aspect of the woman's situation. When someone is sick for a long time, they will try just about anything to find relief. The woman spends all of her money on doctors who not only fail to heal her but actually end up making her sicker. Desperate, ill, and penniless, the woman learns that Jesus will be passing through town, and she bravely conceives a plan: she will venture from the house that has become her prison and seek Jesus' healing touch. It is a simple plan, at least on the surface, and one that is filled with hope and faith. The woman, however, is taking a great risk; if anyone in the crowd recognizes her, her life might be in peril. Her presence in the pushing and shoving crowd would render anyone who comes in direct contact with her ritually unclean.

We can only assume that the bleeding woman covers her face with her veil as she ventures out into the crowded street. Her desire to be healed outweighs the risk of being recognized and contaminating others. The woman does not initially speak to Jesus; rather, she speaks to herself in a sort of interior monologue: "If I but touch his clothes, I will be made well" (Mark 5:28). It is almost like a prayer, a soothing promise she makes to fortify herself in the rushing throng of people who have come to see the popular rabbi, healer, and prophet. As the hemorrhaging woman reaches out to touch Jesus' clothes—or his cloak, in Matthew's version of the story (Matt 9:21)—a miracle happens: "Immediately her hemorrhage stopped; and she felt in her body that she was healed of her disease" (Mark 5:29). In the same instant, however, Jesus, too, feels something: "Immediately aware that power had gone forth from him, Jesus turned about in the crowd and said, 'Who touched my clothes?'" (Mark 5:30). His disciples rightly point out that a giant mob is pressing in on Jesus and how can he possibly know if someone in particular touches his clothes? (Mark 5:31). Ignoring this, Jesus scans the crowd, for he *does* know that someone touched him; he feels "that power had gone forth from him" (Mark 5:30). The connection between Jesus and the woman is "immediate," like an electric shock that passes between the two, and they both sense it.

The woman approaches Jesus "in fear and trembling" and falls down before him and tells him "the whole truth" (Mark 5:33). Her courage to approach Jesus, rather then retreat and disappear into the crowd, is the climax of the story. We cannot know for certain what she says to Jesus; Mark only narrates that the woman tells Jesus the "whole truth." The "whole truth" probably includes mention of her prolonged illness, the failure of doctors to heal her, and the subsequent cure that comes from simply touching Jesus' clothes. Jesus is quick to point out, however, that the woman's cure does not come from simply touching his clothing, but rather, from a much deeper source: "Daughter, your faith has made you well; go in peace, and be healed of your disease" (Mark 5:34).

Jesus' powerful proclamation speaks to the essence of the miracle and the restoration of the hemorrhaging woman. Physicians and their potions fail her; the missing ingredient, it seems, is faith in Jesus. The intimate way in which Jesus addresses the woman, calling her "daughter," is a form of address one might expect from a loving father to his little girl. At this, the reader is reminded of another daughter, who lies lifeless in her bed in the home of her father, Jairus, and who is soon to be roused through the miracle of resurrection.

The hemorrhaging woman might appear as just another face in the crowd and an unlikely recipient of one of Jesus' miracles. For one, she is a woman and a stranger to Jesus, which virtually eliminates the chances of any social interaction between the two given the fact that even men and women of the same family do not speak to each other in public let alone complete strangers of opposite genders. Jesus not only speaks directly to her, but after she is healed, he addresses her tenderly, lovingly, charging her to "go in peace" (Mark 5:34). For another, as we have already seen, the bleeding woman is ritually unclean. She has no business inserting herself into a crowd of people, much less touching Jesus' clothes, effectively rendering all of those with whom she comes into contact unclean. All of these concerns, however, are swept aside, as the readers, both ancient and contemporary, witness the genesis of a miracle, born of suffering, relieved at last through faith.

The Enduring Lessons of the Woman with a Twelve-Year Hemorrhage

In the first of the Buddha's four Noble Truths, he observes that to live is to suffer. One does not have to live very long in this world to know that this is surely true. Try as we might, there is no escaping this aspect of the human condition. Click on your television, log onto your computer, or open a newspaper for the latest news and you will read and see stories of every sort of suffering imaginable: natural disasters, like tornadoes, wildfires, and tsunamis that destroy homes and lives; plane crashes in which there are no survivors; terrorist groups who kidnap and murder innocent people; modern-day plagues that wipe out entire villages. These stories, and many more, capture the headlines and make us shudder with sadness and fear.

At the start of every new semester, I ask my students to make a list of what they consider to be the "Big Questions" in life. I tell them to reflect on those seemingly unanswerable questions that have plagued the lot of humanity since the dawn of time. My intention is to first discuss their questions as a class and then, over the course of the semester, explore what the Bible has to say about these questions. Year after year, I find that most lists are basically the same. My students ask the tough questions that we *all* wonder about: Why am I here? What happens to us after we die? Is there a God? Why do we suffer? This final question, the question of suffering, is for most of us the most pressing because it touches us personally; we see it, feel it, and try to wriggle out of its cruel grasp whenever it grabs hold of us or someone we love. Suffering is at the heart of the story of the woman with a twelve-year hemorrhage: the manner in which she endures her suffering and her relentless search for a way to overcome it are, for us, her most enduring lessons.

Suffering is a complex topic, and while it is preferable for most of us to jump to the end of the hemorrhaging woman's story so that we may marvel at the miracle of her cure, we must first walk with her through twelve long years of pain and alienation. To do that, we must first reflect on the nature of suffering, including what the Bible has to say about this most painful reality.

In my book *What the Bible Really Tells Us: The Essential Guide to Biblical Literacy* (2011), I take direct aim at the question of suffering, pointing out that while we are familiar with the suffering that results from our own poor choices—if you drink too much whiskey, you'll get a headache; if you cheat on your spouse, you might end up in divorce court—we question the suffering that enters our lives from sources beyond our control, like life-threatening diseases and car accidents. When caught in the grip of such suffering, it is normal to wonder why this is happening to us. The question *Why?* leads to more questions: Am I being punished? Is God testing me? Am I supposed to learn something from this experience or is my misery simply a consequence of being human in a less-than-perfect world? When it comes to suffering, our most central question is this: If God truly loves me, how can God allow me (or anyone) to suffer? Theologians often classify such questions as having to do with something called *theodicy*; that is, how can we reconcile a God that is all-knowing, all-loving, and all-powerful (attributes typically associated with God) with a world riddled with suffering, despair, and death? There are a few books in the Bible that deal with the conundrum of theodicy, but the most popular is the book of Job.

Job is described as "blameless and upright, one who feared the LORD and turned away from evil" (Job 1:1). Despite his faithfulness to God, Job suffers unimaginable losses. First, Job is divested of his wealth and livelihood; next, his ten children all die in a freak storm on the same day; and finally, Job suffers serious health problems that render him incapacitated. How could God allow such terrible things to happen to such a good man? According to the book of Job, all of this misery is part of a Divine plan to test the fortitude of Job's faith. Job, outraged at the injustice of it all, soon challenges God to offer an explanation for his suffering. In response, God makes a dramatic appearance in the eye of a storm (Job 38–42), reminding Job of the wonders and mysteries of creation but never answering Job's honest question, *Why?* While many people turn to the book of Job for comfort in their own suffering, relating in some way to Job's misfortunes, they will not find a satisfying answer to the question of *Why?*. Generally speaking, in the Hebrew Bible, suffering is viewed as a mystery, beyond the understanding of we mere mortals. Still, because of the testing of Job, some also come to view their suffering as a test.

If we read Job alone, the theological message seems to be that we must learn to accept the suffering that invariably comes into our lives, for this is what Job ultimately does. But the woman with a twelve-year hemorrhage takes a different approach. She spends everything she has on doctors who actually make a bad situation worse. Now that she is penniless and sick, isolated and viewed as religiously unclean, we might expect her to pull the covers over her head and give up, and who could blame her? But the hemorrhaging woman is a warrior who refuses to give up; if medicine cannot heal her, perhaps it is time to look for a miracle. As we read about her persistence and tenacity in finding a cure for her condition, we are lifted up from the mire of self-pity and despair that may mark our own suffering, and we are inspired to carry on.

In the Gospels, Jesus transforms the way suffering is traditionally understood. Most people during the first century believe that suffering is a form of Divine punishment or, as in the case of Job, that God is testing them. This is particularly true when it comes to illness. Jesus seems to indicate that neither is the case. Jesus does not view illness or death as a punishment but as an occasion to reveal God's love.

> As he walked along, he saw a man blind from birth. His disciples asked him, "Rabbi, who sinned, this man or his parents, that he was born blind?" Jesus answered, "Neither this man nor his parents sinned; he was born blind so that God's works might be revealed in him." (John 9:1–3)

Notice that in this passage, the disciples assume that the blind man or his parents have offended God in some way and that those sins result in the man's blindness. People during biblical times have a rather obsessive preoccupation with their genealogies, and for good reason. The Bible is filled with long lists that trace various family members back through many generations. These ancestral records of who's who are *not* in the Bible merely to frustrate college students with their unpronounceable names; keeping track of your relatives—including any possible sins they may have committed—is a way to explain one's present suffering. It is a common assumption, for example, that if you are a good and God-fearing person but then suddenly fall ill, then some long-dead ancestor who transgressed is to blame. Sins stick to our souls like bad karma; they do not disappear in the shadow of the grave but can linger in the present for three or four generations, causing every form of sickness and other maladies, including blindness, lameness, and, we can assume, hemorrhages.

> I the LORD your God am a jealous God, punishing children for the iniquity of parents, to the third and the fourth generation of those who reject me, but showing steadfast love to the thousandth generation of those who love me and keep my commandments. (Exod 20:5–6)

From the above, we see a clear choice between suffering and peace. To love God is to experience the latter; rejecting God inflicts pain and suffering on future generations. Explaining the source of suffering, it seems, is as easy as reviewing one's family tree in search of ancestral trespasses. This view, that suffering can be the result of someone else's sin, puts the pain of the present into meaningful perspective and virtually eliminates the question of *Why?*

Another common belief held by most people during the time of Jesus is that suffering can be the result of demonic possession. Demons pop up everywhere in the New Testament (appearing some 586 times), wreaking havoc, inflicting pain, and causing suffering. These demons function under the direction of their leader, the Prince of Demons, Satan. By the time of Jesus, the hazy, indistinct image of Satan that appears only briefly in the Hebrew Bible is featured in glaring Technicolor in the New Testament as a formidable adversary and arch-nemesis of Jesus. It is possible, then, that the hemorrhaging woman might be viewed as a social outcast not only because she is religiously impure, but because she is possessed by a demon.

According to the Gospels, demons and their ringleader, Satan, are no match for Jesus, for Jesus defeats them at every turn. Perhaps the bleeding woman has heard of Jesus' prowess as a healer and exorcist, for news travels quickly from one small town or village to another. It is unclear whether or not the woman thinks her condition is caused by the workings of a demon, neither can we assume that she thinks her illness is retributive, based on some undisclosed sin of a long-dead relative. We know only that in the past, she placed her faith in physicians, who took her money but did not restore her health. Perhaps she has reached a point of despair, and all she has left is her faith. She does not sit passively by and wait for her illness to overtake her, however; instead, she turns her faith into action. It takes a great deal of courage for her to step out into the crowd and hope for a miracle, but this is exactly what she does.

Her courage pays off, and when the hemorrhaging woman receives her miracle, we rejoice alongside her. We can envision the healed woman returning to her home, her place of refuge but also the place of her exile. We can't help but wonder what she is thinking as she crosses the threshold, feeling the glorious glow of health after so many years of suffering. Are there friends and family members who cast aside the concerns regarding ritual purity and remained in contact with her during her illness with whom she can now share her joy? Or, does she return to the silence of her home, left alone to ponder her interaction with Jesus? We do not know the answers to these questions, but her illness and subsequent miracle reminds us to be mindful of those who are in physical, emotional, or psychological pain, particularly those who have been suffering for a protracted period of time. People in chronic pain, for example, often report that their friends and relatives, over time, become insensitive to their pain and often blame the patient for not finding that magic pill that will make it all go away.

In writing this chapter, I took this lesson to heart and questioned my own mindfulness. Just yesterday, as I took my daily walk around the small town in which I live, I watched as an old woman climbed aboard a bus, bent over her cane, grunting with each step, her body in a twist of arthritic agony. Moments later, a teenage girl hurried past me, earbuds in her ears, wiping away tears with the back of her hand as she looked straight ahead. Sometime later, I paused, as is my custom, along the water's edge and watched the sun as it slid slowly down behind low, thin clouds, turning them to a bright orange, and then, to a soft pink. As I marveled at the sunset, I also thought about a close friend of mine who is battling a fierce depression with little success.

I realized that so often, when we come face-to-face with suffering, our tendency is to look away, as we tell ourselves that such a thing would never happen to us; but even as we glance away, a still, small voice whispers the truth: *It can happen to you.* When we are faced with a serious illness, particularly if there is no cure on the horizon, as in the case of the bleeding woman, we expect those in our inner circle of friends and family to come to the rescue. We assume that our loved ones will reach out to us and offer us comfort and help us to sort out the many emotions and difficult practicalities that come with being sick. Quite often, however, we are shocked and surprised to find that once the diagnosis is shared, some of our most intimate friends and beloved family members essentially run for the hills. Of course, this only adds to our suffering as we feel the hollow, sinking sense of loss.

When you are seriously ill, your life is filled with losses as you learn to let go of many of the things you once did but now are unable to do. When those near and dear to us fail to visit, offer words of comfort, or listen to us as we try to make sense out of what is happening to us, we feel abandoned and alone. Of course, most people who have had this experience will also marvel at the people who show up with open hands, ready to help. Oftentimes, it is the person we least expect who steps up to paddle beside us as we navigate the murky waters of illness and loss.

The many valuable lessons that the hemorrhaging woman teaches us, including patience, courage, endurance, hope, and belief in miracles, can help us in our own inevitable suffering, but these lessons also call us to become healers in our own unique way, with our words, our actions, and our compassion. Though it is certainly easier to run for the hills and pretend that someone we love is really all right, even when they are not, the story of the hemorrhaging woman inspires us to be that person who shows up when someone we love is in pain.

The hemorrhaging woman's miracle is uniquely tied to Jesus' healing ministry. Jesus does not walk away from the tide of humanity that surrounds him, imploring him to heal a sick child, a lame beggar, or a blind man. Instead, Jesus wades into the undertow of misery, doing what he can to heal, comfort, and improve lives. The story of the bleeding woman summons believers to take up Jesus' challenge to try to ease the suffering of others—even one's enemies—in his name. For his followers, suffering takes on a moral imperative as they are to carry on his ministry of love, healing, and hope. The hemorrhaging woman's suffering and her cure act as a sort of compass, pointing the followers of Jesus in the direction of that neighbor, friend, or loved one who is suffering. Their suffering, our suffering, is profoundly connected to Christ's suffering.

"For I was hungry and you gave me food, I was thirsty and you gave me something to drink, I was a stranger and you welcomed me, I was naked and you gave me clothing, I was sick and you took care of me, I was in prison and you visited me." Then the righteous will answer him, "Lord, when was it that we saw you hungry and gave you food, or thirsty and gave you something to drink? And when was it that we saw you a stranger and welcomed you, or naked and gave you clothing? And when was it that we saw you sick or in prison and visited you?" And the king will answer them, "Truly I tell you, just as you did it to one of the least of these who are members of my family, you did it to me." (Matt 25:35–40)

Finally, the story of the woman with a twelve-year hemorrhage teaches us to be resolute in seeking relief from our suffering. Whether we are facing the pain of illness, the sorrow of grief, the sting of rejection, or any other form of suffering, we must explore every possible avenue for healing. Though we may grow weary, we must not despair. Through faith, courage, and hope, we too can experience the miracle of restoration.

5

Mary Magdalene: Supporter

A Woman of Substance

Matt 27:55–61; 28:1–10; Mark 15:40–41, 47; 16:1–11;
Luke 8:1–3; 24:8–11, 22–24; John 19:25; 20:11–18

B ut Mary stood weeping outside the tomb. As she wept, she bent over to look into the tomb; and she saw two angels in white, sitting where the body of Jesus had been lying, one at the head and the other at the feet. They said to her, "Woman, why are you weeping?" She said to them, "They have taken away my Lord, and I do not know where they have laid him." When she had said this, she turned round and saw Jesus standing there, but she did not know that it was Jesus. Jesus said to her, "Woman, why are you weeping? For whom are you looking?" Supposing him to be the gardener, she said to him, "Sir, if you have carried him away, tell me where you have laid him, and I will take him away." Jesus said to her, "Mary!" She turned and said to him in Hebrew, "Rabbouni!" (which means Teacher). Jesus said to her, "Do not hold on to me, because I have not yet ascended to the Father. But go to my brothers and say to them, 'I am ascending to my Father and your Father, to my God and your God.'" Mary Magdalene went and announced to the disciples, "I have seen the Lord"; and she told them that he had said these things to her. (John 20:11–18)

NEXT TO the mother of Jesus, Mary Magdalene is perhaps the most well-known woman in the New Testament. Her popularity in recent years is due in large part to the 2003 blockbuster detective novel by Dan Brown, *The Da Vinci Code*, which was made into a film of the same name in 2006 and directed by Ron Howard. *The Da Vinci Code*, among other things, posits that Jesus and Mary Magdalene are married and even have a child together (a daughter named Sarah). As a professor of biblical studies who regularly teaches courses on women in the Bible, I remember the flood of e-mails and phone calls that followed the release of Brown's book—and then a second flood after the release of the film. The faithful and faithless alike were eager to get the lowdown, the "real story" from someone like me, who might help them to "know for sure" if Dan Brown is telling the truth. Reminding people that Dan Brown is a writer of *fiction* and that his book is a *novel* did not stop the flow of questions such as Were Jesus and Mary Magdalene *really* married? Did they have a child together? Is any of what Dan Brown writes based on the Bible? If so, where?

There were some, of course, who were quite offended by the idea that Jesus was married, with a child no less! Some religiously conservative groups, journalists, preachers, scholars, and many others were quite up in arms about it all. Many boycotted the book, and later, the film, and Brown even received death threats. There were others, however, who found the notion of a married Jesus with a child interesting and plausible, if not provocative. In speaking to individuals and to groups during this time, I first reminded them that Brown's story is just that: a *story*. In my professional opinion, however, any book or film that interests or, as the case may be, infuriates people enough to actually sit down and read the Bible is a good thing.

The fact that people can have such strong reactions to books like *The Da Vinci Code* or films like *The Passion of the Christ* (2004) indicates a problem—a very real and pressing problem: the pervasive lack of biblical literacy. This is a subject I address in my book *What the Bible Really Tells Us: The Essential Guide to Biblical Literacy* (2011). Learning how to read the Bible and becoming familiar with the people, places, events, and the timeless lessons it imparts helps us to separate fact from fiction. All those people who read Brown's book or saw Ron Howard's movie and felt compelled to call me for the "real story" would not have had to do so had they been familiar with the Bible. They would have known that nowhere in the Bible does it state or even hint at the notion that Jesus is married to anyone, much less Mary Magdalene.

Most of my readers, however, are already quite familiar with the Bible, and you may be wondering at this point why I mention the problem of biblical illiteracy in a chapter about Mary Magdalene. The reason is simple: Of all the women in the Bible, with the possible exception of Eve, Mary Magdalene, who in the Gospels is depicted as a very powerful woman, is generally misunderstood and misrepresented, and biblical illiteracy is to blame. Even today, in my college classroom or when I speak to church groups, if I ask, "Who is Mary Magdalene?" invariably someone raises a hand and answers, "She was a prostitute and Jesus healed her." For centuries, Mary Magdalene has been painted as a reformed sinner and prostitute from whom Jesus cast out seven demons. This image of Mary, sketched and drawn, whittled and chiseled by countless artists, priests, and preachers throughout the ages, has served as a positive image of redemption: the fallen woman rehabilitated by Jesus. But inspiring as this sort of story may be, it is a totally false one. Mary Magdalene appears in all four of the canonical Gospels, but never once is she referred to as a prostitute, or even a sinner of any kind.

The "seven demons" Jesus casts out of her (Luke 8:2; Mark 16:9) most likely refers to a seizure disorder, like epilepsy, or any number of mental illnesses, such as schizophrenia. People during Jesus' day have little or no understanding of the etiology of neurological or mental disorders, instead attributing such maladies to demonic possession. It is likely, then, that Mary suffers from one of these disorders and that Jesus heals her.

So who is responsible for this false image of Mary as a prostitute? As I briefly mention in chapter 2, an accusing finger can be pointed at the sixth-century pope Gregory the Great, who is obviously a not-so-great student of the Bible. Pope Gregory delivered a public sermon that would for centuries confuse the stories of three completely unrelated biblical figures: Mary Magdalene; Mary, the sister of Martha, whom I discuss in some detail in chapter 1; and an unnamed female sinner from Luke's Gospel (7:37–50). The sad result of his mistake is that Mary Magdalene has been branded a repentant prostitute ever since. Had the faithful been able to actually read the New Testament for themselves, they would have recognized Gregory's blunder. Of course, during the sixth century, coupled with the high illiteracy rate, people were actually discouraged from reading the Bible because of the dangers of "private interpretation," a valid concern, but surely not the only concern. With the Bible and its interpretation securely resting in the holy hands of a select few, order and control were maintained.

Pope Gregory may have initiated the confusion, but Mary's tarnished image was perpetuated through the ages due to biblical illiteracy. In fact, it is not until 1969, the era of peace, love, and hippies, that the Catholic Church officially acknowledges Gregory's error, but even since that acknowledgment, her image as sinner extraordinaire lingers indelibly for many today. The time has come for us to discard this blemished, inauthentic portrait of Mary Magdalene and explore the truth about her.

The Bible provides no clear personal details of her age, status, or family, but here's what we *do* know. Her name, Mary Magdalene, provides us with our first real clue, suggesting that she comes from the town of Magdala, located less than 120 miles north of Jerusalem near the Sea of Galilee and mentioned in the New Testament and in certain Jewish texts. And, usually, when a town or village is mentioned in connection with a woman's name in the Bible, it indicates that she is a woman of wealth or higher social status. It is also important to mention that whenever Mary's name is mentioned along with those of other women, her name almost always appears first, a biblical convention indicating her prominence.

Magdala (Aramaic) or, sometimes, Migdal (Hebrew) is located on the western side of the Sea of Galilee between Tiberius and Capernaum. The town itself is mentioned only in the Gospel of Matthew: "After sending away the crowds, he [Jesus] got into the boat and went to the region of Magadan" (15:39). Most scholars assume that "Magadan" refers to Magdala. The town's full name is Magdala Tarichaea (roughly translated as "tower where fish are salted"), and not surprisingly, the town is known for its salted-fish industry. This detail provides yet another clue to Mary's identity. The fishing industry in ancient Israel is a highly profitable one. We know that Israel's salted fish is much sought after and that it is exported in and around the Mediterranean. Thus Magdala is probably an affluent town, and Mary, assigned the town's very name in biblical references to her, likely comes from a family of means. Interestingly, the Apostles Peter, James, and John also come from a prosperous fishing village, Bethsaida.

The Jewish historian Josephus describes Magdala as a thriving fishing village with a sizeable population. Recent excavations seem to support Josephus's description, revealing a large, prosperous Roman city including a rather lavish first-century synagogue, one of only seven synagogues unearthed in Israel that date to the time of Jesus. One of the most amazing artifacts unearthed inside this synagogue is the "Magdala Stone" probably used as a *bimah* (a large table used for reading the Torah). The stone is carved on all sides, except the bottom, and features a sculpted menorah, the oldest ever discovered in Israel.

Mary's "rich girl" status seems to be supported elsewhere in the New Testament. For example, in Luke 8:1–3, we learn that Mary is one of several women who travel with Jesus and the Twelve and who help to finance his ministry.

> Afterward, he journeyed from one town and village to another, preaching and proclaiming the good news of the kingdom of God. Accompanying him were the Twelve and some women who had been cured of evil spirits and infirmities, Mary, called Magdalene, from whom seven demons had gone out, Joanna, the wife of Herod's steward Chuza, Susanna, and many others who provided for him out of their resources. (Luke 8:1–3, NAB)

This may come as a surprise to some. But, then, how many of us have ever stopped to consider the *practicalities* of Jesus' mission? Where do Jesus and his disciples sleep, for example? How do they afford to eat? Who does their laundry? And if none of them are gainfully employed, who pays for food, lodging, and clothing for what appears to be a fairly large group of travelers? According to Luke, at least in part, Jesus' female followers help to finance his ministry.

If Mary does, in fact, come from a wealthy town and an affluent family—and our deductions to that effect would suggest that Peter, James, and John, too, come from wealthy families—then this may significantly alter the way in which we view Jesus' followers. In the ancient world, wealth equals power and social status, both of which are viewed as blessings from God. Traditionally, most of us are taught that Jesus is a poor man, from a poor family, and that his followers are mostly poor fishermen. Modern scholarship, however, indicates that Jesus and his family are hardly poor. He grows up in the Galilee, living in Nazareth and then Capernaum. The Bible describes the occupations of both Joseph and Jesus using the word *tekton*, which means they are what we would today call "construction workers." This means they might work as stonemasons, ironworkers, artisans, or any number of other specialties under the umbrella of this general designation *tekton*. It might also mean that they are carpenters, but since wood is scarce in this region, this is unlikely. Whatever their specialty (most scholars believe they are probably stonemasons), a *tekton* is a respectable occupation and not associated with being destitute or poor, but rather, middle class. Many scholars point to the city of Sepphoris, a Roman city about an hour's walk from Nazareth as evidence that Jesus and his family are not poor. During Jesus' lifetime, the city is part of an active building project instigated by Herod Antipas, and many of the workers come from neighboring towns and villages, especially Nazareth. The workers are paid well for their labors, and if Joseph and Jesus are indeed involved in this project, the young Jesus likely comes into contact with a wide range of people, including wealthy residents, Roman officials, and other workers.

Using Mary Magdalene, Peter, James, and John (followers of Jesus whom we know come from wealthy towns) as examples, let us shift our "traditional" paradigm slightly from a group of poor people following a poor preacher from town to town. What do any of these people have to lose, since they already have nothing? Now, imagine four rich and fairly powerful people who have a great *deal* to lose, who put their considerable reputations on the line in order to follow the intelligent, charismatic rabbi from the Galilee—who is from a similar social class, and so they relate to him and understand the complex teachings of the Kingdom of God. This in no way suggests that *all* of Jesus' followers are wealthy, for his ministry demonstrates that he reaches out to all sorts of people. His disciples probably mirror this and are likely a mix of rich, poor, and everyone in between. But if Mary forfeits a comfortable life in Magdala in order to follow Jesus, this possibility makes her story only more intriguing, and her discipleship more admirable.

Mary's most important role in the Gospels comes at the end of the story, during Jesus' arrest, crucifixion, and resurrection. The Gospels differ in these events, but they all agree on the fact that Mary Magdalene is there through it all. Let us consider each canonical Gospel in turn, beginning with the earliest account of Jesus' Passion and resurrection found in the Gospel of Mark, written in about 70 CE. According to Mark, Jesus is tortured, mocked, and abandoned by his followers, and he dies alone. During this tragic chain of events, however, the author mentions that there *are* some who remain with him, if at a distance.

> There were also women looking on from a distance; among them were Mary Magdalene, and Mary the mother of James the younger and of Joses, and Salome. These used to follow him and provided for him when he was in Galilee; and there were many other women who had come up with him to Jerusalem. (Mark 15:40–41)

Notice that Mary Magdalene's name comes first in Mark's litany of Jesus' female followers who stay with him during what is surely a terribly tragic time for all of them. In Mark, this is the first mention of women supporters that includes women from both the Galilee and from Jerusalem. Conversely, Luke mentions only the Galilean women near the start of Jesus' ministry, and his list of named women, other than Mary Magdalene, differs from Mark's (Luke 8:1–3). Both Luke and Mark, however speak of the women as "providing for" Jesus, which indicates financial support. The presence of the women helps to ameliorate the visceral pain the reader feels, imagining Jesus in his last horrific hours knowing that he is not alone after all. Mark narrates that Joseph of Arimathea goes to Pilate and requests the body of Jesus; his request is granted and Jesus is placed in Joseph's rock-hewn tomb; Joseph then secures the tomb by sealing it with a large stone (Mark 15:42–46). In chapter 1, I discuss first-century burial practices and note that Jewish law dictates that the dead are to be buried within twenty-four hours, and all burials take place outside the city. The body is washed, perfumed, and wrapped in linen. Joseph does not afford Jesus these basic rites but hastily wraps the body in a linen cloth before placing it in the tomb (Mark 15:42–46). During the time of Jesus, the deceased are either buried in shallow graves or, as in the case of Jesus, placed in rock-hewn tombs carved out of local limestone.

Ironically, Joseph of Arimathea is a member of the Sanhedrin, the ruling body that condemns Jesus. To counteract this somewhat negative portrayal of Joseph of Arimathea, Mark mentions that Joseph is a "Kingdom person" (Mark 15:43), which may explain why later Gospel writers view him as a secret follower of Jesus (Matt 27:57; John 19:38). More recent biblical scholarship points to a small but malignant faction within the Sanhedrin, led by the high priest Caiaphas (appointed by none other than Pilate), who condemn Jesus. Joseph of Arimathea's motive for requesting Jesus' body, according to Mark, has to do with his desire to remove the body from the cross before the Sabbath (Mark 15:42).

What do I mean when I say that Mark presents Joseph of Arimathea as a "Kingdom person"? As the Kingdom is central to Jesus' Movement—and we can assume that Mary Magdalene and most, if not all, of Jesus' followers are also "Kingdom people"—let me say a few words about it. Although I mention the Kingdom in other chapters, I understand that some readers may not be reading the chapters of this book "in order." I will therefore briefly explain what the Kingdom means in the Gospels. Jesus speaks repeatedly about the imminent arrival of the Kingdom of God, which to him is an earthly reality. Most people today assume that the Kingdom of God means Heaven, but this is not the case. For Jesus, the Kingdom is closely tied to his apocalyptic view of the end of days, which he believes is on the horizon and will usher in a new world order. This idea of a harmonious, transformed world (the Kingdom) that replaces an evil and corrupt present age is central to apocalyptic thought.

Where does the notion of the end of days (the "apocalypse") come from? Jewish and Christian apocalyptic writing is a literary genre that grows out of a period of political unrest, religious factionalism, foreign domination, and tremendous social change. There are several apocalyptic books in the Bible, including the book of Daniel, the Gospel of Mark, and, of course, the book of Revelation, but the largest body of apocalyptic writings can be found in the Jewish intertestamental literature, written during the three-to-four-hundred-year gap between the Hebrew Bible and New Testament. The Dead Sea scrolls, from Qumran in Israel—home of the Essenes, an ancient Jewish sect—and the Nag Hammadi documents from the Nile Valley (both discovered in 1947) are examples of two vast libraries that come to us from the intertestamental period, but there are hundreds more.

Of course, some scholars hold that it may have actually been the Gospel writers who are the apocalyptic thinkers and that they merely insert their thoughts about the end of days into some of Jesus' teachings. While we can never be 100 percent certain that the words we read in the Gospels are Jesus' exact words, I think we can assume that they are fairly close. And if this is the case, Jesus and his followers clearly believe that the end is near. God's reign will inaugurate a new beginning and the Jewish people will at last be free of foreign occupation (in this case, the Romans) so that the fruits of justice can flourish. It stands to reason that if Jesus and his Apostles are apocalyptic thinkers, then Mary and the other women disciples are too.

With this brief description of the Kingdom of God, let us return to Mark's Gospel. We now have Jesus' body wrapped in a shroud and placed in the tomb of Joseph of Arimathea. Only three women—Mary Magdalene; Mary, the mother of James the younger and Joses; and Salome—witness this hasty burial (Mark 15:40). After the Sabbath, the trio of women return to anoint Jesus' body with spices, and on the way, they discuss their concerns regarding the removal of the large stone that blocks the entrance to the tomb (Mark 16:4). When they arrive at the tomb, however, they find that the stone is already rolled away and Jesus' body is no longer in the tomb. Instead, they encounter a young man, dressed in white, who informs the terrified women that Jesus has been raised (Mark 16:5–6) and he instructs them to tell Peter and the other disciples that Jesus is on his way to the Galilee where they will see him (Mark 16:7). Mark's original Gospel ends with Mary Magdalene and the other women saying nothing to anyone: "So they went out and fled from the tomb, for terror and amazement had seized them; and they said nothing to anyone, for they were afraid" (Mark 16:8).

Later editors, unsatisfied with Mark's original ending, attempted two different endings, usually referred to as the "shorter ending of Mark" and, not surprisingly, the "longer ending of Mark." Mary Magdalene appears only in the latter. Most scholars agree that the longer ending of Mark was added around the second century and echoes elements from the other canonical Gospels and additional New Testament writings. In the longer ending of Mark, the resurrected Jesus appears first to Mary Magdalene, and this time, she tells "those who had been with him," but they do not believe her (Mark 16:9–11). Jesus makes another appearance to two un-identified disciples, and when they report this to the rest of the group, as with Mary Magdalene's report, no one believes them (Mark 16:12–13). The risen Jesus finally appears to the eleven and rebukes them for their lack of faith (Mark 16:14).

For our purposes, we are interested in the differing images of Mary Magdalene in both Mark's original ending and the longer ending. We must first comment on Mark's original, somewhat abrupt ending in which the women witness the empty tomb, run away in fear, and do not say any-thing to anyone (Mark 16:8). The men abandon Jesus in his hour of need and now, the women, who at least remain with him during his Passion, extinguish the one glimmer of hope that there is someone who will be courageous enough to spread the Good News and thus continue Jesus' mission after his death. This ending is in keeping with the manner in which Mark presents the Apostles throughout his Gospel: as witnesses who never seem to fully understand the coming of the Kingdom. Most scholars feel that Mark's reason for presenting the Twelve in this way is really a literary device aimed at the reader to challenge us: The Kingdom is at hand. What will *you*, the faithful reader, do about it? This abrupt ending in Mark is in concert with what always seems to me a rushed Gospel. Mark's Gos-pel conveys a sense of urgency that the author clearly feels. For Mark, the end is near, and the Kingdom is at hand, so we must act! The longer ending mitigates, to some degree, this sense of urgency. Safely removed from the fractious times in which Mark writes his Gospel, the editor or editors during the second century, with the knowledge that the Kingdom is, at present, unrealized, pen a more palatable ending that features Mary Magdalene as the first witness to the resurrection.

Moving to the Gospel of Luke, written in about 85 CE, we find that Luke, like Mark, writes that there are those who watch Jesus' crucifixion from a distance. In Luke, this includes a large, unspecified crowd that disperses after Jesus' death and certain women from the Galilee and Je-sus' "acquaintances" (Luke 23:48–49) who stand at a distance, lingering after Jesus dies. Mary Magdalene is presumably among the crowd, and though Mark specifically names her, Luke does not. As in Mark, Joseph of Arimathea requests the body of Jesus and he places it in a rock-hewn tomb. In Luke's version, Joseph of Arimathea is a member of the council that condemns Jesus, but he "had not agreed to their plan of action" (Luke 23:50–51). Luke's description of Joseph as a "good and righteous man" who is awaiting the Kingdom of God (Luke 23:50–51) is more favorable than Mark's description of Joseph as one who simply wants the body off the cross before the Sabbath (Mark 15:42). In Luke, the women from the Galilee who watch Jesus' execution from a distance are also present at his burial. They return, as in Mark's Gospel, to anoint the body after the Sabbath, and it is clear that Mary Magdalene is among them (Luke 23:55; 24:1,10). This time, the women encounter the empty tomb and *two* men in "dazzling clothes" (as opposed to Mark's "young man in a white robe") and they are terrified. The men speak to the women and remind them of Jesus' words:

> Why do you look for the living among the dead? He is not here, but has risen. Remember how he told you, while he was still in Galilee, that the Son of Man must be handed over to sinners, and be crucified, and on the third day rise again. (Luke 24:5–7).

The women return to Jesus' other followers and relate what they have seen, but they are not believed; Peter inspects the empty tomb for himself, however, and seeing the burial linens no longer attached to the body of Jesus, "he went home, amazed at what had happened" (Luke 24:10–12).

In the Gospel of Matthew, written in about 90 CE, Matthew makes reference to the women who follow Jesus from the Galilee, but Mary Magdalene is the only familiar name among the women Matthew mentions: "Mary Magdalene, Mary, the mother of James and Joseph, and the mother of the sons of Zebedee" (Matt 27:55–56) are among those who remain at the cross and bear witness to the gruesome crucifixion, while the male disciples flee and go into hiding, fearing that the authorities may arrest them because of their association with Jesus. Of course the women are seen in the company of Jesus as well, but they steadfastly remain with their friend throughout his Passion.

According to Matthew, Jesus' crucified body is removed from the cross and placed in the tomb of Joseph of Arimathea (Matt 27:57–60). Matthew notes that Joseph of Arimathea is a rich man and "a disciple of Jesus" (Matt 27:57), which supports the notion that the Jesus Movement is not a poor-man's revolution, but at the very least, a middle-class movement. Matthew notes that Mary Magdalene and the "other Mary" (presumably the mother of James and Joseph) hold a vigil at the tomb. They have just witnessed the murder of their leader and friend, and it is difficult to conceive of the pain, grief, and trauma they have endured, yet they courageously keep watch over the tomb (Matt 27:61). Both of these "Marys" return to the tomb after the Sabbath and encounter an angel in white (Matt 28:1–7). As they leave the empty tomb in "fear and great joy," something amazing happens.

> Suddenly Jesus met them and said, "Greetings!" And they came to him, took hold of his feet, and worshipped him. Then Jesus said to them, "Do not be afraid; go and tell my brothers to go to Galilee; there they will see me." (Matt 28:9–10)

Matthew concludes with Jesus' commissioning of the remaining eleven disciples (Matt 28:16–20).

In John's version of Jesus' death and resurrection, Mary Magdalene commands a more central role. She remains at the foot of the cross, along with two or three women, depending on the way in which it is read: "Meanwhile, standing near the cross of Jesus were his mother, and his mother's sister, Mary the wife of Clopas, and Mary Magdalene" (John 19:25). Some scholars insist that John is referring to three women: Mary, the mother of Jesus; her sister, Mary of Clopas; and Mary Magdalene. Others claim there are four women: Mary, the mother of Jesus; her sister (Jesus' aunt, who is unnamed); Mary of Clopas; and Mary Magdalene. The latter makes more sense, since it is unlikely that parents would name two of their daughters "Mary."

These women, whether three or four strong, are not watching from a distance, as do the women in the Synoptics. They are at the very base of the cross, and Jesus even speaks to them from the cross (John 19:26–27). As in the Synoptics, following Jesus' death, Joseph of Arimathea takes the body of Jesus and quickly wraps it in a linen shroud and lays it in a tomb. In John, Joseph is a secret follower of Jesus and is assisted by Nicodemus with the proper anointing and preparation of Jesus' body (John 19:38–40). Nicodemus is a character unique to John. He is introduced in John 3:1–21 as a Pharisee and leader of the Jews who engages in a nighttime conversation with Jesus and again in John 7:50–51, where he urges justice in the case of Jesus. His reappearance at the burial of Jesus may indicate that he, like Joseph of Arimathea, is a secret follower of Jesus.

In John, the tomb is in a garden and Mary Magdalene alone returns to the tomb while it is still dark outside and notices the rock has been moved (John 20:1). She runs to inform Peter and the unnamed "beloved disciple" and they race to the tomb; finding it empty, the two men go home (John 20:2–10), but Mary remains behind, weeping at the tomb (John 20:11). She encounters then not one but two angels who ask her why she is weeping, and she replies, "They have taken away my Lord, and I do not know where they have laid him" (John 20:13).

Just as she says this, Jesus appears, but she mistakes him for the gardener—that is, until he says her name (John 20:14–16). Why does she think Jesus is the gardener? Scholars have come up with many elaborate and some not-so-elaborate explanations for this, but the most obvious seems to be that traumatized, in a state of grief, eyes swollen with tears, and in darkness, Mary encounters Jesus. Jesus is the last person she expects to see, so she assumes he is the gardener. Who else would be in the garden at this pre-dawn hour? But when Jesus speaks her name, then she knows that this is truly her beloved friend and teacher. It is a very powerful moment, and she alone is witness to this Easter miracle.

When Mary recognizes Jesus, she exclaims, "Rabbouni!" a term that has been variously translated as "My teacher" or "My beloved teacher," but it may simply mean "Teacher" (John 20:16). She reaches out to embrace him, but Jesus says, in the original Greek of John's Gospel, *me mou uptou*, which means "Do not cling to me" or "Do not hold on to me" (John 20:17). Some New Testament scholars and scholars of ancient Greek claim that the use of the verb translated into English as *cling*—"do not *cling*"—is normally used in *Koine* Greek only in the context of an intimate embrace between husband and wife. And while some, of course, find such a line of argument specious, others feel that, taken together with Mary's prominent role in the Gospels as a disciple, this is enough to indicate a genuinely intimate relationship between Jesus and Mary Magdalene—something I will discuss further presently. One other possible explanation for the use of this verb, which seems the most plausible to me, is that the author is seeking to highlight the enormity and uniqueness of the event. Mary is, after all, encountering a *resurrected* Jesus. In any case, after her encounter with the risen Jesus, "Mary Magdalene went and announced to the disciples, 'I have seen the Lord'; and she told them that he had said these things to her" (John 20:18).

When I use the expression "intimate relationship" in reference to Jesus and Mary Magdalene, I use it in a broad sense, as there are, of course, different levels of intimacy. The word "intimate" itself ranges in meaning. It can signify familiarity (I have, for example, an intimate knowledge of my home), tenderness, affection, or even sexual intimacy. If Jesus and Mary share an intimate relationship, just how intimate are they? There are some who assert that they are lovers, or even married, and that the single reference in John 20:17 (*me mou uptou*) "proves" it. The vast majority of scholars, however, disagree.

Still, the Bible isn't the only source we have for Mary, and those who insist that Jesus and Mary are more than friends point to these other sources to fortify their claims. In 1945, at Nag Hammadi in southern Egypt, two brothers come across a large, sealed clay jar. Inside, they discover a cache of ancient papyrus books called *codices* (singular, *codex*). Papyrus, made from the papyrus plant, is a sort of ancient type of writing paper. Unfortunately, it is not very durable, and most papyri disintegrate in a matter of years, but these are fairly well preserved. The codices, all Christian in nature, were purposely hidden away in a field near what was once a monastery. As most ancient Christian texts have been lost or in some cases purposely destroyed as heretical, this discovery is exceptional. Popularly known as the Nag Hammadi Library, the discovery includes such treasures as the Gospel of Thomas, the Gospel of Philip, and the Gospel of Mary Magdalene. Most scholars agree that these are *Gnostic* texts, composed by unknown authors between the first and second centuries CE. *Gnostic* is from the ancient Greek word for "knowledge" (*gnosis*), and Gnosticism has roots that predate Christianity. The individuals or groups responsible for many of the Nag Hammadi documents constitute one of the many groups that emerge roughly around the second century CE. There are many types of "Christian Gnosticism" during this time period, and their beliefs are far too diverse and complex to fully explore here. Very simply, they believe that the essential truth of life is accessible to human beings, and knowledge of self is knowledge of God. They generally reject the various Christian dogmas that developed in the centuries after Jesus' death.

Mary Magdalene is frequently mentioned in the Nag Hammadi documents, and she is presented as one of Jesus' more prominent disciples. For example, she is included in Jesus' discussions with the other disciples, and she has a keen intellect. When the other disciples are confused or misunderstand Jesus' teachings, Mary "gets it." In the Gospel of Philip, Mary Magdalene is an important character and her relationship to Jesus is a very close one. Those who hold that Jesus and Mary Magdalene are more than simply friends and comrades often cite the following passage. The text under consideration, however, is riddled with holes, probably caused by ants. Scholars refer to these holes or gaps in the text as *lacunae*, and I have preserved the lacunae below, indicated with bracketed ellipses.

And the companion of the [. . .] Mary Magdalene [. . .] loved her more than all the disciples, and used to kiss her often on her [. . .]. The rest of the disciples [. . .]. They said to him, "Why do you love her more than all of us?" The Savior answered and said to them, "Why do I not love you like her? When a blind man and one who sees are both together in darkness, they are no different from one another. When the light comes, then he who sees will see the light, and he who is blind will remain in darkness." (Gospel of Philip 63:32–36)

Writers such as Dan Brown, whom I mentioned earlier, draw heavily on many of the Gnostic texts in creating their stories about Jesus and Mary Magdalene, and many readers assume that these Gnostic texts are actually from the Bible, when nothing could be further from the truth. We are once again confronted with the problem of biblical illiteracy, and while use of the Gnostic texts can be entertaining in the context of a novel, sometimes readers reach erroneous conclusions. By this I mean that many readers draw straight lines between certain passages in a particular novel and the Bible, assuming that what they are reading in a book of fiction is somehow biblically based. Still others conclude that if Dan Brown (or any other novelist) writes about something, then it must be true. In Brown's case, he asserts that Jesus and Mary Magdalene are a married couple with a child. Of course, those of us in the field of biblical studies have known about the Gnostic scriptures for decades; it is only when they are trotted out for the general public and sensationalized in a book or film that we see a sort of backlash. People who have never even read the Bible or any of the Gnostic texts jump to premature conclusions, in this instance, that Mary Magdalene and Jesus are more than "just friends."

In the introduction to this book, I mention the so-called Jesus Wife fragment, that tiny scrap of papyrus with writing in Coptic and dated to the fourth century CE. Harvard Divinity professor Karen King has deciphered and authenticated the text, and, like the Gospel of Phillip, the text has several gaps. Very basically (for a fuller description of the Jesus Wife fragment, refer to the introduction) the text reads, "Jesus said to them, 'My wife . . . She will be able to be my disciple . . .'" Of course, the text does not definitively state that the Jesus who concerns us even *has* a wife, and *if* he does have a wife, she is not identified.

When my students ask me what I think about all of this—that is, in my professional opinion, who I think Mary Magdalene really is—I am hesitant to answer because anything I may offer is largely conjecture. When pressed, I offer my *best guess*, based on the definitive information that we *do* have. In my opinion, I believe that Mary Magdalene is an older, wealthy widow who serves as Jesus' comrade, confidant, and friend. That she is present and bears witness to the two most pivotal events in the Gospels, Jesus' crucifixion and resurrection, demonstrates that she is a courageous and steadfast disciple. We must be mindful of the fact that during Jesus' day, it would have been socially unacceptable for a young, single woman to travel around the countryside with a group of (mostly) men; a wealthy older widow helping to provide financial support for a group of missionaries, however, would not have been out of the question.

With all of this information presented thus far—biblical, non-biblical, and archaeological—we can begin to learn more about Mary Magdalene and the central role she plays in the Jesus Movement and ultimately, in the birth of Christianity. St. Augustine (fourth century CE) calls Mary "the Apostle to the Apostles," an indication that even in the early centuries of Christianity, her role as leader and Apostle is recognized and respected. Through a careful reading of the Gospels and other sources, we have begun to recover the true image of Mary Magdalene as Jesus' trusted friend and Apostle.

> But they were grieved. They wept greatly, saying, How shall we go to the Gentiles and preach the gospel of the Kingdom of the Son of Man? If they did not spare Him, how will they spare us? Then Mary stood up, greeted them all, and said to her brethren, Do not weep and do not grieve nor be irresolute, for His grace will be entirely with you and will protect you. But rather, let us praise His greatness, for He has prepared us and made us into Men. When Mary said this, she turned their hearts to the Good, and they began to discuss the words of the Savior. (Gospel of Mary Magdalene 5:1–4)

Mary Magdalene's Enduring Lessons

As with most religious figures, Mary Magdalene is the subject of many stories, myths, and legends. Perhaps the most popular of these legends comes to us from the Middle Ages, in a book titled *The Golden Legend*, written by Jacobus de Voragine. *The Golden Legend* tells the story of Mary Magdalene's life after the death and resurrection of Jesus. According to Jacobus de Voragine, Mary lives a contemplative life as a hermit alone in a cave for thirty years and is attended to by angels. While this and other legends about Mary Magdalene are fanciful and intriguing, they point to the fact that she was a major figure in Jesus' life and remains a central figure in the Christian faith. Of course, it is not surprising that among the many stories told about her, the one that remains indelibly associated with Mary is that she was a reformed prostitute! And this fallacy points us in the direction of her most enduring lessons.

At the start of this chapter, I discussed the problem of biblical illiteracy, connecting the problem with the damaging effects that resulted from a single sermon preached by Pope Gregory the Great. Unaware that he conflates the stories of three unrelated Marys in the New Testament and mistakenly labels Mary Magdalene a penitent prostitute, he forever tarnishes the image of the second most important woman in the New Testament (the mother of Jesus occupies the number one slot in this particular category!). I purposely use the phrase "he forever tarnishes" because despite the official recognition of Gregory's blunder by the Catholic Church in 1969, the general public, many of whom dutifully practice their Christian faith, still cling to the false image of Mary as a redeemed sinner, not out of some sort of sexist malice, but out of ignorance.

In preparation for writing this chapter, I spent the better part of two years asking individuals and groups, including my own students, what they know about Mary Magdalene. Regardless of age, gender, education, or religious affiliation, the overwhelming majority of people still think that *the Bible* describes Mary Magdalene as a rehabilitated prostitute! As I mention at the opening of this chapter, biblical illiteracy is partly to blame, but there are other reasons why this negative portrayal of Mary persists. One of these reasons has to do with image. Our image refers to the way in which other people perceive us, based on the way we look, talk, walk, and dozens of other attributes that coalesce to create a perception of who we are to others. Images may be grounded in reality or they can be complete fabrications. Sometimes, people purposely cultivate a particular image; perhaps they want to go into show business, appear successful to their neighbors, sell more cars, or attract a desirable mate.

There are all sorts of reasons people seek to cultivate certain images, and make no mistake, we all do it. For example, we all have our "professional" image, that image that we show to our colleagues and coworkers. So creating a particular image is not necessarily something bad. The problem arises when others perpetuate a false image of us, which is exactly what happens to Mary Magdalene. Once this false image is created, it seems to take on a life of its own. There are countless works of art, for instance, that feature Mary Magdalene scantily dressed with her breasts exposed; some of these paintings depict her as having red hair (red hair is often connected with evil in the ancient world). There are stories, poems, songs, and countless sermons throughout the ages that help to forge this false image of Mary. The end result is that for the better part of history, she is known not as Jesus' intimate and caring friend, but as a whore!

Of course, no matter what we say, who says it matters. In many ways, Mary's sullied reputation throughout history stands as a testimony to the power of speech, particularly when the speaker is someone in a position of authority and trust, as in the case of Pope Gregory. We can argue that perhaps Pope Gregory makes an honest mistake and that he is simply confused; we could also argue that all of those paintings, poems, and sermons about "Mary Magdalene the prostitute" have one thing in common: they are grounded in ignorance. Conversely, there are those who flatly reject this stance. Indeed, there are many who feel that Mary's reputation as a prostitute has been perpetuated throughout history as a way to negate her important role in the life of Jesus and in the evolution of Christianity. This is a complicated topic, and one that could, and has been, the subject of many books. But what happened to Mary Magdalene, however it happened, is worthy of our thoughtful consideration because the way in which we present ourselves, the image we show to the world, matters. Equally important is the way in which we help to promote the image of another, through our words, thoughts, and deeds. This is the essential takeaway lesson Mary Magdalene's story imparts to us.

Our vision of Mary Magdalene as Jesus' trusted friend and Apostle teaches us a second enduring lesson: love and friendship come in many forms. The vast majority of modern readers understand this concept in theory and in practice. For example, it is not at all unusual today for men and women to be "just friends." Like most people, I have a wonderful stable of friends that is a veritable garden of diversity. The people I trust and love come from many different backgrounds and sweep the spectrum of age, race, nationality, gender, education, sexual orientation, religious affiliation, and much more. But in the restrictive, patriarchal system that governs first-century Judaism, the relationship between Mary Magdalene and Jesus falls into a wholly unique category that I refer to as "unconventional liaisons." In the male-dominated society of first-century Judea, the interactions between men and women are strictly proscribed. In general, men associate with other men and women associate with women. Jesus seems to bypass what contemporary audiences view as an oppressive and often misogynistic system, openly fraternizing with all sorts of people, men, women, saints, and sinners alike. Today, thankfully, the United States, *in general*, encourages diversity and advocates the acceptance of all people. Because of this, we often fail to grasp the magnitude of Jesus' actions and behavior. He is, in every sense of the word, a maverick when it comes to his radical acceptance of *all* people. Everyone is equal in his eyes and all are invited to sit with him at the table of the Kingdom.

In the dangerous world of oppressive Roman rule and Temple intrigue, however, one has to step lightly and choose friends carefully. With watchful eyes all around, Jesus' accepting attitude is admirable, but still, he must be careful; it is difficult to fully trust anyone outside his inner circle of friends. Even within this close-knit group, one of them, Judas, betrays him. In this context, we can assume that Mary's friendship and support probably means a great deal to Jesus. Theirs is an unconventional relationship, but not entirely unprecedented in the Bible. For example, in the Hebrew Bible, the relationship between the prophet Elisha and an unnamed woman from Shunem, referred to only as the "Shunammite woman" (2 Kgs 4:8–37; 8:1–6), represents a highly uncommon liaison. Elisha and the Shunammite woman share a friendship so deep that she has a guest room built especially for Elisha so that he can sleep comfortably during his many visits to her home. When tragedy strikes and the Shunammite woman's young son dies unexpectedly, she turns to Elisha for help. Because of their friendship, the prophet, with the help of God, resurrects the boy (2 Kgs 4:32–37).

In the New Testament, Jesus' love for his friends Martha and her sister Mary (see chapter 1) represents another example of an unconventional liaison. Jesus frequents their home and enjoys meals with the sisters, and when their brother Lazarus dies after a brief illness, we witness yet another resurrection story as Jesus brings the dead man back to life. Mary Magdalene, as part of Jesus' inner circle, shares Jesus' belief in the equality of all God's creatures and calls us to emulate this egalitarian virtue.

In the opening of this chapter, I point out that Mary Magdalene is a powerful woman who has for centuries been misrepresented and misunderstood. In simply reading her story as it appears in the Gospels, together with the dual lessons of mindfulness regarding history's erroneous image of her and the somewhat unconventional liaison between Mary and Jesus, we see her with fresh eyes. This means that we cast away the old, inaccurate image of Mary as a reformed prostitute in favor of the truth. The real Mary Magdalene serves as a role model for men and women alike. Her courage, unflinching friendship, and steadfast belief in Jesus offer us hope in this precarious and uncertain world.

6

Tabitha: Supporter

Widow's Rising

Acts 9:36–42

Now in Joppa there was a disciple whose name was Tabitha, which in Greek is Dorcas. She was devoted to good works and acts of charity. At that time she became ill and died. When they had washed her, they laid her in a room upstairs. Since Lydda was near Joppa, the disciples, who heard that Peter was there, sent two men to him with the request, "Please come to us without delay." So Peter got up and went with them; and when he arrived, they took him to the room upstairs. All the widows stood beside him, weeping and showing tunics and other clothing that Dorcas had made while she was with them. Peter put all of them outside, and then he knelt down and prayed. He turned to the body and said, "Tabitha, get up." Then she opened her eyes, and seeing Peter, she sat up. He gave her his hand and helped her up. Then calling the saints and widows, he showed her to be alive. This became known throughout Joppa, and many believed in the Lord. (Acts 9:36–42)

HE STORY of Tabitha is found in Acts of the Apostles, the second of two volumes attributed to the anonymous author known as Luke and written around 85 CE. One of the most riveting books in the Bible, Acts is often a neglected text in both the classroom and pulpit, eclipsed by the more popular Gospels, which detail the ministry of Jesus. Like the Gospels, Acts is written in narrative prose and contains a succession of stories that describes a somewhat romanticized version of the early Church. Because it is less familiar to readers than the Gospels, let me just say a few words, as a sort of prelude to our discussion of Tabitha, about the text itself, including its structure, main characters, and general themes.

Acts begins with the ascension of Jesus to Heaven and the birth of a new religion, led by the Apostle Peter. The first seven chapters present an idealized version of the early Christian community and the preaching of the Good News throughout all of Judea. These early supporters of the Jesus Movement are generally referred to as followers of "the Way" (Acts 9:2; 18:25; 19:9, 23; 22:4; 24:14, 22), or less often, as *Nazarenes* (Acts 24:5) rather than as *Christians*. Acts 8–12 focuses on preaching and events in Samaria, and the rest of the text features the spreading of the Gospel throughout the Mediterranean, ending with Paul's arrest and imprisonment in Rome. Peter and Paul are central figures in Acts. Paul (formally known as Saul of Tarsus) is a Pharisee who begins as a persecutor of the followers of the Way and then experiences a dramatic conversion event on the road to Damascus.

> Meanwhile Saul, still breathing threats and murder against the disciples of the Lord, went to the high priest and asked him for letters to the synagogues at Damascus, so that if he found any who belonged to the Way, men or women, he might bring them bound to Jerusalem. Now as he was going along and approaching Damascus, suddenly a light from heaven flashed around him. He fell to the ground and heard a voice saying to him, "Saul, Saul, why do you persecute me?" He asked, "Who are you, Lord?" The reply came, "I am Jesus, whom you are persecuting. But get up and enter the city, and you will be told what you are to do." (Acts 9:1–6)

For the rest of his life, Paul becomes a relentless missionary, traveling to various cities in the Roman Empire, founding "house churches," and converting mostly former Gentiles to the Jesus Movement. Many of these house churches are presided over by women.

Peter, on the other hand, remains largely in and around Judea and Samaria, performing miracles, evangelizing, and bringing others into the fold

(Acts 2:41; 4:4; 5:14; 6:7). Though scholars debate the historicity of much of Acts—for example, the image of Paul in Acts differs somewhat from the portrait he paints of himself in his letters—the text *does* provide a glimpse into the formation and life of the early Church and its nascent theology. Luke accomplishes this through his excellent narration and through the use of speeches—a common feature of Greco-Roman historical writing of Luke's day—purportedly from the lips of Peter, Paul, Stephen (who is the first Christian martyr), and others.

In addition to this very brief introduction to Acts of Apostles, it seems prudent to also say a few words about the "resurrection stories" in the Bible, of which Tabitha's story is one. I will give only a brief summary of these other resurrection stories, but I will refer to them as they relate to Tabitha's tale.

There are three resurrection stories in the Hebrew Bible associated with the prophets Elijah and Elisha. The first occurs when the great prophet Elijah stays at the home of the widow of Zarephath and her son, keeping them from starving in the midst of a drought by miraculously providing food for them (1 Kgs 17:14). Sometime later, the widow's son falls ill and dies and Elijah raises him from the dead (1 Kgs 17:17–23). Elijah's successor, Elisha, befriends a wealthy woman in Shunem, and when her son dies suddenly, Elisha successfully revives the boy (2 Kgs 4:32–36). Even in death, Elisha's power to resurrect the dead continues. In 2 Kgs 13:21, the burial of a dead man is underway but is interrupted by a band of marauders. As the funeral party runs for cover, the mourners hastily toss the corpse of the dead man into Elisha's grave, and "as soon as the man touched the bones of Elisha, he came to life and stood on his feet."

In the New Testament, most of the resurrection stories are found in the Gospels. During Jesus' ministry, he raises three people from the dead. In Mark, Jesus raises the deceased daughter of a Temple official, named Jairus.

> He took her by the hand and said to her, "Talitha cum," which means, "Little girl, get up!" And immediately the girl got up and began to walk about (she was twelve years of age). At this they were overcome with amazement. (Mark 5:41–42)

The story of Jairus's daughter has much in common with the story of Tabitha, which we will explore later. In any case, Jairus's daughter and Tabitha are the only two female characters to have been raised from the dead; the rest are all male.

In Luke 7:11–15, Jesus raises the son of the widow of Nain as he is being carried off for burial.

> Then he came forward and touched the bier, and the bearers stood still. And he said, "Young man, I say to you, rise!" The dead man sat up and began to speak, and Jesus gave him to his mother. (Luke 7:14–15)

This is reminiscent of the raising of the sons of the widow of Zarephath and the Shunammite woman. All three women are nameless, associated only with the town in which they live. The woman from Zarephath and the bereaved mother from Nain are both widows, and in all three stories, the dead sons are "only" sons.

Perhaps the most spectacular resurrection story in the Gospels is the raising of Lazarus in John 11. I discuss this story in some detail in chapter 1, but very briefly, Lazarus is a friend of Jesus who falls ill and dies. Jesus is on a journey when he receives the news, and returning to Lazarus's hometown of Bethany, he raises him from the dead after four days in the tomb (John 11:39–44).

Outside the Gospels, the only other resurrection stories appear in Acts. In addition to the raising of Tabitha, Paul resurrects a young man named Eutychus who falls from a window to his death after falling asleep during one of Paul's long-winded discussions (Acts 20:7–9). Talk about boring someone to death! In any case, Paul simply takes the dead man into his arms, and Eutychus comes back to life (Acts 20:7–12). Armed with this short summary of other resurrection stories in the Bible, let us now turn to the story of Tabitha.

Tabitha's story begins, oddly enough, with her death. A well-known and respected member of the community in the town of Joppa, Tabitha dies from an undisclosed illness. From the very first verse in which she is mentioned, we garner several important facts about her. First, she is referred to as a *disciple*: "Now in Joppa there was a disciple whose name was Tabitha" (Acts 9:36). Scholars are quick to point out that Tabitha is the only woman in the New Testament who carries this distinctive designation. This is not to say, however, that she is the only female disciple in the New Testament, for there are many others, including several profiled in this book, but she alone is specifically named as such. Second, she is introduced as a woman with two names, "Tabitha" and "Dorcas"; both names are usually translated as "gazelle." Commentators offer various opinions as to why Luke includes both names, but the most obvious seems to be tied to one of the over-arching themes of Acts, namely, the inclusion of Gentiles in the fledgling Christian community. "Tabitha" is her Aramaic name (Aramaic, of course, is the spoken language of the Jews during this time period), and "Dorcas" is her Greek (Gentile) name. Finally, we learn that Tabitha is "devoted to good works and acts of charity" (Acts 9:36). Her devotion and good works seem primarily directed at the plight of the local widows, or the poor in general (Acts 9:39, 41).

Luke does not narrate the length of Tabitha's illness, but it seems to be brief: "At that time she became ill and died. When they had washed her, they laid her in a room upstairs" (Acts 9:37). "At the time" seems to refer to a period of time in which Peter is in the vicinity, healing a man named Aeneas, a bedridden paralytic from neighboring Lydda (Acts 9:32–34). Such "pairing stories" featuring male and female characters are common in Luke–Acts. For example, in Luke 1:5–23, the priest, Zechariah, receives an angelic birth announcement foretelling the birth of his son, John the Baptist, while in Luke 1:26–38, the same angel, Gabriel, appears to Mary and announces the birth of Jesus.

It is significant that Luke mentions what happens to Tabitha shortly after her death. She is washed, presumably by the widows for whom she cares, and "laid in a room upstairs" (Acts 9:37). The image of the upper room is evocative, not only of the place where Jesus celebrates a final meal with his disciples, but also of two resurrection stories in the Hebrew Bible, mentioned earlier. The prophet Elijah raises from the dead the son of the widow of Zarephath (1 Kgs 17:17–24), and in 2 Kgs 4:18–37, Elisha raises the Shunammite woman's deceased son; both resurrection stories take place in an upper room.

The story of Peter's healing of Aeneas apparently reaches nearby Joppa: "Since Lydda was near Joppa, the disciples, who heard that Peter was there, sent two men to him with the request, 'Please come to us without delay'" (Acts 9:38). The identity of "the disciples" is unclear, but they appear to be members of Tabitha's community, possibly fellow disciples of a house church in Joppa. In any case, we can imagine that buoyed by the news of Peter's healing touch, they cling to the hope that perhaps Peter can use his miraculous healing powers to restore Tabitha to life. The disciples send two men to fetch Peter and he comes at once. Escorted to the upper room, Peter encounters some of the beneficiaries of Tabitha's charitable work: "All the widows stood beside him, weeping and showing tunics and other clothing that Dorcas had made while she was with them" (Acts 9:39). It is unclear why Luke chooses to use Tabitha's Greek name here, but the scene is very moving as the widows cluster around Peter, consumed with grief and loss. They clutch in their hands the garments Tabitha made for them, showing them to the Apostle, treasured objects that attest to Tabitha's philanthropy and goodness.

There is considerable debate concerning the recipients of Tabitha's charitable works. On the one hand, the specific mention of the widows might mean that Tabitha's concern is for their benefit alone. On the other hand, the widows may be one group among many who have benefited from her assistance and they are simply singled out in the story of her death. Some even speculate that the widows are professional mourners, common during this time period, who have come to cry and keen, possibly for a fee. This speculation makes sense in light of what happens when Peter arrives at the scene: greeted by the wailing widows, Peter promptly "put all of them outside" (Acts 9:40). He might consider a group of hired mourners a nuisance and dismiss them from the room in order to concentrate on the task before him. This third speculation seems less sturdy, however, when we consider Peter's behavior *after* he raises Tabitha.

> Peter put all of them outside, and then he knelt down and prayed. He turned to the body and said, "Tabitha, get up." Then she opened her eyes, and seeing Peter, she sat up. He gave her his hand and helped her up. Then calling the saints and widows, he showed her to be alive. (Acts 9:40–41)

In the manner of the prophet Elisha, who raises from the dead the son of the Shunammite woman (2 Kgs 4:32–33), Peter clears the room, prays, and then commands that Tabitha "get up" (Acts 9:40). There are also some striking similarities between Jesus' raising of Jairus's daughter and Peter's resurrection of Tabitha. Before raising the girl, Jesus encounters a mob of mourners in the girl's home and he "put them all outside" (Mark 5:40). In the same way, Peter also banishes the wailing widows before setting to work to raise Tabitha (Acts 9:40). Commentators often note that the Aramaic command Jesus gives to the dead girl, "Talitha cum" (Mark 5:41), is similar and even sounds a lot like the command Peter gives to Tabitha, "Tabitha, get up" (Acts 9:40). In both stories, a hand is extended; Jesus takes the deceased child's hand before he revives her, while Peter takes Tabitha's hand after she awakes, as if to steady her (Mark 5:41; Acts 9:41).

Having accomplished his miracle, Peter recalls the banished widows *and saints* to witness the revived Tabitha: "Then calling the saints and widows, he showed her to be alive" (Acts 9:41). There are two important things to note about Acts 9:41 that help to answer the question regarding the nature of the group on the receiving end of Tabitha's benevolence. First, the widows in question are probably *not* professional mourners. If they were professional mourners, their services would no longer be needed and Peter would not invite them back into the room after Tabitha's resurrection. Second, Luke mentions "the saints" who are also invited to witness the aftermath of the miracle of Tabitha's resurrection, but just who are "the saints"? In the New Testament, a saint is not someone who dies and is later beatified and canonized by the Church, but rather a living individual who devotes himself or herself to the worship of God. If we postulate that certain saints and widows are present when Tabitha dies, we might conclude that Tabitha's charitable works are done in conjunction with the saints and that together, they are perhaps members of one of the small house churches typical of early Christians. The mention earlier of "the disciples" (Acts 9:38) who are also somehow connected to Tabitha fortifies this supposition, as they might also be members of the house church.

All of this information, taken together, paints for us a portrait of a lively community of followers of the Way who work on behalf of those less fortunate. Tabitha's particular role seems primarily concerned with the care of widows, and Tabitha herself may also be a widow, for there is no mention of her husband, who would surely be present during her illness and death. It is precisely this sort of community that is presented as *ideal* in the beginning of Acts.

> Now the whole group of those who believed were of one heart and soul, and no one claimed private ownership of any possessions, but everything they owned was held in common. With great power the apostles gave their testimony to the resurrection of the Lord Jesus, and great grace was upon them all. There was not a needy person among them, for as many as owned lands or houses sold them and brought the proceeds of what was sold. They laid it at the apostles' feet, and it was distributed to each as any had need. (Acts 4:32–35)

Caring for those less fortunate is a biblical imperative with roots in the Hebrew Bible. "Less fortunate" refers to those who are oppressed or deprived of basic human rights. This class of people is referred to by several names, but the most common is *anawim*, from the Hebrew and meaning "bent down" or "being low." Widows and orphans are most often cited. Without the protection of a male figure, widows and children are vulnerable and often exploited. God admonishes his people to care for them (Exod 22:22–24), but there is widespread neglect and even abuse. In the Gospels, Jesus denounces such neglect. He is on the side of the needy and publicly proclaims himself as the fulfillment of Isaiah's messianic vision (Is 61:1–2).

"The Spirit of the Lord is upon me,
because he has anointed me
to bring good news to the poor.
He has sent me to proclaim release to the
captives
and recovery of sight to the blind,
to let the oppressed go free,
to proclaim the year of the Lord's favor."
And he rolled up the scroll, gave it back to the attendant, and sat down. The eyes of all in the synagogue were fixed on him. Then he began to say to them, "Today this scripture has been fulfilled in your hearing." (Luke 4:18–21)

Jesus echoes Isaiah's concern for justice and reaches out to those on the fringes, including the sick, the poor, and the outcast.

Like Jesus, Paul, a central figure in Acts, feels it is incumbent upon the faithful to provide for those less fortunate (Acts 11:29–30; Gal 2:10; Rom 15:25–27). Followers of the Way are to treat each other with fairness, generosity, and respect (Acts 2:42–47). Paul's desire to include Gentiles in the Jesus Movement (Acts 15; Gal 2:1–9) demonstrates a spirit of inclusion, a distinctive aspect of Jesus' mission: "There is no longer Jew or Greek, there is no longer slave or free, there is no longer male and female; for all of you are one in Christ Jesus" (Gal 3:28).

Tabitha and her community model Jesus' concern for those less fortunate in caring for the widows. Her ministry is a unique one and unprecedented in the Bible: a woman caring for other women in need. The love and gratitude the widows feel for Tabitha is shown in the way they grieve over her passing, something I shall delve into in more detail in the Enduring Lessons section. Peter restores Tabitha, and in his so doing, "many believed in the Lord" (Acts 9:42). One of Luke's central concerns is the way in which the Church grows, through spreading of the Gospel, the work of the Spirit, and the inclusion of Gentiles. Through Peter's miraculous intervention, a woman is raised from the dead to continue her charitable work, and others who hear of the miracle come to a new life in Christ. While Tabitha's story is usually read with an eye to the actions of Peter, we would be remiss not to appreciate the special ministry of this remarkable woman.

Tabitha's Enduring Lessons

Tabitha's story teaches us many enduring lessons, but in this section, I shall focus on only two: the nature of grief, and the miracle of resurrection. Let us begin with a discussion of the common twin foes that beset all of humankind: death and grief.

Tabitha's death prompts us to reflect upon the nature of grief and its meaning. I must preface this particular section of Tabitha's enduring lessons with a brief personal note. I have been an author for many years, and my first book was actually one I never wanted to write. *Surviving the Death of a Sibling: Living Through Grief When an Adult Brother or Sister Dies* was published in 2003, prompted by the passing of my only brother, who died after a brief illness in the prime of his life at the age of forty-three. I loved him very much, and his death devastated my family and unleashed a torrent of grief so profound, I did not think I could endure it. I consider *Surviving the Death of a Sibling* to be my seminal work, not only because it was really the first book to examine the unique experience of bereaved *adult* siblings, but also because it launched a ministry of sorts for me.

I have spoken to a variety of audiences, large and small, about the nature of bereavement (and other grief-related topics) over the many years since my brother's death; I have facilitated a grief support group for bereaved adult siblings; and I continue to write articles, conduct workshops, and occasionally teach courses about this very important topic. I even wrote another book about grief (*Grief Dreams: How They Help Heal Us after the Death of a Loved One*; 2005). My work with grieving people, particularly other bereaved adult siblings, has been one of the most rewarding experiences of my life. I have learned many things about grief, and sadly, I have experienced many more losses since the death of my brother, but my studies and work in the area of grief and loss have helped me to grow personally and spiritually.

The Bible is filled with stories of loss, suffering, death, and grief. When I teach such stories, I make certain that students do not gloss over the tragic circumstances at the center of it all, for it is their natural inclination to do just that. For example, most of my students have heard the story of Jesus' crucifixion and death so many times that they are somewhat numb to the raw realities of profound pain, horror, and the agonizing grief felt by his family, friends, and followers. When I teach this material, I try help students imagine what Jesus is going through, but also to ponder the aftermath of his death for those who loved him. With this brief preamble in mind, let us return to Tabitha's first enduring lesson.

The widows greet Peter as he arrives in Joppa and they are in a state of extreme duress. We do not know how long they have been with Tabitha;

perhaps they cared for her during her illness or maybe they learn of her death and rush to her home to console one another. The text is unclear, but they are there, with others from Tabitha's community (the saints and disciples), deep in the throes of grief. They clutch the tunics and other garments Tabitha made for them, perhaps to comfort themselves through the simple act of touching something connected to their dead patroness. Grieving people often find great comfort in such simple actions. I remember a friend, who had recently lost her father, confessed that when she and her mother were packing up her father's clothing for donation, she kept one of his shirts. "I can still smell his cologne on it," she told me. "I keep it in the back of my closet and touch it sometimes when I'm really missing him."

Many grieving people feel a sense of comfort in holding on to something concrete, like a garment, blanket, book, or brooch that belonged to a deceased loved one. This seems to be the case with the widows. The widows in Tabitha's story also feel the need to show Peter the clothing. We can almost see them proffering the tunics and other garments as they tell Peter, "Look! She made these things for us because she wanted to take care of us! Oh, how we will miss her!" It is almost as if the widows want Peter to view the tangible evidence of Tabitha's benevolence. Perhaps if he knows how much the widows need her, depend on her, and love her, he will try all the more to revive her.

The presence of the bereaved widows in this story reminds us that the experience of grief is a universal and unavoidable consequence of being human. We will all, at one time or another, feel the maelstrom of emotions that accompany the loss of someone we love. These feelings include shock, denial, anger, guilt, depression, remorse, hopelessness, profound sorrow, and much more. The widows, as far as we know, are not Tabitha's relatives, but they have surely come to care very deeply for her. They remind us that grief is not reserved for family members of the deceased alone; indeed, oftentimes those to whom we are most close are friends or colleagues. In fact, there is no mention of Tabitha's family in the story at all. The widows, saints, and disciples who are part of her community are present, however, which leads us to consider the possibility that Tabitha does not have a family beyond her community. Some scholars assert that the name "Tabitha" is actually a slave name, and they postulate that perhaps Tabitha is a former slave. We have no way of knowing this, of course, but in a very real sense, it does not matter, for it is clear that Tabitha is surrounded by people who love her and who greatly grieve her passing. I have observed that those who love deeply grieve deeply.

In the midst of the finality of death and grief, however, Tabitha's story takes a sharp turn with the arrival of Peter, and with him, a glimmer of hope. Our final enduring lesson explores the mystery and miracle of resurrection, what it means in the world of biblical antiquity, and what it means for us today. We begin by briefly looking at the differences between what the Hebrew Bible and New Testament have to say about resurrection in general. In the Hebrew Bible, the best way to summarize the prevailing wisdom regarding resurrection in ancient Israel is to quote from the book of Ecclesiastes.

> For the fate of humans and the fate of animals is the same; as one dies, so dies the other. . . . All go to one place; all are from the dust, and all turn to dust again. Who knows whether the human spirit goes upward and the spirit of animals goes downward to the earth? (Eccl 3:19–21)

The prevailing wisdom in the Hebrew Bible, in general, is that this life is the only life we have.

Though the idea that death is *the end* predominates in much of the Hebrew Bible, there are some later texts, such as the book of Daniel (164 BCE), that demonstrate a belief in the resurrection of the body and even some type of eternal judgment: "Many of those who sleep in the dust of the earth shall awake, some to everlasting life, and some to shame and contempt" (Dan 12:2).

In the New Testament, there is a different view, one that includes a resurrection of the body and an eternal life in Heaven.

> In my Father's house, there are many dwelling places. If it were not so, would I have told you that I go to prepare a place for you? And if I go and prepare a place for you, I will come again and take you to myself, so that where I am, you may be also. (John 14:2–3)

Many Christians assume that after death, our resurrection takes place in Heaven. The Bible, however, as we have seen, narrates several resurrections that take place in the earthly realm, including Tabitha's resurrection.

In all of the resurrection stories, the person dies and remains dead for a period of time until he or she is brought back to life. This leaves us with the uneasy and unanswerable question of where it is that the "temporarily deceased" go, if anywhere. For example, where *is* Lazarus while he lies dead in a tomb for four days (John 11:39) or Tabitha, who lies in her death chamber for an undisclosed number of hours or days?

The Hebrew Bible *does* mention a sort of holding place, a dark, creepy underworld called *Sheol*. In some versions of the Bible, *Sheol* is inaccurately rendered "hell," but *Sheol* is not fully developed and is not the same locale as hell. The general consensus regarding *Sheol* is that the dead dwell for a time there before simply disappearing. Is it possible that Tabitha and others who die briefly, only to be restored at a later time, linger in *Sheol?* We cannot know for certain, but they must go *somewhere*. Since none of those in the Bible who are resurrected ever speak about their experience of death, we are left to wonder.

Perhaps, though, we are missing the point in ruminating about such matters. That is, maybe we should think less about the intricacies of the temporarily dead and more about the miracle of resurrection, or for that matter, miracles in general. This brings us to a more fruitful and meaningful discussion that begins with the basic question What is a miracle? Simply put, a miracle is an extraordinary event; it is supernatural in nature and unexplainable using ordinary reasoning. The resurrection stories are perhaps the most dramatic examples of miracles in the Bible, and, as we have seen, we are at a loss to explain them. But there are also modern miracles that happen every day: people overcome illnesses diagnosed as fatal, they survive terrible accidents, or they triumph over seemingly incredible odds to succeed at something deemed impossible. Ask anyone who has ever held their newborn child in their arms, sighed in the loving embrace of a soul mate, or felt the overwhelming and certain Presence of The One, and they will tell you what a miracle looks like, feels like.

What is the function of miracles in the New Testament? The miracle stories in the Gospels point to Jesus' true identity as the Messiah, the Savior, and the Son of God. There is some confusion concerning his identity during Jesus' lifetime because, let's face it, whether you are a believer or not, Jesus is a rather amazing individual. There is certainly some animosity among some members of the Temple elite, who constantly try to trip him up on matters of the Law or expose him as a charlatan or heretic. When Jesus performs a miracle, it eliminates doubts concerning who he is, but even more than this, miracles function as a means to bring people closer to God.

In Acts, the miracle functions in much the same way as it does in the Gospels, but with a slight difference. The miracle stories in Acts bring people to faith in Jesus. When the Apostles perform miracles in Acts, they do so in the belief that Jesus is working through them. When, for example, Peter heals a lame beggar in Acts 3, the crowds who witness the lame man walking and jumping for joy cluster around Peter in wonderment. Rather than accepting the praise for himself, he instead tells the onlookers that faith in Jesus has given the lame man perfect health (Acts 3:16). According to Luke, it is Christ, then, working through Peter, who restores the lame man.

Tabitha's second enduring lesson is as powerful as the first, for through the experience of grief *and* the miracle of resurrection, we are transformed. When we lose someone we love, our task is not to somehow "get over it," because that is never going to happen. A profound loss changes us profoundly. The task instead is to envision who we have become in light of our loss. We certainly will not simply revert back to our old selves after a period of time, though this is a common misconception among the bereaved. In the darkness and desolation of grief, however, something inside us is waiting to be born. Grief experts often refer to this birthing process as "meaning making." Each of us grieves in our own unique way and each of us will ultimately make meaning out of our loss in our own way, for this is how we heal. Healing does not mean forgetting or letting go; it means transformation.

For some, starting or participating in a charity event in honor of a deceased loved one, such as an ovarian cancer awareness walk done in memory of their mother or a memorial golf tournament in memory of a brother, helps them to make meaning. For others, it may be the birth of some creative process, such as a collection of poetry, a book, or some work of art, such as the creation of the AIDS Quilt. The timetable and the path we choose for meaning making is different for all of us, but the result is the same: we are rescued from the depths of despair and transformed. This does not mean that we suddenly go skipping down the road to a happily ever after; rather, our loss is incorporated into who we have become as a result of the death of someone we love.

In the same way, Christians believe that through the miracle of resurrection we are, in a sense, reborn. In the Gospel of John, following Jesus' death on the cross, Mary Magdalene encounters Jesus in the garden but does not recognize him; in fact, she mistakes Jesus for the gardener (John 20:14–15)! Only when he speaks her name does she recognize him (John 20:16). The resurrected Jesus is somehow different, at least in appearance, from the earthly Jesus (though it's also possible that Mary Magdalene in her overwhelming grief simply fails to recognize him). Perhaps John narrates the garden event and Jesus' transformation as a means to offer Christians a glimpse at their own glorified selves, basking in the light of new life and love in Christ.

Several years ago, someone told me that when a baby is in the process of being born, she thinks she is dying. The hushed, gentle, rocking darkness of the womb is suddenly a frightening place for the child as she is squeezed and pushed downward toward an uncertain light. She emerges, and for the first time in her life, she is wet, cold, and usually screaming as her lungs painfully fill with air. Hands reach out and grab the baby, and she experiences touch for the first time. The sounds and voices, once muffled by the water world in which her every need was provided for, now seem loud and scary as she squints in the brightness of a great, white light. No wonder she is crying! Only when the baby is swaddled and given to her mother does the fear subside; held safe in the loving arms of her mother or father, the baby has been transformed, moving from her water world to the world of noise and light and love. She is not dying after all, but only entering a new phase of being. Perhaps this is what death is like for us. We may feel pain and we may struggle against it, or it may come quickly. As we leave this life, bound for the new adventure that is resurrection, like a newborn, we enter a new world, devoid of the divisiveness, judgment, and strife that mark the earthly realm, to bask in the light of God.

And so it is that this short story of a humble woman who dedicates her life to helping other women offers us the precious promise of new life. Her earthly resurrection stands as a symbol of hope for the living and consolation for those who grieve. The miracle of her life of service, her miraculous return from the dead, and the enduring love of her community in life and in death offer us calm and peace in the face of both of these realities.

Mothers, Murderers, and Missionaries

Elizabeth

Mary of Nazareth

Herodias

Pilate's Wife

Prisca

The Woman at the Well

Here I am, the servant of the Lord;
let it be with me according to your word.
(Luke 1:38)

7

Elizabeth: Mother

Angelic Gift

Luke 1:5–80

In those days Mary set out and went with haste to a Judean town in the hill country, where she entered the house of Zechariah and greeted Elizabeth. When Elizabeth heard Mary's greeting, the child leapt in her womb. And Elizabeth was filled with the Holy Spirit and exclaimed with a loud cry, "Blessed are you among women, and blessed is the fruit of your womb. And why has this happened to me, that the mother of my Lord comes to me? For as soon as I heard the sound of your greeting, the child in my womb leapt for joy." (Luke 1:39–44)

THERE ARE two things that everyone seems to know about Elizabeth: The first, of course, is that she is the mother of John the Baptist. The second is that she is somehow related to Mary, the mother of Jesus. While both of these assumptions are correct, I find it interesting that Elizabeth is remembered largely in the context of other people—in this case, her famous son, John, and her well-known relative, Mary of Nazareth. In this chapter, we will focus on Elizabeth both as an individual and as a central figure in the unfolding story of the coming of the Messiah.

Unique to the Gospel of Luke, Elizabeth's story seems strangely familiar, echoing themes and motifs found in the Hebrew Bible. We will examine these connections as we travel with Elizabeth on her remarkable journey from old age and childlessness to God's promise fulfilled in the birth of a son. Elizabeth's story is part of Luke's infancy narrative, and her unlikely pregnancy is coupled with the unusual circumstances of Mary's pregnancy and the birth of Jesus.

Only two of the four Gospels, Matthew and Luke, offer us an account of Jesus' birth; Mark and John open with an adult Jesus. Though we tend to commingle both of the so-called infancy narratives in Matthew and Luke, the stories are actually quite different. For example, Luke recounts the familiar story of the inn with no room and the shepherds in the field who receive an angelic visitation (Luke 2:8–15), but these and other details are absent in Matthew's version. According to Matthew, magi from the East follow a star that leads them to the Christ child (Matt 2:1–12), but Luke makes no mention of magi or their star. Incidentally, the Christmas carol "We Three Kings of Orient Are" and ceramic, gift-bearing figures under our Christmas trees tell us that the visitors are three wise men, but the exact number of individuals who visit the Christ child is never actually mentioned in the text (Matt 2:1–12). Most scholars believe that the tradition of three wise men arises from the three gifts mentioned: gold, frankincense, and myrrh. The Greek word *magi* (often translated as "wise men," "sages," "astrologers," or "magicians") is a plural but entirely gender-neutral noun, hence we may be talking about as few as a pair of visitors or even many visitors (male, female, or both); we simply do not know. Since Matthew does not mention Elizabeth, we shall lay aside Matthew's infancy narrative and focus on Luke's version.

Luke introduces Elizabeth as the pious and barren wife of a priest named Zechariah. A descendant of Aaron, who is the older brother of Moses and Israel's first priest, Elizabeth has an impressive pedigree. Luke further describes the elderly, childless couple as "righteous before God, living blamelessly according to all the commandments and regulations of the Lord" (Luke 1:6). Not surprisingly, Elizabeth alone is cited as "barren" (Luke 1:7). In the world of biblical antiquity, the failure to produce children is always the "fault" of the woman and male infertility is rarely, if ever, considered to be an issue. Before we proceed, let me just say a few words about "barrenness" and the way in which is viewed during biblical times.

The overwhelming majority of men and women in biblical times marry and have children, not always because they necessarily want to, but because it is expected of them. Families are the bedrock of the community, and it is a strong communal identity that allows Judaism, and eventually Christianity, to flourish. It is highly unusual for women and men to remain single, though the Bible does mention a few, including, for example, Moses' sister Miriam and the prophet Jeremiah, whom God forbids to marry (Jer 16:2). Once wed, women are expected to have many children, and each child is viewed as a cherished gift from God. It is considered unnatural not to want children, and despite a high infant-mortality rate (scholars speculate that as many as half of all children born will die before ever reaching adulthood) and great personal risk (complications during childbirth and postpartum infections are the leading causes of death for women), it is clear that most women very much want to become mothers.

While children are considered great blessings from God, infertility, or "barrenness," is seen as a terrible curse. This means that the barren woman not only feels incomplete in her expected roles as wife and mother, she is also socially ostracized, and her situation is understood as form of Divine punishment. Barrenness is a common theme in the Bible; for example, all of the matriarchs (Sarah, Rebekah, Rachel, and Leah) experience barrenness at one time or another. In fact, this type of story is so common in the Bible that scholars often refer to it as "the barren woman motif" because each story follows a predictable pattern: First, the woman is presented as barren. Second, there is an annunciation, usually through a messenger or angel, that the barren woman will become pregnant and give birth to a son. Sometimes, various attributes of the future son are given. Third, the woman (or in the case of Elizabeth, her husband) expresses disbelief or shock. Finally, the annunciation is fulfilled in the birth of a son.

The story of Elizabeth and Zechariah reminds us of Sarah and Abraham, the elderly barren couple who are the founding parents of the Jewish people. Luke's audience more than likely notes this connection and is probably familiar with other barren couples in the Hebrew Bible.

It is during Zechariah's special offering of incense in the sanctuary of the Temple that he receives an angelic visitation. The incense offering is "chosen by lot" (Luke 1:8–9) and considered to be a great honor. Alone in the most sacred place in God's Temple with a throng of people praying outside, Zechariah is terrified when an angel suddenly appears, but he must put his fears aside for the angel has an important message for him.

> "Do not be afraid, Zechariah, for your prayer has been heard. Your wife Elizabeth will bear you a son, and you will name him John. You will have joy and gladness, and many will rejoice at his birth, for he will be great in the sight of the Lord. He must never drink wine or strong drink; even before his birth he will be filled with the Holy Spirit. He will turn many of the people of Israel to the Lord their God. With the spirit and power of Elijah he will go before him, to turn the hearts of parents to their children, and the disobedient to the wisdom of the righteous, to make ready a people prepared for the Lord." (Luke 1:13–17)

This annunciation is typical in many ways of other angelic announcements in the Bible; for example, the angel proclaims that the child will be male and destined for greatness. But there are a few things about this annunciation—and the child to come—that are quite unique. According to the angel, John will be a *nazirite*. As I mentioned in chapter 2, the word "nazirite" comes from a Hebrew word that means "consecrated." Nazirites are sacred volunteers, dedicated to serve God, and although the nazirite vow (Num 6:1–21) is normally taken for a brief period of time, there are a few men, as I've noted—including the great judge Samson (Judg 13:5); the prophet Samuel (1 Sam 1:11); and, according to the angel, John the Baptist—who will observe this vow for a lifetime. As a nazirite, John is prohibited from drinking alcohol, consuming ritually unclean food, touching dead bodies, and cutting his hair. Although men or women may take this vow, there is no record in the Bible of a female nazirite, with the possible exception of Bernice (see chapter 2), the great-granddaughter of Herod the Great, who takes a religious vow that seems quite similar to the nazirite vow.

The angel, who later introduces himself as Gabriel (Luke 1:19), makes it clear that John, "with the spirit and power of Elijah," will be the *forerunner* of the Messiah (Luke 1:17; Mal 4:5–6; Matt 11:14) thus dispelling any notion that John, himself, is the long-awaited Messiah, as some may believe. John behaves and even dresses like Elijah (Mark 1:6; 2 Kgs 1:8). John's connection to Elijah is significant because in the Jewish tradition, the return of the prophet Elijah signals the arrival of the Messiah (Mal 4:5). According to 2 Kings, Elijah doesn't exactly die; instead, he is whisked away in a chariot of fire: "As they [Elijah and his protégé, Elisha] continued walking and talking, a chariot of fire and horses of fire separated the two of them, and Elijah ascended in a whirlwind into heaven" (2 Kgs 2:11). The assumption is that Elijah is taken into Heaven, which seems to be supported by text, but also by the fact that Elijah can correspond from Heaven with humans on Earth (2 Chron 21:12–15). This means that Elijah is one of two individuals in the Hebrew Bible who seem to simply disappear without actually dying; the other is Enoch, who takes a walk with God and then vanishes (Gen 5:24).

There is much folklore surrounding Elijah's dramatic departure from this world, and it somehow becomes enmeshed in a belief that God will send a Messiah to deliver the faithful from the pain and suffering of this oppressive world, while Elijah will return to Earth just prior to this event. The reappearance of Elijah is hoped for at every Passover Seder, and in most Jewish homes, the door is left ajar for the prophet to enter and a place is set for Elijah at the table. An interesting footnote to all of this is that some apparently think that perhaps Jesus is Elijah (Mark 8:28).

Elizabeth will become the mother of a remarkable son, John, whom scholars usually agree is Luke's primary focus. But is this really the case? Is Elizabeth merely a vessel who brings forth the forerunner of the Messiah? While it is certainly true that Elizabeth's central role is that of John's mother, a closer reading of the story indicates that she is much more. For instance, consider the way in which Luke contrasts Elizabeth with her husband, Zechariah. Both are described as faithful Jews, yet when Gabriel announces to Zechariah the promise of a child, Zechariah does not believe him (Luke 1:18). Because of his lack of faith, Zechariah is rendered mute until after John is born. Elizabeth, on the other hand, demonstrates more faith than her husband, who is a priest! Though advanced in years, far beyond the age of childbearing, Elizabeth does not question God but instead views her unlikely pregnancy as a gift, and she expresses gratitude to God for removing her "disgrace" (Luke 1:25). My students often frown when they read Luke 1:25 because they, like many modern readers, are offended by the notion that infertility is somehow a "disgrace." We must remember, however, that according to Elizabeth's religious worldview, barrenness is a punishment for sin, and for her, to be a sinner is a "disgrace."

The story of Elizabeth is interrupted by the story of Mary of Nazareth, whose angelic visitation parallels Zechariah's visit from the angel Gabriel. This is another example of Luke's fondness for pairing stories using male and female characters in similar circumstances. For example, in Luke 7, we have the story of Jesus curing the centurion's son followed by the raising of the son of the (nameless) widow from Nain. Luke pairs Zechariah and Mary of Nazareth in dual annunciation stories that are remarkably similar. The angel Gabriel appears to Zechariah (Luke 1:11) and then to Mary (1:26–28); Zechariah and Mary receive an unlikely birth announcement from the angel—unlikely because Elizabeth is barren (1:18) and Mary is a virgin (1:34); Gabriel announces the sex and name of the child that is to be born to Elizabeth (1:13) and then to Mary (1:31); the angel reassures both Zechariah and Mary and tells them not to be afraid (1:13, 30); both Zechariah and Mary question Gabriel regarding the improbability of a pregnancy (1:18, 34); and finally, both Zechariah and Mary receive signs confirming the angelic pronouncements: Zechariah is rendered mute until the birth of John (1:20) and Mary receives the seemingly impossible news of her elderly kinswoman's pregnancy, "for nothing will be impossible with God" (1:36–37).

Following Mary's annunciation, she goes "with haste" to visit Elizabeth (Luke 1:39). Luke links the women not only through their miraculous conceptions, but also through blood. Because Luke refers to Elizabeth only as Mary's "relative," we cannot know for certain how they are related, but most commentators suppose they are cousins. In yet another pairing—this time, it is two women—we have a beautiful story of unlikely mothers, one barren and old and the other a mere teenager of fourteen, but both become pregnant through the power of God.

Elizabeth has been in seclusion during most of her pregnancy and she is overjoyed to see the young Mary, and apparently, the unborn John is just as delighted: "When Elizabeth heard Mary's greeting, the child leaped in her womb" (Luke 1:41). Elizabeth, filled with the power of the Holy Spirit, joyfully cries out in a loud voice, "Blessed are you among women, and blessed is the fruit of your womb. And why has this happened to me, that the mother of my Lord comes to me?" (Luke 1:42–43). Elizabeth's recognition of Mary's unborn child as her "Lord" constitutes the first affirmation of Jesus as the Christ in Luke's Gospel. That she is an old, previously barren female ("disgraced") makes her proclamation even more profound and reminds us that the Lord "sets on high those who are lowly" (Job 5:11). Elizabeth endures many years of barrenness and all the attendant emotions that accompany such a condition in first-century Judaism: sadness, humiliation, social stigma, and most of all, bewilderment as to why God has forgotten her. Despite all this, however, she remains faithful (Luke 1:6). It seems only right and fitting that she is the first to recognize Mary as the mother of her Lord. Perhaps her years of suffering have brought her closer to God, as suffering so often does, and sharpened her discernment skills in recognizing the Holy Spirit at work.

Having offered her relative, Mary, two blessings (Luke 1:42), Elizabeth now offers her a third: "And blessed is she who believed that there would be a fulfillment of what was spoken to her by the Lord" (Luke

1:45). Here is something else this pair has in common: they both believe in the power of the Lord. The faith of the women contrasts sharply with the mute Zechariah, silenced because of his lack of faith (Luke 1:20).

Mary's response to Elizabeth is the famous song of praise called the *Magnificat*, or the Canticle of Mary. I will have more to say about this song in the next chapter that deals with Mary of Nazareth, but it is important to point out that there are some significant technical questions regarding the *Magnificat*, including the question about who actually sings it. Some older versions of the New Testament place the song on Elizabeth's lips, while others question whether or not the song is from the hand of Luke at all, suggesting that someone other than Luke writes it and an ancient editor inserts it here. We cannot definitively answer these questions and so, for the moment, we will assume the *Magnificat* is Mary's song of praise to God. Mary stays with Elizabeth for three months, which means that Mary is still a houseguest when John is born, though Luke does not narrate this.

The birth of John is an occasion for communal rejoicing as Elizabeth's friends and family acknowledge the mercy of God (Luke 1:57–58). Luke emphasizes Elizabeth as the central figure.

> Now the time came for *Elizabeth* to give birth, and *she* bore a son. *Her* neighbors and relatives heard that the Lord had shown his great mercy *to her*, and they rejoiced *with her*. (1:57–58; emphasis mine)

Elizabeth gives birth; *she* bears a son; *her* friends and neighbors recognize the Lord's mercy to *her* and they rejoice with *her*. The child's father is not even mentioned until eight days later, when Jewish law mandates that the infant be circumcised. The people assume that the child will be named after his father, which seems to be the custom, though history tells us that it is actually the custom at this time to name the child after his grandfather. Elizabeth remains at the center of the scene, and it is *she* who remains faithful to the stipulation regarding the child's name during the annunciation and it is *she* who corrects the false assumptions of the crowd, who assume that he will be named after his father (Luke 1:59–60).

The confused crowd turns to the still-mute father, who is not mentioned by name. His silence in this scene is striking; the child is over a week old, yet Zechariah is still without speech. Unable to talk, Zechariah must write the child's name, a confirmation of Elizabeth's firm resolve to follow Gabriel's command to name the baby John. Taking a tablet, Zechariah writes, "His name is John" (Luke 1:63). This action seems to be the magic cure for his muteness, the act of faith required to at last release his tongue. The crowd is bewildered, and as Zechariah's tongue is loosened, so too are the tongues of the witnesses to these strange events, who waste no time in spreading the news of what they have seen throughout all of Judea (Luke 1:65–66).

Though Elizabeth fades from the story once she insists that her son be named John, Zechariah is filled with the Holy Spirit and the gift of prophecy (Luke 1:67). Once again, Luke pairs Zechariah and Mary as Zechariah recites a canticle that reminds us of Mary's *Magnificat* (Luke 1:68–79). Both canticles are often linked to the Canticle of Hannah in 1 Sam 2:1–10. Hannah, like Elizabeth, experiences barrenness until God remembers her and blesses her with a son, the great prophet Samuel. Most scholars note that Luke's audience probably recognizes this connection—along with others, including allusions to the story of Abraham and Sarah—and see them as part of a seamless narrative of salvation history that begins in the Hebrew Bible and is fulfilled in the coming of Christ. Elizabeth is, in a sense, the herald of deliverance and hope for a weary world. Indeed, Elizabeth, the once "disgraced" yet ever-faithful servant of God, is not only chosen to deliver the forerunner of the Messiah, she is also the first to deliver the bold proclamation of Jesus as Lord (Luke 1:43).

Elizabeth's Enduring Lessons

Luke chooses to begin his Gospel with the familiar story of a barren woman. Though this motif is well known to Luke's first-century audience, among the many barren-woman stories in the Bible, the character of Elizabeth is unique. Earlier, I mentioned the fact that most scholars connect the story of Elizabeth and Zechariah to the story of Abraham and Sarah in the book of Genesis. While this connection is surely intentional on Luke's part, Elizabeth differs from Sarah in some very significant ways.

When we read the story of Sarah and Abraham, we learn that included in the promises God makes to them is the unlikely assurance that they will have a son (Gen 17:16). For a pair of childless senior citizens, this seems unbelievable, almost preposterous, so much so that Abraham and Sarah burst out laughing at the idea of having a child in their old age (Gen 17:17; 18:12). Of course, God's promise comes to pass and Sarah gives birth to a son, naming him Isaac, from the Hebrew meaning "he laughs." But God's promise does not immediately come to fruition, and Sarah grows impatient. She decides that it is time for her to take the matter into her own hands and devises a plan that will backfire on her. She instructs Abraham to sleep with her maidservant, Hagar, with the belief that somehow, the son born of such a union will, in a sense, be partly Sarah's. We know today, of course, that any child born to Hagar and Abraham is not biologically related to Sarah at all; but in the world of biblical antiquity, where this sort of arrangement is fairly common, there is a very real belief that the child will be related to Sarah (Gen 16:1–2).

Her plan goes terribly wrong, however, and Sarah ends up resenting the pregnant Hagar, who seems to flaunt her pregnancy. The jealous Sarah abuses Hagar so much that Hagar runs away (Gen 16:6). Instructed by God's messenger to return to her mistress (and to Sarah's abuse!), Hagar returns and gives birth to a son, Ishmael (Gen 16:7–16). Twenty-five years after God's initial promise, at the age of ninety, Sarah finally gives birth to her son, Isaac (Gen 21:1–7). After Isaac's birth, and fearing a clash of inheritance issues, Sarah banishes Hagar and Ishmael forever (Gen 21:9–10). Technically speaking, Ishmael is Abraham's firstborn son, not Isaac. This means that Ishmael assumes the rights of primogeniture and is therefore entitled to inherit Abraham's sizeable estate, as is customary during this time period. Sarah is no fool and the only way to prevent Ishmael from inheriting Abraham's wealth is to get rid of him and his mother. This is not a very flattering portrait of the matriarch, and, other than the barrenness and advanced age, Sarah and Elizabeth have little else in common.

Elizabeth endures the "disgrace" of her barrenness, but unlike Sarah, she does not try to manipulate events to remove her barrenness. Instead, she remains "righteous before God, living blamelessly according to all the commandments and regulations of the Lord" (Luke 1:6). We must assume that Elizabeth has spent the better part of her life wondering why God has withheld from her the blessings of children. We cannot help but question how she continues to maintain her faith in a God who is responsible for a lifetime of social stigma and personal longing. It is in this line of questioning that we encounter Elizabeth's most enduring lessons. Elizabeth's story is filled with lessons of hope, love, patience, and faith. I have decided, however, to focus on two key lessons: The first has to do with trust; more specifically, placing our trust in God. For Elizabeth, the second enduring lesson is uniquely tied to the first and centers on the notion of persistence, or perseverance. Elizabeth trusts in God, and even though she experiences a lifetime of barrenness, she nonetheless perseveres in her faith. As we explore these two enduring lessons—trust in God and persistence—as they relate to Elizabeth, we will also reflect upon the way in which these lessons might help us in our own lives today.

Elizabeth does not understand the mystery of God's ways any more than the rest of us, yet she remains faithful, placing her trust in God despite her disgrace. She has no way of knowing that God has great plans for her and also for the son she will bear in her old age. Sarah, on the other hand, does not completely trust in God to follow through on his promise of a son. Tired of waiting, she devises the Hagar pregnancy scheme to, in a sense, force God's hand; but this plan only brings her more misery. I suspect that most of us identify more with Sarah's strategy; that is, doing *something* is preferable to doing nothing. Elizabeth presents us with an alternative approach. Her lesson seems simple: trust in God. Unlike Sarah, Elizabeth does not connive or scheme; she simply places her trust in God and waits. She continues to practice her faith and exercises a great deal of patience, even though she does not understand why God has "disgraced" her in such a visceral way. Her approach may seem counterintuitive to many of us who prefer a more proactive stance, but it is a mistake to think that Elizabeth is doing nothing to alleviate the pain of her present circumstances. Those who place their trust in God find a great deal of comfort and solace, even in the midst of great difficulties. A wise teacher once told me that "faith" should be understood as a verb, and Elizabeth exemplifies this meaning. Luke tells us that Elizabeth lives "according to all the commandments and regulations of the Lord" (Luke 1:6). True faith does not come easy for most of us. It is like almost anything in life that is truly worthwhile: it requires a lot of practice. Elizabeth demonstrates the fruits of this practice; her faith helps to mitigate the longing for a child with the assurance that she is not alone, for God is with her. Her story helps us to understand that God's plan for us may not be the plan we have in mind for ourselves and that sometimes, as in the story of Elizabeth, God saves the best for last.

If Elizabeth's first enduring lesson has to do with trust, or more specifically, placing our trust in God, her second enduring lesson demonstrates to us the rewards of persistence. It is easy to trust in God and to persist in faith when everything is going well, but what about those times when life treats us unfairly? Many of us struggle to remain faithful during times of suffering, particularly, as in the case of Elizabeth, when there seems to be no remedy forthcoming and no end in sight. This ageless struggle is reflected in many of the Psalms, particularly those Psalms that ask the question How long, O Lord? (Ps 13:1). How long must we wait? Elizabeth does not seem to ask this question; rather, she remains steadfast in her faith, and in time, God looks favorably on her (Luke 1:25). Persistent people like Elizabeth have that unique ability to soldier on despite the obstacles, challenges, and difficulties that life sometimes throws in their path. For example, there are people who have lost their homes in fires, floods, tornadoes, or other natural disasters; those who have been wrongly convicted and incarcerated for crimes they did not commit; people who have lost loved ones though death, divorce, infidelity, or abandonment; those who live in chronic pain, either physical, emotional, or both; and people who suffer through countless other calamities that break their hearts, their bones, their bank accounts, and their spirits. Persistent people deal with life's challenges because they have mastered the art of not giving up. When they hit a bump in the road, they do not throw their hands in the air and surrender; rather, they persevere as they creatively search for solutions.

Persistent people are usually successful people, both professionally and personally, because their worldview is one that is overwhelmingly hopeful. They know that in general, we are the author of our own life. Each day, line by line, we write the script and imagine the possibilities. Of course, persistent people experience failure, disappointment, and loss just like the rest of us, but they understand failure, disappointment, and loss as temporary conditions. They know that as long as they persevere in working through a particular problem, they will eventually experience some sort of resolution. For example, in chapter 6, I mention my work in the area of bereavement. I have written two books and many articles about grief, facilitated grief workshops and taught classes on topics related to dying, death, and mourning. Of the many bereaved persons I have met and worked with during the past fifteen years, I have observed that persistent personalities, in general, traverse the complicated landscape of loss with an openness to the process, and anyone who has ever experienced the death of someone they love knows that grieving certainly is a *process*. Persistent people tend to recognize that each individual grieves in his or her own way; and, I have noticed that they are less likely to get "stuck" in one phase of grief or another (often termed "complicated" grief). The majority of participants in the grief group I facilitated were persistent people, which makes a great deal of sense considering the fact that persistent people are probably more likely to seek out a support group in the first place. What stands out most in my mind, however, is that these persistent people were able to envision a time when they would be able to cherish their sibling's memory (the group was for bereaved adult siblings) without feeling the profound sorrow of their present circumstances.

When we think of persistence in terms of faith and the way in which Elizabeth perseveres in her faith despite the fact that God has withheld from her the blessing of a child, we can't help but think of what persistence in faith means in our own lives. Faith, for most of us, requires perseverance. A faith-filled life does not just happen; it must be cultivated and nourished, through such things as prayer and good works. This sort of faith, grounded in trust, will not fail us when it is tested by the inevitable challenges that come into our lives.

In Elizabeth's movement from a barren woman to a woman filled with joy, the twin lessons of trust in God and persistence in faith appear before us like flowers in full bloom. When we read that she is chosen in her old age to give birth to John the Baptist, a child who will grow up to be a good and holy man, we recall the many years of Elizabeth's longing and disgrace. Elizabeth shows us that even in the twilight years of our lives, wonderful, miraculous things can happen to us if we place our trust in God and persevere in faith.

8

Mary of Nazareth: Mother

Jesus' Mom

Matthew 1–2; 12:46–50; 13:54–56; Mark 3:31–35; 6:3;
Luke 1–2; 8:19–21; 11:27; John 2:1–12; 6:42; 19:25–27;
Acts 1:14

A nd Mary said,
"My soul magnifies the Lord,
and my spirit rejoices in God my Savior,
for he has looked with favor on
the lowliness of his servant.
Surely, from now on all generations will
call me blessed;
for the Mighty One has done great things
for me,
and holy is his name.
His mercy is for those who fear him
from generation to generation.
He has shown strength with his arm;
he has scattered the proud in the
thoughts of their hearts.
He has brought down the powerful

from their thrones,
and lifted up the lowly;
he has filled the hungry with good
things,
and sent the rich away empty.
He has helped his servant Israel,
in remembrance of his mercy,
according to the promise he made to our
ancestors,
to Abraham and to his descendants for ever." (Luke 1:46–55)

Mary OF NAZARETH is often regarded as the most important woman in the New Testament and in all of Christianity. Despite her wide appeal and recognition, it is surprising that the New Testament actually has very little to say about Jesus' mother. Much of what we *think* we know about Mary actually comes from sources outside the New Testament, as is the case with many of the women profiled in this book.

Perhaps the most important text outside of the Bible in which Mary of Nazareth is mentioned is the Infancy Gospel of James, sometimes referred to as the Protevangelium of James (Pr Jam). The earliest manuscript containing the Infancy Gospel of James can be dated to around the third century, but most other manuscripts were written much later, generally between the tenth and sixteenth centuries. The Infancy Gospel of James contains legends and stories about Mary, including the identity of her parents, Anna and Joachim, who are not mentioned at all in the New Testament. The text also contains stories of Mary's miraculous conception, her birth, childhood, marriage to Joseph, and the virginal conception and birth of Jesus. While most scholars (me included) do not consider the Infancy Gospel of James to be an authoritative source for information about Mary of Nazareth, we cannot disregard it entirely. In this chapter, I will refer to it with great caution, largely as it relates to references of Mary in the canonical Gospels.

Before we begin, I feel that it is necessary to clarify the two main reasons why I refer to the mother of Jesus as "Mary of Nazareth." First, depending upon how you count them, there are between seven to ten Marys in the New Testament, which is not surprising considering "Mary" is the most popular female name among Jewish women living in first-century Judea. Most scholars agree that roughly one in five women are named Mary (in Hebrew, *Miriam* or *Miriamne*), so my first reason is a practical one: "Mary of Nazareth" distinguishes this Mary from the other Marys in the New Testament. The second main reason I refer to her as Mary of Nazareth has more to do with the way I have come to know her over the many years, and especially, more recently. I have thought about her, studied and researched her life, lectured about her, and, if I am being totally honest here, prayed to her. My understanding of Mary of Nazareth as a remarkable woman is not confined to her very important role as the mother of Jesus. Indeed, I have come to know her as an intelligent, faith-filled, and extraordinarily courageous woman in her own right. I have mentioned elsewhere in this book that when a woman's name is mentioned in connection with a town or village (for example, Mary of Magdala, aka Mary Magdalene), this is the Bible's way of letting the reader know that the woman is special; perhaps she is wealthy, socially prominent, highly regarded, or sometimes, all three. Referring to Jesus' mother as Mary of Nazareth is my way of acknowledging her specialness as we begin to view her both as the mother of Jesus and as an impressive individual in her own right.

Mary of Nazareth is the second of two mothers presented in this second part of the book, "Mothers, Missionaries, and Murderers." We will examine her role as she appears in three pivotal scenes in the Gospels, the first of which is in the so-called infancy narratives found only in Luke and Matthew. (The other two Gospel writers, Mark and John, begin their stories of the life of Jesus with an adult Jesus about to embark on his earthly ministry.) The second important scene, common to all the Synoptic Gospels, occurs when Jesus' family hears rumors that Jesus has "gone out of his mind" (Mark 3:21). Apparently, Jesus' preaching irritates a few of his neighbors who knew him before his ministry, and some hostilities arise. Mary is among a small contingent who attempt to bring him home and defuse the situation (Mark 3:31–35; Luke 8:19–21; Matt 12:46–50). The third crucial scene in which Mary appears is during Jesus' crucifixion. There is great deal of confusion in the Gospels regarding exactly who is present at the crucifixion, largely due to the fact that there are several women named Mary. Scholars continue to argue about the identities of these Marys, especially in the Synoptics, but John's Gospel is very clear about the presence of Jesus' mother during his crucifixion (John 19:25–27).

In addition to these three pivotal appearances, Mary of Nazareth is mentioned in several isolated instances, including an incident in Luke when Mary and Joseph accidentally leave the young Jesus behind at the Temple during one of the family's pilgrimages to Jerusalem (Luke 2:41–51). Mary is also present during the wedding feast at Cana alongside Jesus, a story that is unique to John's Gospel (John 2:1–12), and there is a brief reference to Mary in Acts, where she is featured in the company of many of Jesus' followers in the aftermath of his death (Acts 1:14).

With this brief introduction in mind, let us take a closer look at Mary of Nazareth, beginning with the infancy narratives in Luke and Matthew. Mary is a pious, young Jewish girl living with her family in the village of Nazareth, located in the southern part of a region known as the Galilee. She is a virgin and engaged to a man named Joseph, from the house of David (Luke 1:26–27). Her life is like that of most young women during this time period, and so far, there is nothing that would set her apart from her peers. Mary can look forward to a very predictable future: she will marry, have children, maintain her household, and rear her children in the Jewish tradition. In an instant, however, Mary's predictable and insulated world vanishes, and into this very ordinary life, something extraordinary happens.

According to Luke, God sends the angel Gabriel, the same angel who visits Zechariah in Jerusalem to announce the birth of John the Baptist (Luke 1:11–19), to visit Mary in Nazareth. Luke's version of Mary's birth announcement and pregnancy is entwined with that of her kinswoman, Elizabeth (the subject of chapter 7), but Mary's reaction to the sudden appearance of the angel is quite different from Zechariah's astonished reaction. Whereas Zechariah is "terrified; and fear overwhelmed him" (Luke 1:12), Mary is described as only "perplexed" (Luke 1:29). Zechariah, a priest, expresses doubt and skepticism when the angel reveals that Elizabeth will give birth to a son. Because of his lack of belief, he is rendered mute for the duration of Elizabeth's pregnancy (Luke 1:18–20). When Mary questions Gabriel concerning the feasibility of her conceiving and giving birth to a son given the fact that she is a virgin (Luke 1:34), instead of being rendered mute like the incredulous Zechariah, she has her questions answered and receives an offer of proof.

> The angel said to her, "The Holy Spirit will come upon you, and the power of the Most High will overshadow you; therefore the child to be born will be holy; he will be called Son of God. And now, your relative Elizabeth in her old age has also conceived a son; and this is the sixth month for her who was said to be barren. For nothing will be impossible with God." (Luke 1:35–37)

Convinced that the angel and his announcement are the real deal, Mary of Nazareth submits to the Lord, thus demonstrating her obedience to God (Luke 1:38).

Following the annunciation, Mary sets out on a journey "with haste" to visit her relative Elizabeth (Luke 1:39). The angel offers the elderly Elizabeth's pregnancy as a sort of confirmation that all of this is really happening, and Mary wastes no time in ratifying the facts. It is unclear just how Mary and Elizabeth are related, but as I mention in chapter 7, most commentators suppose they are cousins, though Luke does not expressly state this. Luke makes Mary's journey seem like a brief excursion into the Judean hills: "In those days Mary set out and went with haste to a Judean town in the hill country" (Luke 1:39), but having spent a great deal of time in Israel myself, I can attest to the fact that this is no easy trip, particularly for a pregnant woman. Mary's home in Nazareth is about ninety miles from the town of Ein Karem, the home of Elizabeth. The terrain is rocky and difficult to traverse. We can assume that Mary travels by donkey, but

Luke does not provide the details of her mode of transportation and so it is entirely possible that she walks. It is unlikely that she travels alone, but again, Luke is silent on the question of whether or not she has traveling companions. In any case, she probably travels between eight to ten miles per day, making this about a ten-day journey. Even for a healthy teenager (Mary is about fourteen), the trip is a challenging one.

When Mary arrives at Ein Karem (the town's name means "spring of vineyards," and the town is known for its terraced vineyards), she greets Elizabeth and the child in Elizabeth's womb "leaped for joy" (Luke 1:41, 44). Mary responds with the *Magnificat* (Luke 1:46–55), a canticle that closely resembles Hannah's hymn in 1 Sam 2:1–10 (I shall have more to say about the *Magnificat* in the Enduring Lessons Section). Mary remains with Elizabeth for three months and then returns to Nazareth (Luke 1:56).

According to Luke 2:1, shortly before Jesus' birth, Caesar Augustus orders a worldwide census that requires all the people to return to the place of their birth in order to be counted. Since Joseph is from Bethlehem, he takes the very pregnant Mary with him to comply with the census (Luke 2:1–5). Most scholars are quick to point out that there is no evidence outside Luke to support a census at this time, but it is entirely possible that locally, perhaps, a census is conducted. In any case, the rest of the story is well known among most Christians: Bethlehem is crowded to the rafters with people registering for the census and thus there are no available accommodations for travelers like Mary and Joseph. Mary and Joseph take refuge in a stable, during which time Mary goes into labor and gives birth to Jesus; she then wraps the child to keep him warm, and settles him in a feeding trough, or manger (Luke 2:5–7). Alerted to the birth of the Messiah by a heavenly host of angels, some local shepherds make their way to the stable: "So they went with haste and found Mary and Joseph, and the child lying in the manger" (Luke 2:16). The shepherds convey their fantastic tale of angels filling the night sky to others, including Mary, and she "treasured all these words and pondered them in her heart" (Luke 2:19).

Luke reminds us that Mary and Joseph are religious Jews who faithfully circumcise Jesus eight days after his birth (Luke 2:21) and then present him at the Temple. While at the Temple, they encounter a holy man named Simeon, to whom "it had been revealed . . . by the Holy Spirit that he would not see death before he had seen the Lord's Messiah" (Luke 2:26). Simeon blesses the little family and then, with prophetic authority, he speaks only to Mary.

"This child is destined for the falling and the rising of many in Israel, and to be a sign that will be opposed so that the inner thoughts of

many will be revealed—and a sword will pierce your own soul too."
(Luke 2:34–35)

Luke does not record Mary's reaction to Simeon's sober prophecy, but we can imagine that some of it might be troubling news for the young mother to hear. Given the circumstances of Jesus' conception and birth, followed by Simeon's confirmation of Jesus as the Messiah, Mary must surely know that her son is no ordinary infant. His destiny, however, is far in the future, and Mary must attend to the day-to-day needs of her baby. Following Jesus' presentation at the Temple, the family returns to Nazareth, and thus Luke's version of the infancy narrative comes to a close (Luke 2:39). Luke's introduction of the young Mary of Nazareth offers us an insight into a unique sort of first-century female. She is pious, obedient to the will of God, discerning, independent, and brave—qualities she will need in the months and years that lie ahead.

Matthew's infancy narrative differs significantly from Luke's version of events. In Luke, Mary is a central figure who boldly questions the angel, Gabriel, decides on her own to travel a long distance to visit her relative Elizabeth, and, though hugely pregnant, courageously travels to Bethlehem with Joseph and gives birth unassisted in a stable! In Matthew's version of events, Mary of Nazareth is a secondary character; the focus is instead on her betrothed, Joseph. Matthew begins in a very straightforward manner.

Now the birth of Jesus the Messiah took place in this way. When his mother Mary had been engaged to Joseph, but before they lived together, she was found to be with child from the Holy Spirit. Her husband Joseph, being a righteous man and unwilling to expose her to public disgrace, planned to dismiss her quietly. But just when he had resolved to do this, an angel of the Lord appeared to him in a dream and said, "Joseph, son of David, do not be afraid to take Mary as your wife, for the child conceived in her is from the Holy Spirit." (Matt 1:18–20)

The unwed and pregnant Mary presents a problem for her righteous husband, Joseph, but it is an even bigger problem for Mary. If Joseph rejects her, the penalty for premarital sex is death by stoning (Deut 22:13–21). Before we proceed, however, a brief clarifying note regarding first-century Jewish marriage customs seems in order. Matthew writes that Mary and Joseph are *engaged* but that they do not yet live together (Matt 1:18); later, he refers to Joseph as Mary's *husband* (Matt 1:19). Is Joseph Mary's fiancé or her husband? During this time, a Jewish marriage is a three-step process, beginning with the engagement. The couple's parents arrange most marriages, often when the future bride and groom are mere young-sters. Long engagements are not unusual and are, in fact, the norm. A year before the actual marriage ceremony, the couple is considered betrothed; they do not yet live or sleep together, but this second step is binding and the only way out at this point is either through divorce or death. The final phase of marriage is the actual ceremony, at which point, the couple enjoys all of the rights of marriage, including cohabitation and sexual relations. Mary and Joseph are in that one-year period of betrothal when Mary becomes pregnant.

Unlike the angel in Luke, the angel in Matthew's version is unnamed. Matthew's angel appears in a dream to Joseph, which is quite different from Gabriel's face-to-face appearance to Mary in Luke. Like Mary, Jo-seph is pious and obedient; the angel tells Joseph, who is from the house of David, to marry his betrothed, and he obeys, thus making Mary, and by extension Jesus, also a member of the house of David (Matt 1:24). Mat-thew, writing for a primarily Jewish audience, is concerned with connect-ing Jesus with Jewish messianic expectations; namely, that the Messiah is from the house of David and that he is born in Bethlehem, the hometown of King David (Mic 5:2; 1 Sam 16:1–13).

Matthew is the only Gospel that includes the story of the wise men (or *magi*) and their quest to find the Christ child after following a star from the East (Matt 2:1–2). Unfortunately, they make a stop in Jerusalem to ask for directions and word gets back to King Herod that there is a newborn King of the Jews (Matt 2:3–7). I have discussed Herod the Great on sev-eral occasions in this book (see for example chapter 2) and will therefore say only a few words about him here. Herod the Great rules Roman-occupied Judea from about 37 to 4 BCE. His engineering and political prowess are unrivaled for the time period, but so too is his reputation for brutality and paranoia. Highly susceptible to rumors, when Herod learns of a potential threat to his throne from the newborn Messiah in Bethle-hem, he wants very badly to get his hands on the infant Jesus. He asks the magi to return to him once they locate the child so that Herod may go to him and "pay him homage" (Matt 2:8).

Following their star, the magi find Jesus and Mary in Bethlehem: "On entering the house, they saw the child with Mary his mother; and they knelt down and paid him homage" (Matt 2:11). Warned in a dream not to reveal the whereabouts of Jesus, the magi return to their country, ignoring Herod's request that they report back to him regarding the whereabouts of Jesus (Matt 2:12, 8).

Once again, in a series of dreams, Joseph is told what to do. Herod, seeking to destroy Jesus, orders the massacre of all the children of Bethlehem two years old or younger (Matt 2:16). Warned, again in a dream, Joseph takes Mary and Jesus to Egypt for safekeeping (Matt 2:13–15). Upon Herod's death, once more an angel appears to Joseph in a dream and commands him to bring the child and his mother back to Judea, and Joseph brings the little family back home, settling them in Nazareth (Matt 2:19–23).

Matthew's Mary is a one-dimensional version of the woman presented in Luke. Gone is the animated, thoughtful, and intelligent woman from Luke's Gospel who boldly questions Gabriel and who daringly travels through the hill country on a ten-day trek to the home of Elizabeth. In Matthew's infancy narrative, Mary never utters a word and Matthew often neglects to mention Mary by name, referring to her instead as "the child's mother" (Matt 2:13,14, 20–21). Both Gospels agree on key points, such as the power of the Holy Spirit (Matt 1:18, 20; Luke 1:35), the virginal conception (Matt 1:23; Luke 1:34–35), and the recognition of Jesus as Savior (Matt 1:21; Luke 1:32–33). In our attempt, however, to get a sense of what Mary of Nazareth is *really* like, Luke's infancy narrative helps us to better understand Mary as a person, alongside and apart from her role as Jesus' mother.

Aside from the infancy narratives in Luke and Matthew, there is only one other story about Jesus' childhood in the New Testament. The story is brief, but it offers us a wonderful opportunity to witness Mary dealing with a twelve-year-old Jesus. As is their custom, Mary and her family travel from Nazareth to Jerusalem to celebrate the Passover feast. The brief mention of this trip as something that Mary does every year alerts us to two important details about Mary (Luke 2:41). First, as I have already noted, Mary is an observant and religious Jew. It is not uncommon during this time period, *for people who can afford it*, to travel with friends and neighbors to Jerusalem to celebrate the various Jewish festivals. Traveling, then as now, is expensive. It is clear from Luke that Mary regularly makes the roughly 90- to 120-mile journey to Jerusalem with her relatives and friends from Nazareth (Luke 2:41–44), which brings us to our second important detail about Mary: she is *not* poor. The standard portrait of Jesus, his family, and his disciples implies poverty, but this is likely *not* the case. I discuss the probable economic status of Jesus and his followers in some detail in chapter 5, and there I question the common belief that Jesus and his disciples are all poor people. And if we believe Luke, then Mary of Nazareth is not poor either. In fact, according to the Infancy

Gospel of James, Mary's father, Joachim, is an exceedingly wealthy man (Pr Jam 1:1).

When Mary and her family travel to Jerusalem, they travel as part of a large group. It is likely that the strong, younger men lead the pack, vigilant with their spears and keen eyesight, on the lookout for robbers, snakes, and other possible calamities that might cause problems for the group. The elderly, the infirm, and the children, who might move a bit slower then the rest of the pilgrims, bring up the rear. In other words, families do not necessarily remain together as they travel. Children, for example, prefer to be with other children and likely play together and enjoy the trip under the watchful gaze of dozens of adoring grandparents. Mary and Joseph do not worry about the welfare of Jesus, for he is traveling with his neighbors, people who know, love, and care for him. When the group of pilgrims assembles to return to Nazareth, Mary and Joseph assume that Jesus is in the rear, with the other children; but he is not. He has instead decided to stay behind at the Temple.

> When the festival was ended and they started to return, the boy Jesus stayed behind in Jerusalem, but his parents did not know it. Assuming that he was in the group of travellers, they went a day's journey. Then they started to look for him among their relatives and friends. (Luke 2:43–44)

Unable to locate Jesus, Mary and Joseph return to Jerusalem and spend *three* days searching for him. We can only imagine the worry and fear Mary and Joseph feel as they search in vain for Jesus. When they finally find him, Jesus is in the Temple "sitting among the teachers, listening to them and asking them questions. And all who heard him were amazed at his understanding and his answers" (Luke 2:46–47).

When Mary sees Jesus, she is no doubt relieved, but also "astonished" (Luke 2:48). Mary does not care that the precocious Jesus is holding his own in the company of wise teachers, and her emotions burst forth as she scolds him: "Child, why have you treated us like this? Look, your father and I have been searching for you in great anxiety" (Luke 2:48). When Jesus responds to her, saying, "Why were you searching for me? Did you not know that I must be in my Father's house?" Mary and Joseph do not understand (Luke 2:49–50). It is interesting to contrast Mary's use of the word "father," an apparent reference to Joseph, with Jesus' use of the word; it is almost as if Jesus is correcting her, reminding her of his *true* father. The scene concludes with the family's return to Nazareth, and Luke notes that Mary "treasured all these things in her heart" (Luke 2:51). After the initial fear and shock of losing Jesus and the anxiety of searching for him, Mary puts all of that aside and she is able to treasure the memory of her son in the house of his Father.

The next story featuring Mary appears in various versions in all three of the Synoptic Gospels. Jesus' ministry is underway, and news reaches his family that Jesus has "gone out of his mind" (Mark 3:21). Jesus' siblings and Mary appear on the scene and attempt to bring him home (Mark 3:31–35; Luke 8:19–21; Matt 12:46–50).

> Then his mother and his brothers came to him, but they could not reach him because of the crowd. And he was told, "Your mother and your brothers are standing outside, wanting to see you." But he said to them, "My mother and my brothers are those who hear the word of God and do it." (Luke 8:19–21)

Most of the scholarly conversation about this relatively uneventful scene centers on the identity of the purported siblings. I use the word "purported" here because there are many opinions concerning the identity of the individuals who show up alongside Mary. There are several instances in which they are named, either singularly (Gal 1:18–19) or in a group (John 2:12; 7:3–5; Acts 1:14). In Mark, when Jesus is teaching in the synagogue in his hometown, people think he is a "smarty-pants" and rudely question his identity: "Is not this the carpenter, the son of Mary and brother of James and Joses and Judas and Simon, and are not his sisters here with us?" (Mark 6:3). Matthew's version of the same event differs slightly: "Is not this the carpenter's son? Is not his mother called Mary? And are not his brothers James and Joseph and Simon and Judas? And are not all his sisters with us?" (Matt 13:55–56). Before I discuss the men and women who accompany Mary, it is important to note the manner in which the two Evangelists refer here to Jesus. In Mark's version, written in about 70 CE, he calls Jesus "the carpenter" and makes no mention of Joseph, referring to Jesus only as "the son of Mary" (Mark 6:3). Matthew, writing some thirty years later, calls Jesus "the carpenter's son" and calls his mother "Mary" (Matt 13:55).

Some scholars claim that referring to Jesus as "the son of Mary" is a first-century insult and insinuates that he is illegitimate. Others contend that Mark's use of the phrase in the context of what is happening in the text alludes to the fact that Mary is a widow. While we have no way of knowing if this phrase is intended to be an insult, we do have ample evidence to support the idea that Mary is a widow. There is a tradition in many texts outside of the New Testament, including the Infancy Gospel of James, that Joseph is an old man and a widower with grown children when he marries Mary (Pr Jam 8:13). The New Testament itself seems to indicate that Joseph dies when Jesus is still a youngster for he drops out of sight after the incident in the Temple when Jesus is twelve years old (Luke 2:41–51). At the wedding feast at Cana, when Jesus turns water into wine, Mary is in attendance, but Joseph is not mentioned (John 2:1–11); neither is he present during Jesus' crucifixion when Mary is remanded to the care of the beloved disciple, something that would not be necessary if Mary had a living husband (John 19:25–27).

In returning to the scene under consideration, in general, there are five main arguments regarding the identity of the individuals who accompany Mary and their relationship to Jesus. The first argument contends that James, Joseph (Mark uses his nickname, "Joses," which is like our use of the nickname "Joey" for someone named Joseph), Judas, and Simon are, in fact, Jesus' brothers and that Jesus also has at least two sisters (the plural form for "sister" is used in both Mark and Matthew). This assumption is supported by Mark's and Matthew's use of the Greek word for brother, *adelphos* (plural, *adelphoi*) and the Greek word for sister, *adelphē* (plural, *adelphai*). Other commentators deny this assumption and argue that sometimes the Greek words for brother and sister are used to mean cousin (argument number two); therefore, the individuals in question are actually Jesus' cousins. There is, however, a Greek word for cousin, *anepsios*, and it is not used in Mark 6:3 or Matthew 13:55–56. The third argument asserts that the siblings are actually Jesus' stepbrothers and sisters, the children of Joseph by a previous marriage or marriages. Since life expectancy for men is much higher than for women during this time period, it is not at all uncommon for widowers to remarry two or three times. If this is the case with Joseph, Jesus' stepsiblings would be older than Jesus and therefore would have the right to essentially tell him what to do. This explains their presence on the scene; they have come along with Mary to tell Jesus that he must return home. Birth order is strictly observed, and younger siblings or stepsiblings would not take it upon themselves to dictate the behavior of an older brother or sister.

A fourth argument is perhaps the most simple. Some commentators hold that the words "brother" and "sister" are used for people who are not necessarily one's sibling. A good example of this is the use of the word "brethren" (Rom 12:12, KJV). Even today, I often hear my male students greet one another, using the term "brother" when they are simply friends.

The last argument I will mention here (for there are many more!) is the fact that in John's Gospel, Jesus commends the care of his mother to the beloved disciple (John 19:26–27). As I mentioned earlier, it is clear by this time that Mary is a widow, and if this is the case, why would Jesus place Mary in the care of a non-relative if Mary has other children?

Let's return to the scene. Mary hears rumors about Jesus (Mark 3:21) and believes he may be in danger. She is a concerned parent who is likely worried about Jesus' safety, and with good reason. Luke mentions that people in Nazareth are outraged with Jesus' teachings and try to hurl him off a cliff (Luke 4:29–30)! Once again, Mary is fearless as she ventures into potentially hostile territory to check on the welfare of her son.

The final, pivotal scene that specifically mentions Mary is during Jesus' crucifixion. The Synoptic Gospels do not specifically identify Jesus' mother among the retinue of women who remain with Jesus during his crucifixion. John, however, is quite explicit.

> Meanwhile, standing near the cross of Jesus were his mother, and his mother's sister, Mary the wife of Clopas, and Mary Magdalene. When Jesus saw his mother and the disciple whom he loved standing beside her, he said to his mother, "Woman, here is your son." Then he said to the disciple, "Here is your mother." And from that hour the disciple took her into his own home. (John 19:25–27)

John mentions four women at the cross: Jesus' mother, his aunt (Mary's unnamed sister), another Mary who is the wife of Clopas, and Mary Magdalene. Mary of Nazareth is mentioned first, occupying the central place among the women. In addition to the three Marys present at the cross is a mysterious figure known only as the "beloved disciple," to whom Jesus bequeaths his mother. There is a long-standing tradition that the beloved disciple is the Apostle John, but many scholars reject this supposition and put forth other contenders for the role, including some of the other Apostles, Jesus' friend Lazarus, and even Mary Magdalene. The truth is, we simply do not know the identity of the beloved disciple and it must therefore remain a mystery. In this final scene, we witness the strength of Mary's character, as a woman and as a mother.

Roman crucifixion is a particularly brutal form of execution designed not only to inflict extreme pain, but also to humiliate the individual and his family. The Romans also consider crucifixion a type of deterrence, and bodies of the crucified are often left on the cross for days and even weeks, serving as grotesque warnings to potential troublemakers. Fearing that they might suffer a similar fate, Jesus' male disciples disperse and go into hiding shortly after his arrest; most of Jesus' female followers, however, remain with him, including his mother.

Mary's presence at such a frightening and traumatic event is difficult to imagine. Her beautiful son is beaten, bruised, and bleeding. She stands by, helpless in the face of Jesus' suffering, and must watch as he slowly dies before her eyes. John situates her at the foot of the cross, close enough to hear Jesus speak. In the midst of this horror, this unfathomable tragedy, Mary draws on the wellspring of faith that has always guided her life; she remains steadfast and courageous when most of us would likely flee or collapse in fear and grief. Her presence, her strength, and, most of all, her deep love for her son help Jesus in his hour of greatest need. This is the Mary that we have come to know: determined, faithful, and brave.

Mary of Nazareth's Enduring Lessons

Before I began to write a single word about Mary, a friend asked me what I planned to say about her. Before I could answer, she added, "Is there anything about her that hasn't already been said?" In conducting research for this chapter, I had to agree with my friend in that people have written about Mary of Nazareth from just about every possible angle. Mary is the most worshipped and venerated woman in all of Christendom. Countless stories, paintings, icons, sculptures, and songs about Mary abound; what more could I add?

Later that same day, I reread every passage that features or refers to Mary of Nazareth in the New Testament. I spent time thinking about the meaning of the stories and why the authors decided to include them in the first place. I took off my scholar's cap and simply read the words. While we can never be completely certain that the stories of Mary, written a generation or two after the fact, accurately reflect the events of her life, we do know that traditionally, her character is well known among the earliest Christians. For me, the simple act of rereading what the four Evangelists say about Mary has given me a greater insight into who she is as a person, and I have infused these insights throughout this chapter. She is consistently presented as intelligent, courageous, faithful, determined, and contemplative. As a mother, she is loyal, strong, fearless, loving, and protective.

Of the many enduring lessons Mary imparts to us, I have chosen to focus on only two. The first enduring lesson is really an attempt to answer the question What does it mean to say yes to God? That is, what can we learn from Mary's decision to submit to the will of God? The second enduring lesson explores the meaning of courage and the way in which it can enrich and quite literally change our lives. I have often described Mary of Nazareth as a woman of great courage; as we look at her life, can *we* learn how to live life more courageously?

As we embark on the first enduring lesson, let us return for a moment to the infancy narrative in Luke. Gabriel appears to Mary with an announcement that she will conceive a child through the power of the Holy Spirit. The one thing that we often miss in this story is the fact that Mary has a choice; she can tell the angel to go away, that she is not interested, or she can say yes to God. Recall that Mary does not immediately say yes; first, she asks, "How can this be, since I am a virgin?" (Luke 1:34). To Mary, to anyone, this seems impossible. The angel must explain how it will be done.

> The Holy Spirit will come upon you, and the power of the Most High will overshadow you; therefore the child to be born will be holy; he will be called Son of God. (Luke 1:35)

We have no way of knowing how long it takes for Mary to come to a decision, but the text seems to indicate that she is pondering the matter. As if sensing her deliberations, Gabriel offers her a sign.

> And now, your relative Elizabeth in her old age has also conceived a son; and this is the sixth month for her who was said to be barren. For nothing will be impossible with God. (Luke 1:36–37)

After some consideration, Mary says yes: "Here am I, the servant of the Lord; let it be with me according to your word" (Luke 1:38). Notice the words Mary uses here. When she says yes to God, Mary humbles herself to serve God. In much the same way, on the eve of Jesus' crucifixion, while praying on the Mount of Olives, Jesus prays, "Father, if you are willing, remove this cup from me; yet, not my will but yours be done" (Luke 22:42). Interestingly, an angel also visits Jesus: "Then an angel from heaven appeared to him and gave him strength" (Luke 22:43). Both Mary and Jesus submit to the will of God, even as God's will is unclear.

What does it mean for Mary to serve God? When she travels to see Elizabeth, she recites a canticle that very much resembles Hannah's song in 1 Sam 2:1–10.

> "My soul magnifies the Lord,
> and my spirit rejoices in God my Savior,
> for he has looked with favor on
> the lowliness of his servant.
> Surely, from now on all generations will
> call me blessed;

for the Mighty One has done great things
for me,
and holy is his name.
His mercy is for those who fear him
from generation to generation.
He has shown strength with his arm;
he has scattered the proud in the
thoughts of their hearts.
He has brought down the powerful
from their thrones,
and lifted up the lowly;
he has filled the hungry with good
things,
and sent the rich away empty.
He has helped his servant Israel,
in remembrance of his mercy,
according to the promise he made to our
ancestors,
to Abraham and to his descendants forever." (Luke 1:46–56)

The *Magnificat* is the longest oratory uttered by a woman in the entire New Testament, and I am always surprised that it was not excised by the Roman censors, under whose watchful eyes all of the Gospels were composed. Mary's *Magnificat* tells us a great deal about what it means *to Mary* to say yes to God. Perhaps the most important thing to note in Mary's sudden outburst of song is the idea of reversals: the lowly will be elevated; the haughty will be scattered; powerful rulers will fall; the hungry will be fed; and the rich will walk away penniless. These are some powerful ideas, but they are ideas that Jesus repeatedly speaks about during his ministry when he proclaims the coming of the Kingdom of God. Remember that Jesus is an apocalyptic thinker who believes that the present age is coming to an end and a new world order is about to unfold. In the Kingdom, there will be no more war, no more suffering, no more grief; peace and harmony will reign in God's Kingdom.

Jesus' beliefs about the coming of the Kingdom are shared by many; indeed, Mary's people have waited a long time for the Messiah, the one who will rescue Israel from the clutches of the Roman Empire and liberate them so that all people may enjoy a new life in the Kingdom. Mary's song is not an example of some sort of passive piety, but a powerful call to active resistance against tyranny and oppression. Jesus' Apostles and disciples share Jesus' vision of this new world, and we have every reason to believe that Mary, herself, is a Kingdom person. This assumption is clear in the words of the *Magnificat* alone, but many scholars maintain that Mary of Nazareth is an active participant in Jesus' ministry. Her presence, along with Jesus, at the wedding feast at Cana (John 2:1–12); her arrival on the scene when Jesus' authority is questioned (Mark 3:31–23; Luke 8:19–21; Matt 12:46–50); and her powerful presence at the foot of the cross (John 19:25–27) indicate that Jesus' mother is also one of his disciples. According to Acts, following Jesus' death, Mary of Nazareth remains an active part of the post-resurrection community, awaiting the arrival of the Kingdom.

> Then they returned to Jerusalem from the mount called Olivet, which is near Jerusalem, a Sabbath day's journey away. When they had entered the city, they went to the room upstairs where they were staying, Peter, and John, and James, and Andrew, Philip and Thomas, Bartholomew and Matthew, James son of Alphaeus, and Simon the Zealot, and Judas son of James. All these were constantly devoting themselves to prayer, together with certain women, including Mary the mother of Jesus, as well as his brothers. (Acts 1:12–14)

Mary of Nazareth teaches us that saying yes to God is something that is proactive. We stand up to be counted among those who are on the side of the needy, the downtrodden, the poor, and the afflicted. When we say yes to God, we are saying yes to an active pursuit of justice; we are saying yes to a faith-filled life; and we are saying yes to God's plan for us, even when we do not understand just what that plan may entail. But saying yes to God does not automatically make our lives easier. Doing the right thing, treating others fairly, and loving our enemies are just a few examples of Jesus' teachings that many find difficult. When I removed my scholar's cap and simply reread Mary's story, I remember thinking how much her life changed once she said yes to God. Before she said yes to God, Mary could count on a relatively mundane and safe life. She would have married, had children, and lived a life of relative comfort. But Mary made another choice, one that changed the course of her life and the course of human history.

As we reflect upon Mary's choice to say yes to God, we cannot help but admire her courage at such a young age—which brings us to Mary of Nazareth's second enduring lesson: the true meaning of courage and the way in which it can change our lives. As we begin to think about all of this, let us return to the annunciation scene in Luke's Gospel. Most of us are so familiar with this story that we fail to sufficiently engage our imaginations, thus missing the shocking nature of this unprecedented event. When I discuss this story with students, I first ask them this question: "What would you do if you were sitting alone in your room, and out of nowhere, an angel suddenly appeared?" Most admit that they would be terrified; some state that they would probably scream or try to run away. At the very least, they would call for help. But Mary does none of these things; in fact, although she is "perplexed" (Luke 1:29), she is unafraid. She listens, contemplates, and then says yes, knowing that there is a distinct chance that she might lose Joseph and face a possible death by stoning (Deut 22:13–21). Making my students aware of the possible consequences of saying yes to God in this situation, I then ask them, "How many of you would say yes?" Very few hands are raised in affirmation.

This is the first example of Mary's great courage, which is evident throughout the Gospels. Other examples include her impromptu and dangerous journey to visit Elizabeth (Luke 1:39–56); her daring escape into Egypt by night under the murderous threats of King Herod, who seeks to destroy her infant son (Matt 2:13–14); her trip into hostile territory in an attempt to rescue her son and bring him home when she learns of rumors that threaten his safety (Mark 3:31–35; Luke 8:19–21; Matt 12:46–50); and her presence at the foot of the cross during Jesus' crucifixion (John 19:25–27). Even her involvement in the Kingdom movement requires a great deal of courage. Mary's Roman oppressors do not look kindly on those who proclaim that a new world is on the horizon, ruled not by maniacal Roman emperors, but by God.

Demonstrating courage does not mean that we are not afraid; in fact, courage is often defined as doing the right thing in the face of fear or danger. There are dozens of passages in the Bible that adjure us to not be afraid.

> The LORD is my light and my salvation;
> whom shall I fear?
> The LORD is the stronghold of my life;
> of whom shall I be afraid? (Ps 27:1)

Mary seems to be courageous by nature, which is probably one of the reasons why God chooses her in the first place. I find it noteworthy that Mary's courage is, in one way or another, always connected to her son. This speaks to a universal reality among mothers: even the meekest woman will quickly rise to the occasion and demonstrate great courage when her child is threatened.

Mary speaks to us today and calls us to live life courageously. Her actions inspire us to release the old fears that hold us back from living a fuller, more purposeful life. Remember that courageous people are not necessarily fearless; rather, they are people who push past their fears and embrace a new way of being in the world. Whether you are a person who resists change, or someone who believes that they will never find true and lasting love, or someone who is dealing with physical or emotional pain, Mary of Nazareth, whose life is filled with much suffering, teaches you and all of us to be courageous as we cope with the inevitable pain that enters every human life. This, of course, is not easy to do; but Mary's courage, grounded in faith, serves as a model for us, helping us to persevere even when we grow weary with the effort.

Many years ago, when my daughter, Annie, was about five years old, she became obsessed with Mary. She loved it when we would drive past a house with a statue of Mary in the front yard, something that is fairly common in southern New England where my daughter grew up. She had a Mary keychain, a glow-in-the-dark figurine of Mary, and even a little purse with an image of Mary of Nazareth on the front. She loved to hear stories about her, sang songs about her, and asked me endless questions about her. The Mary she loved and admired then was not the Mary she would later read about in school and hear about in sermons at church. In her five-year-old imagination, Mary was a beautiful young woman who wore a blue dress and held the baby Jesus in her arms. My little girl is a grown woman now, but Mary still holds a special place in her heart. Like my daughter, the Mary I thought I knew is much different from the Mary I know today. Mary of Nazareth is a complex compilation: She is the thoughtful teenager who carefully deliberates before committing to something big (Luke 1:34). She is the loving mother and visionary disciple who looks forward to the arrival of the Kingdom and a world free of pain and strife (Luke 1:46–55). And, finally, she is the courageous woman whose life is forever changed the moment she says yes to God.

9

Herodias:
Mother and Murderer

Off with His Head!

Mark 6:17–18; Matt 14:1–11; Luke 3:19–20; 9:7–9 NAB

Herod was the one who had John arrested and bound in prison on account of Herodias, the wife of his brother Philip, whom he had married. John had said to Herod, "It is not lawful for you to have your brother's wife." Herodias harbored a grudge against him and wanted to kill him but was unable to do so.

Herod feared John, knowing him to be a righteous and holy man, and kept him in custody. When he heard him speak he was very much perplexed, yet he liked to listen to him. She had an opportunity one day when Herod, on his birthday, gave a banquet for his courtiers, his military officers, and the leading men of Galilee. Herodias's own daughter came in and performed a dance that delighted Herod and his guests. The king said to the girl, "Ask of me whatever you wish and I will grant it to you." He even swore [many things] to her, "I will grant you whatever you ask of me, even to half of my kingdom." She went out and said to her mother, "What shall I ask for?" She replied, "The head of John the Baptist." The girl hurried back to the king's presence and made her request, "I want you to give me at once on a platter the head of John the Baptist." The king was deeply distressed, but because of his oaths and the guests he did not wish to break his word to her. So he promptly dispatched an executioner with orders to bring back his head.

He went off and beheaded him in the prison. He brought in the head on a platter and gave it to the girl. The girl in turn gave it to her mother. (Mark 6:17–28)

OF ALL THE WOMEN in the New Testament, perhaps none is more reviled than Herodias. Credited as the mastermind behind the beheading of John the Baptist in two of the four canonical Gospels, Herodias is depicted as vengeful, manipulative, brutal, and cruel. A quick glance at her infamous family tree gives us little reason to doubt the negative commentary about her, but as always, there is more than one way to read her story.

Herodias is the granddaughter of Herod the Great (74–4 BCE), the infamous evil king who orders the "slaughter of the innocents" in Matthew's Gospel (2:16). I have referred to Herod the Great and members of his family in previous chapters, particularly in chapter 2, but I will offer a fuller treatment of the infamous family here, in the context of Herodias. King Herod can be best described as a sociopathic genius. A gifted engineer and builder, he is responsible not only for the expansion of the Second Temple but many other building projects, including the desert fortress of Masada; the fortress near Bethlehem aptly named the Herodium, which some archaeologists believe to be his tomb; the Antonia fortress in Jerusalem; and the port of Caesarea Maritima. In addition to his success as a builder, he is a politically savvy diplomat whose support of Rome results in his appointment as King of Judea in 40 BCE. Herod's genius, however, is eclipsed largely by his brutal self-interest and pernicious paranoia, and he destroys anyone who threatens his absolute power, including members of his own family. Herod executes one of his wives, Miriamne I (Herodias's grandmother), whom he apparently truly loves, in a fit of jealousy. Years before, he murdered Miriamne's grandfather, Hyrcanus, whom Herod felt was a threat to his throne, and Miriamne's brother, Jonathan, a mere youth and all of seventeen. Herod orders Jonathan to be drowned because of the boy's popularity among the people as a priest. It would seem that Miriamne has good reason to despise her husband, and, according to Josephus, despise him she does.

Miriamne nonetheless has five children with King Herod: two daughters, and three sons. The youngest son dies while he is away at school in Rome. The remaining two sons, Alexander and Aristobulus, the latter of whom is Herodias's father, harbor a deep contempt for their father for murdering their mother and do little to hide their feelings. The King's paranoia makes him highly susceptible to rumors about Alexander and Aristobulus, whom he fears will betray him, so he has them executed. After her father's death, King Herod raises Herodias until his own death, some three years later.

Before he dies, Herod the Great arranges the marriage of Herodias to his brother, her uncle, Herod II, sometimes referred to as Herod Philip

I or, less frequently, Herod Beothus. The Gospels of Mark and Matthew refer to husband number one simply as Philip, but most scholars feel that this erroneously confuses Herod II with his half-brother, Philip the Tetrarch, who is sometimes referred to as Herod Philip II. If all of this seems a little confusing, that is because it *is* confusing! The Herods are a complicated family, and we have conflicting historical reports and conflicting biblical accounts about them. In this chapter, I will try to keep things as simple as possible concerning the Herodian dynasty, which is not to be confused with the Herodian political party mentioned in the Gospels (Mark 12:13). While our focus remains fixed on the actions of Herodias, it is nonetheless important to know something about her family as it helps us to understand what motivates her. Indeed, it seems that in the case of Herodias, the proverbial apple does not fall far from the dysfunctional family tree.

When Herod the Great dies, he divides his territories among his three surviving sons and they each become the ruler or *Tetrarch* of a particular area. The title *Tetrarch*, meaning "the ruler of a quarter," is somewhat perplexing given the fact that we are talking about three sons, not four. There are various explanations and theories surrounding the use of the term *Tetrarch* in the Gospels, the most plausible of which is that over time, the term *Tetrarch* is used loosely, more as an honorific or as a synonym for "king," a term sometimes used when referring to Herod Antipas (Mark 6:14, 22, 25–26), another of Herod the Great's sons, by wife Malthace.

The Jewish historian Josephus records that Herodias and Herod II have a daughter, Salome. In some texts, the daughter is referred to as Salome, but in others, she bears her mother's name, Herodias. For our purposes, we will assume that her name is Salome and we will refer to her biological father as Herod II. I have and will continue to rely on Josephus quite a bit in this chapter, but remember that Josephus is a Jewish defector to Rome, so we must view Josephus's history with equal amounts of credulity and suspicion. His description of the Herodian Family Dramas is generally considered to be quite reliable, however, and he is enormously helpful in filling in some of the gaps in Matthew, Mark, and Luke regarding Herodias's story.

According to Josephus, Herod II's brother (who, of course, is also named Herod!) falls in love with Herodias. The brother is usually referred to as Herod Antipas, Tetrarch of Galilee and Perea. Herod Antipas is an interesting individual, possessing all of the unsavory character traits of his father, minus his father's genius. Most readers remember Herod Antipas as the Herod whom Jesus calls "that fox" (Luke 13:32) when he learns that Antipas is seeking to apprehend him. Also in the Gospel of Luke, following Jesus' arrest, Pilate sends Jesus to Herod Antipas for another trial (Luke 23:6–16).

In any case, we must question whether or not this is a story of "true love" between Herodias and Antipas. Many scholars are suspicious of Herodias's motives and view her as an opportunist, eager to trade in her less-successful husband for the more powerful Antipas. We may never know her exact motives, but we do know that there are a few glitches in their scheme to marry, not the least of which is the most obvious: Herodias and Herod Antipas are already married to other people. Herodias, of course, is married to Herod II, and Josephus tells us that she divorces him in order to marry his brother. Antipas's situation is apparently more delicate. His politically sensitive marriage to Phasaelis, the daughter of the Nabatean King Aretas, preserves a fragile alliance between the two rulers. When Antipas divorces Phasaelis in order to marry Herodias, King Aretas is not too pleased with the situation. In fact, he is so furious that a war between Antipas and Aretas ensues in which Aretas is the victor.

Of course, Herodias is a woman accustomed to getting what she wants, and she finally gets her man. But even when Herodias gets what she wants and weds Antipas, her husband's half-brother, who is also her uncle, their problems are far from over. According to Jewish law, their marriage is considered incestuous: "If a man takes his brother's wife, it is impurity; he has uncovered his brother's nakedness; they shall be childless" (Lev 20:21). It is this blatant disregard for the Law that prompts John the Baptist to condemn their union. John's denunciation of their marriage sets into motion a torrent of events that results in his beheading. With this brief synopsis in mind, let us take a closer look at Herodias and compare what the Synoptic Gospels have to say about her.

According to Mark, written in about 70 CE, Herod Antipas hears of Jesus' many wondrous deeds and ponders the local gossip about Jesus' "true" identity.

> King Herod heard about it, for his fame had become widespread, and people were saying, "John the Baptist has been raised from the dead; that is why mighty powers are at work in him." Others were saying, "He is Elijah"; still others, "He is a prophet like any of the prophets." (Mark 6:14–15)

Suffering from a guilty conscience because he is the one who orders the execution of John the Baptist, Antipas is convinced that Jesus is a resurrected John (Mark 6:16), which is a rather intriguing assumption given the fact that Jews generally do not believe in reincarnation. Matthew is in agreement with Mark in that Antipas believes that Jesus is a resurrected John the Baptist, but Matthew goes a bit further. In Matthew, Antipas attributes Jesus' "powers" to the fact that the beheaded John now lives in Jesus (Matt 14:2). In Luke, written in about 85 CE, Antipas is aware of what some are saying about Jesus—that he is a risen John, or Elijah, or one of the prophets (Luke 9:7–8)—but Antipas does not seem to suffer from the guilty conscience described in Mark, nor does he agree with what others are saying about Jesus' identity. In Luke, Antipas seems more interested in simply meeting Jesus (Luke 9:9). Interestingly, Luke makes no mention of Herodias in his brief version of events (Luke 9:7–9), which is a bit puzzling considering his low opinion of the Herods. In any case, because Luke does not include Herodias in his narrative of the events surrounding the beheading of John, we shall confine our inquiry to Mark and Matthew, comparing and contrasting what each has to say about the circumstances of John's death and Herodias's role in it. I have chosen to use the New American Bible (NAB) in this chapter for all New Testament references because I feel it is the best English translation of Herodias's story.

Both Mark and Matthew give the reader a backstory of the events leading up to the gruesome murder of the Baptist; consequently, this is also where the reader is first introduced to Herodias. As I have already mentioned, John the Baptist upbraids Antipas for his incestuous marriage to Herodias (Mark 6:18; cf. Matt 14:4), and we must assume that John is probably making a very public pronouncement against the couple's unlawful marriage. Such a public airing of her dirty laundry infuriates Herodias probably as much as the couple's blatant disregard of the Law offends the religious sensibilities of many of Antipas's subjects.

According to Josephus, "Herodias took upon her to confound the laws of our country, and divorce herself from her husband while he was still alive, and was married to Herod [Antipas], her husband's brother" (*Antiquities* 18.5). Josephus's description of the event, among other things, calls into question the overall legality of Jewish divorce. Josephus seems to indicate that it is forbidden for a woman to divorce her husband, but is this really the case? While it is true that passages in the Hebrew Bible seem to indicate that only men can initiate divorce (Deut 24:1–4; Jer 3:8), documents uncovered from a Jewish military outpost in Elephantine, Egypt (sixth to fourth century BCE) clearly show that Jewish women not only initiate divorce but also retain the possessions they bring to the marriage after the divorce. Additionally, the Elephantine documents reveal that there are even special provisions in cases involving abuse. We might conclude that perhaps the pious majority may shun divorce, but Herodias is nonetheless able to legally divorce her first husband, and she does. For

John the Baptist, it is her *remarriage* to Antipas that seems to be the more serious offense.

Josephus's statement is equally confusing when he asserts that Herodias divorces her first husband "while he was still alive." Are we to assume that women are allowed to divorce only dead husbands? That would make no sense. But what does Josephus mean when he writes that Herodias divorces her husband "while he was still alive"? This may be a vague reference to the Jewish law of levirate (Deut 25:5–10), which decrees that a surviving brother must marry his dead brother's widow, should the brother die childless. The levirate law further stipulates that the firstborn son between the brother's widow and the surviving brother will be recognized as the son of the dead brother, with all of the rights and privileges afforded a firstborn son, including the rights of inheritance. Perhaps Josephus's words "while he was still alive" are intended to highlight the fact that this is *not* a situation that requires the law of levirate, the only instance when a woman is permitted to marry her husband's brother, but is instead a willful disregard for the Torah's injunction against such a union.

Returning to Mark and Matthew's Gospels, in Mark we find Herodias so outraged at John's very public exhortation regarding the legality of her marriage that she wants to kill him: "Herodias harbored a grudge against him, and wanted to kill him but was unable to do so" (Mark 6:19). Mark's statement seems odd; if Herodias wants to have the Baptizer killed, why doesn't she simply arrange for his execution? This would have been within her means as Antipas's queen and totally in keeping with her family's tendency to kill anyone who gets in their way. Mark provides us with the answer: her husband fears John, and although he does confine the Baptizer to prison in an effort to silence him, Antipas recognizes that John is a holy man and therefore protects him (Mark 6:20). Moreover, according to Mark, "When he [Antipas] heard him, he was very much perplexed, yet he liked to listen to him" (Mark 6:20). Mark seems to be saying that Antipas is captivated by John's charisma, even as the Baptizer's teachings are beyond the Tetrarch's grasp. Perhaps this is Mark's way of distancing Antipas from his wife's grudge, for in Mark's version of events, Herodias's intractable hatred is contrasted with her husband's almost affable curiosity regarding John.

In Matthew, however, it is *Antipas* who wants to execute John, and the only thing he fears is a possible riot of those who consider John a prophet (Matt 14:5). Absent is any mention of Herodias's grudge or Antipas's passing interest in anything the Baptist might have to say. Matthew, whose audience is primarily Jewish, is interested in making connections to the Hebrew Bible. In Matthew, John the Baptist evokes images of Israel's great prophets who must contend with despotic kings like Antipas. The vast majority of scholars also assert that Matthew uses the story of John the Baptist as a means to foreshadow Jesus' unjust arrest and subsequent execution at the hands of Pontius Pilate.

In Mark, shutting up the Baptizer in prison is obviously not enough for Herodias. We can almost see her, clenching her fists and pacing the floor as she nurses her grudge against her accuser. Both Mark and Matthew agree that the tides of fate suddenly turn in her favor when Antipas throws for himself what appears to be a stag birthday party (Mark 6:21; Matt 14:6). During the celebration, Salome surprises her stepfather/great-uncle and his cronies with a dance (Mark 6:21–22; Matt 14:6). We do not know what sort of dance she performs, but we *do* know that it impresses Antipas so much that he swears an oath to give the girl whatever she asks including half of his kingdom (Mark 6:22–23; Matt 14:6–7).

Commentators seem to be of two minds when it comes to this dance. Some (the minority) argue that Salome is probably a young girl when she performs her dance and that Antipas's praise should be understood in the context of a proud parent. Those who reside in this camp rightly argue that as a Herodian princess, it is unlikely that Salome would provide "party entertainment" for a group of men. Slave girls or professional dancers, many of whom are prostitutes, usually provide this sort of entertainment. Others (the majority) argue that Salome is a young woman whose erotic dance fans the flames of lust in Antipas and his party pals—so much so that he offers her anything her heart desires. We do not know the age of Salome at the time of her dance and we have no description of the type of dance, though some commentators believe it may be the Dance of Seven Veils, an ancient sort of striptease dedicated to the fertility goddess Ishtar. Others suggest that it may be a sort of ballet with pantomime that tells a story, a type of dance popular in Rome around this time period, but all of this is merely conjecture. Neither the Bible nor Josephus provides a clue regarding the dance itself; we have only the giddy, reckless reaction of an aroused Antipas. His reaction, if taken seriously, requires us to dismiss the notion that Antipas is reacting as a "proud parent" because his "little girl" entertains his party guests with an adorable dance and side with the commentators who assert that Salome's dance is likely a sensual one.

After her dance, Salome exits the adulation of Antipas and his party guests to seek her mother's advice.

She went out and said to her mother, "What shall I ask for?" She replied, "The head of John the Baptist." The girl hurried back to the

king's presence and made her request, "I want you to give me at once
on a platter the head of John the Baptist." (Mark 6:24–25)

Mark affirms that Herodias is not in the room during the dance, but Salome knows just where to find her. When she asks her mother, "What shall
I ask for?" (Mark 6:24), Herodias does not need time to ponder: "The
head of John the Baptist" (Mark 6:24). Mark notes that Salome immediately rushes back to the party, and curiously, her request is even more
gruesome than her mother's. Not only does she ask for the head of John
the Baptist, she further stipulates that the execution take place "at once"
and that the severed head of John *be served on a platter* (Mark 6:25).

Matthew omits many of the details in Mark, though the outcome
is still the same: John is beheaded and his head is served on a platter. In
Mark, Herodias is clearly in another room, perhaps watching her daughter dance from a distance. Following the dance, Salome rushes from the
banquet room to her mother. In Matthew, there is no rushing back and
forth; Salome is merely "prompted by her mother" (Matt 14:8) to request
the head of John. Is Herodias an invited party guest in Matthew's version?
It is impossible to tell, but if she is, then she is a blatant witness to her
daughter's dance. Salome's request for John's head in Matthew differs only
slightly from Mark's version.

"Give me here on a platter the head of John the Baptist." (Matt 14:8)

"I want you to give me at once on a platter the head of John the
Baptist." (Mark 6:25)

Not wanting to renege on his oath, which in the ancient world is binding, Antipas, though "deeply distressed," *promptly* dispatches a soldier to
behead the Baptist (Mark 6:26–27), thus following Salome's command to
execute John "at once" (Mark 6:25). Matthew follows Mark with Antipas
honoring his oath and guests. Antipas is simply "distressed" in Matthew,
and although Matthew leaves out the urgency of Salome's request, omit-
ting the words "promptly" and "at once" (Mark 6:26–27), the beheading
takes place forthwith (Matt 14:9–10). In both Matthew and Mark, the
head of the Baptist is given to Salome on a platter and she then presents it
to her mother (Matt 14:11; Mark 6:28).

As we read this story carefully, it seems almost too seamless. The
dance, Antipas's reaction, and the dialogue between mother and daughter
raise suspicion. Specifically, is it possible that the dance is part of a carefully constructed plot between mother and daughter to get the head of the

Baptist on a platter? Could Herodias anticipate her husband's reaction to the dance? We can't help but imagine that perhaps Herodias and her daughter have conversations about John the Baptist and his humiliating accusations concerning Herodias's marriage to Antipas. The ease of the discussion between mother and daughter following the dance and Salome's added demands in Mark of an *immediate* execution and ghastly request that the head be presented on a platter lead us to wonder if perhaps Herodias and Salome have discussed this before. It is possible that Salome is also embarrassed by John's public denunciations of her mother's remarriage or, at the very least, maybe she sympathizes with her mother's desire to have him killed so as to permanently silence him. Moreover, perhaps the plot takes shape with the announcement that Antipas is throwing a party, providing the perfect opportunity for several days of mother-daughter planning before the party. Based on the text, we cannot rule out the possibility of a plot nor can we say for certain that there is one. Still, it is worth considering.

Mark's final comment on the whole tragic scene has to do with John's Apostles, who arrive to take his body and lay it in a tomb (Mark 6:29). Matthew also has John's Apostles removing the body and burying it—perhaps in a tomb, though Matthew does not provide this detail. Unlike Mark, however, in Matthew, after John's Apostles bury their leader, "they went and told Jesus" (Matt 14:12).

In summary, as we wade through the story of Herodias in Mark and Matthew, the first thing we notice is that Matthew offers us a similar, but edited version of Mark's account. Taken together, along with the historical information provided to us courtesy of Josephus, Herodias emerges as a murderous villainess—a rare type of female character in the Bible. The glaring omission of her story in Luke and John is thought-provoking and leads us to ask this question: If only two of the four Evangelists include the story of Herodias, are we getting only half of the story? The details provided by Mark are questionable, so much so that Luke (85 CE) and John (95 CE) do not record them at all while Matthew (90 CE) pares down the story and makes it slightly more palatable than Mark's version (70 CE). Though Josephus views Herodias with unabashed disdain, he makes no mention of the party, the dance, or the oath. Josephus cites Antipas and Antipas alone as the man behind the execution of John. This leads some scholars to argue that Mark's story (and Matthew's version of it) is nothing more than a fictitious tale that emerges around the very real historical event of the beheading of John the Baptist.

After the beheading of John, Herodias is never again specifically mentioned in the Gospels. In Luke, following Jesus' arrest, Pilate sends him to

Antipas for interrogation (Luke 23:6–12), and Herodias may have been present during that interrogation, but Luke does not mention her name.

Herodias's ultimate fate is one she no doubt finds as humiliating as John the Baptist's public denunciation of her marriage to Antipas. According to Josephus, in a very complex chain of events, Herodias's brother, Agrippa I, enjoying the patronage of the Roman emperor, Gaius, acquires more land in Palestine and thus becomes more powerful than Antipas. Josephus reports that this makes his sister, Herodias, extraordinarily jealous. She now regards the once-irresistible Antipas as little more than chopped liver! Because of Agrippa's good fortune and Herodias's profound envy, she hounds Antipas to appeal to Rome for more power. He eventually gives in to her nagging, but this proves to be his undoing. Agrippa I sends information to the emperor accusing Antipas of stockpiling weapons for use against Rome, and whether or not this accusation is true, Gaius strips Antipas of his tetrarchy and his Roman citizenship, banishing him from the empire. Because Herodias is Agrippa's sister, he allows her to remain under his care, but Herodias appears to choose banishment with her husband. Do not be misled, however, by this perceived sense of loyalty to her husband. When Antipas is banished and Herodias is given the opportunity to retain her possessions and remain under her brother's care, she writes an offensive letter to the emperor, so infuriating him that Gaius rescinds his offer and banishes Herodias too.

Josephus reports that the couple is exiled to Spain, comforted only by their memories of the good ol' days of murder and mayhem. And so the curtain falls on the story of Herodias, remembered in history as the evil and greedy social climber who marries her husband's brother and who uses her own daughter to satisfy her grudge against John the Baptist.

Herodias's Enduring Lessons

If the stories of Herodias in Mark and Matthew are accurate, what sort of enduring lessons can we learn from a woman like Herodias? Sometimes, the Bible teaches us what *not* to do through the words and actions of certain characters. Herodias, then, sets for us a bad example; indeed, her first enduring lesson reminds us of the dangers of disordered power and greed. Driven by the desire for more, she ignores the religious laws that stipulate acceptable marital relationships and divorces one brother in order to marry the other. Her second enduring lesson flows from the first and has to do with the toxic effects of grudge-holding. Her simmering hatred for John the Baptist boils over into a murderous rage in which she enlists the help of her own child to carry out her malicious intentions.

As we begin our enduring lessons, it is helpful to briefly examine the small stable of female executioners in the Bible in order to see how their actions relate—or do not relate—to the story of Herodias. This enables us to view her behavior through the historical lens of the biblical authors, and usually, this view tends to differ from the contemporary lens through which we moderns tend to look at many of the stories about women in the Bible, particularly those stories about the bad girls.

Notice that I use the word "executioners" to describe these women, for this will be our focus. There are other stories of women who kill, although they are arguably few in number. Most such deaths are unintentional, such as the woman who accidentally smothers her baby in the night when she rolls on top of him (1 Kgs 3:16–22). A woman may kill in order to survive, as in the gruesome story of the two starving mothers in 2 Kgs 6:26–29 who resort to cannibalism, boiling and eating the flesh of one woman's son. Such women, of course, are not of the same caliber as women executioners. Counted among the thin ranks of female murderesses, Herodias is often lumped together with other female killers, including Judith, Jael, and Jezebel—but is this a fair comparison? A brief summary of Judith, Jael, and Jezebel will help to answer this preliminary question.

We begin with Judith, found in the book that bears her name. Incidentally, the book of Judith is an official part of the canon in Catholic versions of the Bible. In Protestant versions of the Bible, Judith can be found in a special section between the Hebrew Bible and New Testament called the Apocrypha (from the Greek meaning "hidden" or "esoteric"), but it is not considered an official part of the Protestant canon. In any case, when Judith's little town of Bethulia is under siege by the Assyrians, the men of the town fail to defend it (Judith 1–7). Surrounded by the Assyrians, Bethulia is on the brink of starvation and the citizens are dying of thirst when Judith, who is described as a beautiful and pious widow, steps forward with a plan to save her people. She uses her beauty and brains to beguile the Assyrian general, Holofernes, who is quite taken with her. When he invites her into his tent for dinner, with plans to seduce her, he ends up drinking too much and passes out on his bed. Courageous Judith lops off the head of Holofernes with his own sword as he lies in a drunken stupor, puts the severed head into her bag, and returns to her people (Jud 13:2–14, NAB). In the morning, when the Assyrian soldiers realize that their leader has been murdered, they scatter in a panic and the Jews are able to defeat them. Judith receives a favorable review in the Bible and is lauded as a great heroine.

And then there is Jael. Judges 4–5 details an Israelite victory over the Canaanites. Led by the great judge Deborah, the Israelites are the underdogs in the battle against a far superior Canaanite army led by a general named Sisera. Once routed, Sisera deserts his post and flees to the tent of Jael. Thinking her tent a "safe haven," he does not know that Jael has kinship ties, through her husband, to the Israelites, and Sisera's place of refuge will turn out to be his tomb. He asks Jael for water, and she gives him milk, which makes him sleepy. Already exhausted from killing all those Israelites, he falls asleep and Jael seizes the opportunity. With a hammer in one hand and tent peg in the other, she drives the tent peg through Sisera's skull, killing him (Judg 4:21).

While Judith and Jael technically commit murder, it is a mistake to draw connections between their actions and the actions of Herodias, at least as far as the biblical writers are concerned. Judith's and Jael's actions are seen as heroic largely because of *context*; that is, they fight on the side of the LORD against Israel's enemies. In the case of Herodias, however, the murder is personal. And unlike Judith and Jael, Herodias makes sure that others do her dirty work for her, namely, her own daughter and the unnamed executioner Antipas dispatches to behead John the Baptist. While the connections to Judith and Jael are dubious, at best, there is one female murderess to whom we can connect Herodias: the Bible's favorite bad girl, the evil queen we all love to hate named Jezebel.

The wife of wicked King Ahab, Jezebel is an imported bride from Phoenicia and a non-Jew. In general, the biblical authors dislike foreign women because they introduce their husbands to foreign gods, often influencing them to forsake Yhwh in favor of imported but forbidden deities, which seems to be the case with Ahab (1 Kgs 16:29–33). Jezebel stirs up trouble wherever she goes, and for reasons that are not totally clear, she launches a killing campaign against the prophets of Israel (1 Kgs 18:4). When the powerful Israelite prophet Elijah tries to stop her, she threatens his life. Like Herodias, Jezebel harbors a grudge against Elijah and tries to have him killed, but under the protection of Yhwh, Elijah is able to escape her murderous grasp. Jezebel does, however, manage to arrange the execution of another innocent man, a man named Naboth (1 Kings 21). The execution of Naboth offers us a definitive link between Jezebel and Herodias.

What follows is an abbreviated version of the events leading up to the execution of Naboth. When King Ahab wishes to plant a little vegetable garden on a plot of land next to the palace compound, he finds that the land belongs to Naboth, who refuses the king's offer of a better vineyard or cash in exchange for the property. Because the land has been in Naboth's family for generations, it is sacred, and he cannot, by law, sell it (1 Kgs 21:1–3). Disappointed at Naboth's decision not to sell, Ahab returns to his palace to sulk (1 Kgs 21:4). When Jezebel learns of this, she takes matters into her own hands and sends letters in Ahab's name to the elders of Naboth's village, accusing him of cursing God and the king, offenses punishable by death (1 Kgs 21:8–10). Thanks to Jezebel's trickery, Naboth is falsely convicted of blasphemy and treason, and he is executed. Ahab then confiscates the dead man's property (1 Kgs 21:15–16). Like Herodias, Jezebel uses manipulation and deceit to arrange the execution of Naboth. Jezebel and Herodias also both ignore the religious stipulations set forth in the Torah: John the Baptist points out Herodias's unlawful marriage to her husband's brother (Lev 20:21), and Naboth reminds Ahab that he cannot sell his land due to a Torah injunction that forbids the selling of ancestral property (Lev 25:34).

Jezebel's actions, like Herodias's actions, are of a personal nature. Jezebel seems motivated by a desire to assuage her pouting husband's disappointment regarding his plans to plant a vegetable garden, while Herodias hopes to permanently silence the Baptist's humiliating public critique of her marriage. Judith and Jael are hailed as national heroines, for their murders are for the greater good of the nation and take place in the context of a war. Their executions are regarded as justified. Jezebel and Herodias, on the other hand, behave cruelly, and selfishly, with a total disregard for the other. There is a final thread that connects all four of our women executioners: All of the women dehumanize their victims.

In my college classroom, as my students study the Bible and ancient history in general, they often remark that "life seems cheap" in a world where slavery, torture, and the execution of innocent people is commonplace. While this is certainly true, we do not have to look very far in our own modern world to see that in many ways, things have not changed much. Today, there are still pockets of slavery of many kinds, ranging from human trafficking to those who work for "slave wages," barely scraping by, to women who become economic hostages in bad marriages. There are many places where the torture and the execution of innocent people takes place on a regular basis. The headlines scream at us, detailing the most recent terrorist attack, latest school shooting, and hundreds of other daily atrocities that pepper modern life. Social media brings each horror up close and personal, and all of it seems overwhelming and at times, hopeless. We can imagine that our brothers and sisters in the ancient world often feel this sort of hopelessness too, and this is one of the many ways in which our world connects with theirs.

When we read the accounts of Herodias in Mark and Matthew, we cannot help but feel a sense of shock, outrage, and profound sadness for the victims in the story. John the Baptist is brutally murdered because he dared to speak the truth, but he is not the only victim in Herodias's scheme. I have already mentioned the fact that Herodias uses Salome as a means to a terrible end, and though John and Salome are the primary victims in this story, there are many more. Think for a moment about John's family, his friends, neighbors, and especially his followers who come to retrieve his headless body in order to bury it. If you have read this book sequentially, then you might recall John's mother, Elizabeth, and the joy she feels when she receives the blessings of a son after so many years of barrenness and longing (chapter 7). We do not know if Elizabeth predeceases her son, but every parent's worse nightmare is realized in the death of a child. Even Jesus is affected by this tragedy, and when he learns of John's murder, "he withdrew from there in a boat to a deserted place by himself" (Matt 14:13). The ripple effect of grief in losing John, a good and holy man, is not emphasized in the Gospels, perhaps because the grief is somehow overshadowed by the horrific, dehumanizing, and senseless circumstances of his death. So it is today when we read about average citizens who are murdered as they innocently shop at a mall or sit in a movie theater or classroom. The individual stories of grief and loss are often lost in the collective terror we feel about the actions of the assailant and the sheer magnitude of the tragedy.

The painful results of Herodias's actions are made all the more difficult when we recognize that it all begins with a grudge. The dangers of grudge-holding point us in the direction of Herodias's second, and very grim, enduring lesson. John the Baptist says something that offends and embarrasses Herodias. There is of course, incontrovertible truth in what he says and this undoubtedly contributes to her anger and sense of outrage. She holds on to these feelings, allowing them to grow and fester within her so that her anger takes on a life of its own and becomes the impetus behind a ruthless murder. Jesus understands the human tendency to nurse a grudge and how, left unchecked, it can grow and consume us.

"You have heard that it was said to those of ancient times, 'You shall not murder; and whoever murders shall be liable to judgment.' But I say to you, that if you are angry with a brother or sister, you will be liable to judgment; and if you insult a brother or sister, you will be liable to the council; if you say 'You fool,' you will be liable to the hell of fire. So when you are offering your gift at the altar, if you remember that your brother or sister has something against you, leave your gift there before the altar and go; first be reconciled to your brother or sister, and then come and offer your gift." (Matt 5:21–24)

Jesus realizes that there are often many steps that lead to murder, beginning with anger, malice, gossip, or insults. He rightly asserts that we should reconcile disagreements and resolve our differences before they get out of hand and harden into the implacability of a grudge, as in the case of Herodias. We must assume that there are other contributing factors, including her upbringing in a family known for its violence and the fact that Herodias intuits, on some level, that John is speaking the truth: her marriage *is* in violation of Jewish law. Most of us at one time or another have felt the creeping, malignant growth of a grudge as it takes up residence in our hearts. We may unwittingly feed the grudge, through blame, playing the role of the victim, and though amassing a jury of friends, relatives, and just about anyone else who will listen to our case and render judgment in our favor.

A grudge is like a feral cat; once you feed it, it is difficult to get rid of it. Even when we have been legitimately wronged by another, holding on to a grudge only serves to further harm us. Grudges are psychologically destructive and can consume a person, driving them to do things that, in their right mind, they probably would never even consider doing. Grudge-holders can become vengeful people, and sometimes they morph into the dreaded "scorekeeper"—individuals who are able to keep track of every real or perceived transgression of another. These transgressions act as fuel for the grudge. Scorekeepers can, with very little effort, recall the tally of offenses and tick them off, one by one, to the perceived (or real) offender. This is a necessary tactic to keep the grudge going. The grudge-holder usually views herself or himself as a victim, which may or may not be the case; but grudge-holders are victims bent on punishing the offender, whether psychologically, usually through the use of verbal barbs that can escalate to physical violence or, in the case of scorekeepers, through a presentation of the aforementioned tally of offenses. The end result, for both the scorekeeper and the (perceived or real) offender, is misery.

Because grudges are so harmful, we must learn to let them go. It sounds so simple, but it is actually quite challenging. Why? Because the only real remedy for grudge-holding is forgiveness. Learning how to forgive others releases us from the terrible burden of being tied to the one who has wronged us. In most cases, the offender has moved on and does not even think about the actions that hurt us. Nursing a grudge, then, really only harms the grudge-holder. Forgiveness, however, does not come easily to most people and requires much practice (I discuss forgiveness in more detail in chapter 2). There are many ways to practice forgiveness, but perhaps the most simple is to conjure an image of the offender in your mind and then repeat these words, over and over: I forgive you and I release you.

While Herodias's most enduring lessons have to do with the negative consequences of greed, disordered power, and grudge-holding, there are several other "inverse lessons" she offers us—lessons in how *not* to behave. Given the historical information we have about her based on Josephus—including the Herod family legacy of cruelty and brutality, her scandalous affair with her husband's brother, her unlawful marriage, and her pathological jealousy of her brother—coupled with the material in Mark and Matthew that cites the manipulation of her daughter to bring about the death of John the Baptist, we learn what it means to be selfish, a disloyal spouse, sacrilegious, a jealous sibling, and a very bad parent.

At the beginning of this chapter, I briefly describe Herodias's family—a family that today, we would term "dysfunctional." An alternative or "sympathetic" reading of her story might be to view her actions as resulting from her traumatizing childhood, one in which her grandfather executes her grandmother and her own father and then proceeds to marry her off to his brother. We know today that children learn from what they see, but we also know that children are remarkably resilient and that growing up in a dysfunctional family, even one marked with violence, does not always mean that a child's destiny is already predetermined. We cannot know for certain the details of Herodias's upbringing or the lasting effects of the trauma she may have experienced as a child. Such concerns, particularly in royal circles, are largely unknown or ignored in the ancient world. And even in a sympathetic reading of her story, we find it difficult to excuse her behavior. But as I mentioned earlier, there is always more than one way to read a given story. In the final analysis, Herodias's story and her enduring lessons offer us a cautionary tale, the subtext of which whispers to us to be vigilant, for evil appears in many guises, assuming many shapes and forms—including those of Herodian princesses.

10

The Wife of Pontius Pilate: Murderer

I Had a Dream

Matt 27:19

W hile he was still seated on the bench, his wife sent him a message, "Have nothing to do with that righteous man. I suffered much in a dream today because of him." (Matt 27:19, NAB)

ILATE'S WIFE, an unnamed woman who appears only briefly in the Gospel of Matthew, is one of the most mysterious women in the New Testament. We have no physical description of her and know almost nothing about her other than the fact that she is credited with a mere two sentences, written in a message to her husband, Pontius Pilate, on the day of Jesus' execution. Some say her message has the power to change the course of history; others gloss over her note and wonder why Matthew decides to include it in his version of the Passion Narrative at all. In this chapter, we will explore Pilate's wife; the strange world in which she lives; her marriage to one of history's most despised men; the meaning of her message; her dream; and the relevance of dreams in general in the ancient world. We will also examine the stories, myths, and legends that develop about her after Jesus' death. Our guiding question is this: Is the wife of Pilate a "good girl" who courageously seeks to intervene and rescue an innocent Jesus from death, or is she a "bad girl" who believes that Jesus should be promptly executed, and she is therefore counted among the guilty circle of villains that include her husband and certain members of the Temple elite who seek to destroy Jesus?

The first thing we can say about Pilate's wife is perhaps the most obvious: she is nameless. Recognized only through her connection to her husband, she takes her place among the vast majority of women in the Bible who are not named. I address the issue of namelessness in the introduction, but we must briefly revisit it here. It is difficult to compose a list, exact in number, of all of the named women in the New Testament. For example, some women are known by two names, as in the case of Tabitha (Acts 9:36–42) who is also known as Dorcas; do we count two names or only one since both names refer to the same woman? Sometimes the woman named is merely a reference to a woman from the Hebrew Bible, as we find in the genealogies of Matthew and Luke. So do we include those names in our final tabulation? Questions such as these make name counting a confusing and challenging task. In general, though, if we count all of the named individuals (male and female) in the Hebrew Bible and New Testament, female names constitute less than 10 percent of the total. This is a small percentage, so we must consider the larger implications of nameless women in the Bible. People without names are more forgettable, and thus their stories are under-read, under-studied, and underappreciated. In an effort to compensate for her lack of a proper name, she is sometimes referred to as "Mrs. Pilate"—but even this is incorrect. First-century Roman women do not generally take their husband's name after marriage. Her lack of a proper name so bothers the later commentators who spin post-biblical yarns about her that a name for her is created: "Claudia

Procula." I will discuss this in more detail later; but for now, let us try to retrace the footsteps of Pilate's wife from Rome to Judea.

We know that Pilate's wife travels from the splendid comfort of her home in Rome to a far-flung corner of the Roman Empire because of her husband's appointment as prefect of Judea around the year 26 CE. There has been some confusion concerning Pilate's exact title because Josephus refers to him as "procurator" while the Gospels refer to him as "governor." Which title is correct? Archaeology gives us the answer. In 1961, archaeologists unearthed a partial inscription on a limestone block at Caesarea Maritima, Pilate's official residence in Judea. Located on a lovely stretch of coastline on the Mediterranean Sea that is today a popular tourist attraction, Caesarea Maritima is the seat of Roman imperial rule in Judea. The artifact, commonly referred to as the Pilate Stone, comes to us from the first century, the time of Jesus and Pilate. The Latin inscription is a dedication plaque for some sort of building called the Tiberieum and constructed by Pilate in honor of Tiberias Caesar Augustus, who rules from 14–37 CE. The fragmentary inscription reads,

> To the Divine Augusti [this] Tiberieum
> . . . Pontius Pilate
> . . . prefect of Judea
> . . . has dedicated [this]

The building no longer exists, but the plaque confirms Pilate's title as prefect of Judea, a title associated with the equestrian rank, which was connected at one time with the Roman cavalry, as the name implies. As prefect of Judea, Pilate has a largely military role; he is to maintain law and order and engage in various other administrative duties associated with the business of the empire. Pilate's title and his military background help to explain many of his actions and much of his behavior, described in some detail by the Jewish historian Josephus.

Josephus reports that upon his arrival in Judea and under the cover of darkness, Pilate installs in Jerusalem the Roman Standards, bearing the image of the Emperor Tiberius (*Antiquities* 18.3.1). Nothing like insulting the locals as soon as you arrive! The Jews, of course, view this as an affront to their religious beliefs that forbid graven images. Pilate is surely aware that he is infringing upon the religious sensibilities of his new "subjects," and so we must question his motives. Is he trying to make a statement about his absolute power? Or is he testing the religious waters of the local Jews, perhaps attempting to ferret out the religious fanatics among them so as to identify them and, if necessary, eliminate them? Though his motives remain a mystery, we do know that his actions provoke a great outcry from the Jews, and even when Pilate responds threateningly, with his considerable troops mustered and brandishing their weapons, the protesting Jews prefer death to the sacrilege. In the end, Pilate has the standards removed, but then he does something even more outrageous. He builds an aqueduct using Jewish funds collected largely for the maintenance of the Temple (*Wars* 2.9.4). When the indignant Jews again gather in protest, Pilate signals to his soldiers, whom he has disguised in plain clothes among the mob, to bludgeon the protestors. Josephus reports that many Jews are killed, either from the brutality of the attack or by being trampled to death as the crowd panics and attempts to flee. Josephus also notes that Pilate's actions serve to silence and terrify the Jews into grudging submission (*Wars* 2.9.4). This image of Pilate as an instigator, who stirs up trouble with the Jews, runs counter to the Evangelists' presentation of him. In general, the Gospels convey a rather genteel version of Pilate, though Luke does allude to Pilate's brutal massacre of some Galileans related to their religious sacrifices, but the circumstances of the incident are unclear (Luke 13:1). We will discuss Matthew's Pilate in some detail later, but for now, we must wonder, Where is Pilate's wife during all of this commotion?

Having left Rome, and presumably her friends and family, to travel to a place that, by Roman standards, is a backward nation of strange people with an odd religion fixated on a single deity, we can imagine that Pilate's wife's first thoughts are of a longing for home. As the wife of a political official and member of the upper class, she is, we can assume, accustomed to a comfortable lifestyle and afforded some level of education, and though she is not allowed to vote or hold office, Pilate's wife is able to offer her husband political advice. There is evidence that Roman women do act as political counselors to their husbands; the best example is that of Livia (58 BCE–29 CE), wife and advisor to her husband Augustus (born Julius Caesar Octavianus; 63 BCE–14 CE). Livia is such a trusted advisor that after Augustus's death, she is deified during her lifetime, becoming Livia Augustus. The infamous message Pilate's wife sends to her husband regarding the fate of Jesus (Matt 27:19) leads us to conclude that she too is accustomed to offering her opinion and advice on political matters to her husband.

As the matron of her home, Pilate's wife, like most upper-class Roman women, is in charge of maintaining domestic order, largely through directing her staff of slaves. She is also in charge of entertaining guests, keeping up her correspondence, and spinning, or the making of clothing—something expected of even the wealthiest Roman women. Since the Romans are known to export their way of life and standard of living, Pilate's compound at Caesarea Maritima likely resembles the sort of home his wife is accustomed to, and, located some seventy miles northwest of Jerusalem, it is quiet and devoid of the noise and clamor of that Holy City.

Historically, we know that Pilate travels to Jerusalem only when necessary—when there is trouble or the possibility of it. Does his wife accompany him during these fractious times, or does she remain safely ensconced in their villa along the sunny shores of the Mediterranean? Of course, we are particularly interested to know if she is actually in Jerusalem during that fateful Passover when she has a disturbing dream about a preacher named Jesus from the Galilee. We do know that Pilate goes to Jerusalem for that Passover, in the spring, sometime during the years 30–33 CE. The city swells with pilgrims, and the possibility of riots and various types of criminal activity increases. It is during this time that the worlds of Pilate's wife and Jesus of Nazareth collide.

I should mention, as a footnote to what follows, that I write this chapter in Jerusalem during the weeks leading up to and in the very midst of the Christian Holy Week and the Jewish Passover, which, this year, fall during the same week. I have been to Jerusalem many times, and now I am on sabbatical from my university and have been living in Jerusalem for several months as I research and write this book. I have studied this Holy City from just about every point of view—religious (mostly Jewish, Christian, and Muslim), political, archaeological, and interpersonal, listening to the stories and opinions of friends, colleagues, and people I have met on the street. There was a time in my career when I felt quite certain that I knew and understood the events that lead to Jesus' crucifixion, rattling off the "facts" in class lectures without even glancing at my notes. Today, however, I am less certain. As this chapter is about Pilate's wife, my focus, naturally, is on her; but I cannot discuss her role in Jesus' death—and the section under which I include her in this book ("Murderers") tips my hand from the get-go: I do believe she has a role in that death—without providing my best-guess scenario of what happens during that Holy Week, over two thousand years ago.

Since Pilate's wife appears only in the Gospel of Matthew, I will focus on Matthew's version of the Passion Narrative, inserting material from the canonical Gospels and other sources, including Josephus, when necessary. According to Matthew, Jesus leaves the Galilee, followed by a large crowd and goes "to the district of Judea across the Jordan" on his trek to Jerusalem (Matt 19:1–2). Theology aside for the moment, we can't help but wonder why Jesus goes to Jerusalem in the first place. Practically speaking, he has already established his ministry in the Galilee and has been quite successful in bringing the message of the Kingdom of God to his countrymen and women. If the Galilee is the heart of his ministry, then why travel to Jerusalem? Quite often, when I pose this question to students, I find that most assume that Jesus travels often to Jerusalem. This assumption, I think, arises from the connection we have in our minds with Jerusalem as the place of Jesus' death and resurrection, but according to both Mark and Matthew, Jesus travels to Jerusalem only *once*—during the final week of his life (Mark 11:1–11; Matt 21:1–10). But what about the other two Gospels, Luke and John? What do *they* have to say about Jesus and Jerusalem?

Contrary to Mark and Matthew, the Gospel of Luke indicates that Jesus visits Jerusalem quite often. According to Luke, Jesus' parents are Torah-abiding Jews who frequently visit the Temple. Jesus is presented at the Temple as an infant (Luke 2:22–23), and apparently the family makes a yearly pilgrimage during Passover, traveling from their home in Nazareth to Jerusalem. On one occasion, Mary and Joseph accidentally leave the then twelve-year-old Jesus behind (Luke 2:41–51) at the Temple (see chapter 8).

In Luke's temptation scene, which occurs before Jesus begins his earthly ministry, Satan brings Jesus to Jerusalem, to the Temple pinnacle, urging Jesus to throw himself to the ground in order to prove that he is indeed the Son of God (Luke 4:9–12). Finally, in Luke 19:28–39, Jesus enters Jerusalem in the same sort of triumphal way as described in the other Gospels (Mark 11:1–11; Matt 21:1–10; John 12:12–19).

According to John's Gospel, Jesus travels to Jerusalem at least four times. The first is for Passover, when he drives away the moneychangers and those selling animals for sacrificial purposes as we see in the Synoptics (John 2:13–17, cf. Mark 11:15–17; Matt 21:12–13; Luke 19:45–46). John situates this event earlier in the life of Jesus, whereas Matthew, Mark, and Luke mention it in conjunction with Jesus' visit to Jerusalem during the final days of his life. According to John, Jesus again travels to Jerusalem for an unknown Jewish festival (possibly Passover or Pentecost) and cures a sick man on the Sabbath, which of course is in violation of the Torah injunction against work of any kind on the day set aside for rest (John 5:1–18; Gen 2:2–3). Apparently, in observation of the Festival of Booths (*Sukkot*) and the Festival of Dedication (*Hanukkah*), Jesus again goes to Jerusalem, inciting his enemies against him (John 7:1–10; 10:22–23). According to John, Jesus' final visit to Jerusalem is in concert with the Synoptics. That is, Jesus makes a triumphal "Palm Sunday" entrance into the city and his enemies feel overwhelmed for "the whole world has gone after him!" (John 12:12–15, 19).

In returning to the question as to *why* Jesus travels to Jerusalem during what will prove to be his last days, we now find the question almost impossible to answer, for it depends on which Gospel we are reading. If we read Luke and John, we might, like my students, conclude that it is Jesus' custom to go to Jerusalem, along with thousands of other pilgrims, to celebrate the various Jewish festivals, especially Passover. Mark and Matthew, however, present us with a more somber version: the culmination of Jesus' ministry comes in his first and last trip to Jerusalem.

Returning to Matthew, the only Gospel that features Pilate's wife, we note that Jesus journeys *up* to Jerusalem (for Jerusalem is on a mountaintop), stopping at various towns and cities along the way, including Jericho, Bethphage, and Bethany, the home of his friends, Mary, Martha, and Lazarus. According to Matthew, Jesus and the Twelve stay in Bethany, presumably at the home of his friends, commuting to Jerusalem from Bethany, which is about two miles away, during Holy Week (Matt 21:17; 26:6). The Twelve seem to meet up with Jesus at the Garden of Gethsemane on the Mount of Olives at day's end to return to Bethany. This "meeting-up" place—well-known, of course, to Judas—is the place of Jesus' arrest (Matt 26:36–56; Mark 14:32–50; Luke 22:39–54; John 18:1–13).

Jesus enters Jerusalem with a great deal of fanfare, so much so that the entire city is in turmoil (Matt 21:10). Having been sent ahead of the crowd, two of the disciples procure a donkey and her colt, just as Jesus directs, and return to him with the animals (Matt 21:1–7). Matthew notes that Jesus' entry into the city is in fulfillment of the prophecy of Zechariah, though scholars contend that the passage below is really a compilation of both Isaiah and Zechariah.

This happened so that what had been spoken through the prophet might be fulfilled:
"Say to daughter Zion,
'Behold, your king comes to you,
meek and riding on an ass,
and on a colt, the foal of a beast of
burden.'" (Matt 21:4–5; Isa 62:11; Zech 9:9)

The disciples place their cloaks on both animals and Jesus sits on them, which seems a little odd. Does Jesus ride *both* the mother donkey *and* her colt at the same time? Mark and Luke mention only a colt, while John has Jesus ride in on a donkey (Mark 11:7; Luke 19:35; John 12:14). Matthew seems very interested in having Jesus fulfill Zechariah's prophecy to the letter, even as it raises the curious question of how Jesus manages to ride two animals at the same time! A quick glance at Zechariah 9:9 makes it clear that there is really only one animal, mentioned two times, thus leading to Matthew's confusion.

> Rejoice heartily, O daughter Zion,
> shout for joy, O daughter Jerusalem!
> See, your king shall come to you;
> A just savior is he,
> Meek, and riding on an ass,
> on a colt, the foal of an ass. (Zech 9:9)

In any case, Jesus' entrance into the city is a grand affair.

> They brought the ass and the colt and laid their cloaks over them, and he sat upon them. The very large crowd spread their cloaks on the road, while others cut branches from the trees and strewed them on the road. The crowds preceding him and those following kept crying out and saying:
> "Hosanna to the Son of David;
> blessed is he who comes in the name
> of the Lord;
> hosanna in the highest." (Matt 21:7–9)

Pilate too has come to Jerusalem to make certain that peace and order are observed during this Passover, fortifying the city with extra troops. Agitators are singled out, watched very closely, and arrested promptly should there be a hint of trouble, and many are crucified. Is Pilate's wife riding alongside her husband as he and his entourage arrive in the city? Does Pilate stand with his wife and witness Jesus' grand processional, taking note of the large crowd of followers? The Gospels do not provide the answers to these questions, but we do know that processionals are considered important occasions for the Romans, particularly military processions, so even if Pilate and his wife do not witness Jesus' royal entry into the city, they are surely made aware of it.

Matthew does not tell us how long Jesus stays in Bethany while visiting Jerusalem by day, but Mark mentions two days (Mark 14:1) and John, six (John 12:1). In Jerusalem, Jesus teaches and preaches along the periphery of the Temple and heals the sick around the Bethesda and Siloam pools. These pools are known for their healing properties, and it seems likely that the sick gather around these two pools in hopes that the waters will cure them. Some scholars assert that the public pools are also used as makeshift *mikva'ot* during the times of Jewish feasts, such as Passover. The *mikvah* (plural, *mikva'ot*) is a stepped purification installation, used for Jewish ritual purification, and the citizens of Jerusalem even open the private *mikva'ot* in their homes to pilgrims who must purify themselves before entering the Temple as there is a shortage of such pools during those crowded festival days.

Jesus also encounters the moneychangers and animal mongers, selling various poor creatures in cages and in stalls for ritual sacrifices. This area, for purity purposes, is not inside the Temple, as Matthew might lead us to believe (Matt 21:12–13) but beyond its holy parameters. When Jesus sees the greedy moneychangers and fetid arena of sacrificial animals, he is sickened and outraged. Turning over their tables, he drives them away (Matt 21:12–13). This action alone should sound the alarm for Pilate, who no doubt has his spies disguised in plain clothes, circulating among the crowd, and reporting back to him. We must question why Jesus is not arrested for this action, since it seems much more menacing than his hailed entry into the city.

Perhaps it is Jesus' healing and teaching activities that render him a marked man. Healing the sick, and teaching his disciples to do the same, muscles in on the Temple economy. It is normally the priest who heals the sick, and like physicians today, there is a fee for their services, but Jesus and his disciples heal for free. Alongside Jesus' ministry of healing is a powerful message, which forms the core of his teaching. He speaks repeatedly about the imminent arrival of the Kingdom of God.

I have mentioned the Kingdom in various places throughout this book, particularly in chapter 5, so I will not explore it in depth here, except to say that Jesus and his followers are apocalyptic thinkers who believe that a transformed world is about to be born. This new world, in part, will liberate the Jewish people from Roman occupation. Jesus and the "Kingdom people" who believe that a radical change in world order is on the horizon are a dangerous threat to Roman imperial rule, and it is no small wonder that Pilate may want to put an end to the Galilean rabbi and his seditious teachings! Moreover, a small slice of the Temple elite, led by the high priest Caiaphas (appointed by Pilate), seems concerned with Jesus' growing popularity and large following. They are threatened by his mass appeal and they conspire against him (Matt 26:3–5).

On the first day of Passover, Jesus sends his disciples into the city to prepare a place for the meal (Matt 26:17–19). They celebrate the meal and then depart for the Mount of Olives, their meeting-up place, where Jesus prays. Presently, a group led by his betrayer, Judas Iscariot, descends upon Jesus and arrest him as his disciples scatter in fear (Matt

26:47–56). The story is familiar to us, yet what follows is difficult to bear, no matter how many times we read it. Jesus is brought first to the house of Caiaphas, where an impromptu trial is held at night during Passover. Scholars question the veracity of such a Jewish trial—and in fact, all of the various trials that appear in the Gospels. The trial under consideration in Matt 26:57–68 is curious given the fact that the Sanhedrin (the Jewish court) does not convene at night. They do not meet in the home of the high priest, but meet instead in the Temple, in an area known as the Chamber of Hewn Stones, and they certainly do not meet during Passover. Perhaps, however, this is a rare instance in which they do. In any case, Matthew relates that Jesus, by and large, refuses to answer their questions, which seems to confirm his guilt.

> But Jesus was silent. Then the high priest said to him, "I order you to tell under oath before the living God, whether you are the Messiah, the Son of God." Jesus said to him in reply, "You have said so. But I tell you: From now on you will see the 'Son of Man seated at the right hand of Power' and 'coming on the clouds of heaven.'" (Matt 26:63–64)

With this, Jesus is accused of blasphemy, spat upon, slapped, and mocked (Matt 26:65–68). Then, he is turned over to Pilate (Matt 27:2).

As I mention earlier, the portrait of Pilate presented in Matthew, and in the Gospels in general, is quite different from the historical accounts of him. For instance, Philo, the Hellenistic Jewish Philosopher and contemporary of Jesus, describes Pilate as abusive and violent, with a history of executing untried prisoners (*Legatio* 38.302). We have already noted that Josephus depicts Pilate as brutal and cruel, detesting mobs and crushing rebellions.

It is very important to underscore the fact that when the Gospels are written, Christianity is an illegal religion. Rome is usually tolerant of the many religions throughout its vast empire, but the Christians are another matter. This is a complicated issue, but the main reason why Christianity is "outlawed" during this time period is because Christians refuse to recognize the Roman emperor as a god. The Roman practice of deifying the emperor after death, as in the case of Caesar, changes with his son, Augustus, who essentially deifies himself in life—becoming *Caesar Divi Filisum*, or "Caesar the Son of God." Most Romans view the veneration of the emperor as more of a civic, rather than religious, duty; they may *publicly* proclaim the emperor as divine, but then they return to their homes and worship their own gods. Christians, however, refuse to worship the emperor in any way—for them, there is only one God. Their refusal to venerate the emperor, however, rankles the Roman authorities, and they declare Christianity illegal. The final book of the New Testament, the book of Revelation, reflects this tense situation between Rome and the nascent Christian faith.

Most scholars agree that the sympathetic portrait of Pilate in the Gospels reflects the dire circumstances of the second half of the first century and the formidable Roman rulers under whose watchful eyes the Gospels are written. This apologetic image of Pilate is meant, among other things, to placate the Roman oppressors in order to gain more freedom for early Christians. This is a challenge, given the fact that the Roman prefect, Pilate, crucifies their God! Making it appear that Pilate does not wish to crucify Jesus but is swayed by an angry mob of Jews may mollify the Roman censors, but make no mistake: It is Pilate, and only Pilate, who is able to condemn and crucify Jesus. To Pilate, Jesus is but a flea on the back of a dog, one of many troublemakers crucified during that Passover. That a small faction of the Temple elite, in cahoots with Rome, plots against Jesus is probably true, but the erroneous portrait we see in the Gospels, making the Jews *en masse* responsible for Jesus' crucifixion, is not only historically inaccurate but has resulted in centuries of anti-Semitism, with far-reaching and deadly consequences.

Keeping all of this in mind, we return to Matthew's version of Jesus' trial before Pilate. When Pilate questions Jesus regarding the accusations leveled against him by the Temple elite, Jesus again remains silent.

> Now Jesus stood before the governor, and he questioned him, "Are you the king of the Jews?" Jesus said, "You say so." And when he was accused by the chief priests and elders, he made no answer. Then Pilate said to him, "Do you not hear how many things they are testifying against you?" But he did not answer him one word, so that the governor was greatly amazed. (Matt 27:11–14)

Pilate is "amazed" that Jesus does not answer the charges brought against him. His silence seems to confirm, at least as far as Pilate is concerned, Jesus' guilt. If we take into account Jesus' behavior since his arrival in Jerusalem, including his "regal" entry into the city, his turning over the tables of the moneychangers and animal vendors, his preaching concerning the coming of the Kingdom, his healing of the sick, and the expanding crowd that follows him, then we can conclude that, to the Romans anyway, Jesus is a problem. Pilate is aware of Jesus' actions since his arrival in the city, and there is nothing Pilate hates more than a riot among the Jews.

For this reason alone, Pilate might eliminate Jesus. Taken together with Jesus' refusal to refute the charges against him, Pilate assumes that Jesus also considers himself the King of the Jews, a royal title from the Romans last given to Herod the Great.

There is plenty of ammunition Pilate can use against Jesus, not that Pilate needs it in order to execute him, for Pilate does as he pleases. In Matthew, however, Pilate appears as somewhat of a weakling: an indecisive leader who is torn and who does not really want to execute Jesus. In hopes of placating the crowd, stirred up by Jesus' enemies and on the verge of a riot, Pilate invokes a special favor given to the Jews during festival time: the release of one prisoner of their choosing. Pilate presents two options: Jesus Barabbas, a terrorist, convicted of murder and insurrection (Mark 15:7) whose name means Jesus "Son-of-the-father" (Barabbas) or the other Jesus, the *true* Son of the Father, who claims to be the King of the Jews. The irony of the names of the prisoners is not lost on Matthew's intended audience. Most scholars question the historicity of the "prisoner release program" mentioned in Matthew (also in Mark 15:6 and John 18:39, but absent in Luke), as there is no record of such a program ever existing outside of the Gospels. That Pilate would even entertain the release of a known insurrectionist like Barabbas is highly unlikely, especially when the city is brimming with Passover pilgrims from all over the country. This, of course, does not mean that it is untrue, only that we should read it, and for that matter, both the Jewish trial and the trial before Pilate, critically.

The scene is chaotic. Matthew reports that Pilate bargains with the unruly crowd, offering clemency to the convicted terrorist Barabbas, in hopes that they will choose to release Jesus instead. Into the midst of all this insanity steps Pilate's wife with her ominous message.

> While he was still seated on the bench, his wife sent him a message, "Have nothing to do with that righteous man. I suffered much in a dream today because of him." (Matt 27:19, NAB)

The note to her husband makes it clear that Pilate's wife is aware of the court proceedings currently underway, supporting the notion that she accompanies him to Jerusalem for Passover. Is she watching the events unfold from the wings? It would seem so. That she feels free to interrupt her husband's judicial deliberations with a message that essentially tells him what to do indicates that she is the sort of wife, like Livia, who is accustomed to giving her husband counsel.

Let's take a close look at this message because historically, it is largely misunderstood. I chose to use the translation from the New American Bible as it most closely aligns with the original Greek, especially with respect to the manner in which Pilate's wife identifies Jesus. In her message, she instructs her husband to "have nothing to do" with Jesus, which is another way of saying, "Don't get mixed up in this affair." She wants Pilate to end the trial quickly before the unruly crowd gets out of hand.

Pilate's wife refers to Jesus as a "righteous man." Some translators render the word "righteous" to read "innocent," which is a mistranslation and changes the meaning of the message. In her opinion, Jesus is *not* innocent. The words "righteous" and "innocent" are not synonymous, not now and not then. In describing Jesus as a "righteous man," Pilate's wife concurs with her husband's supposition that Jesus is guilty. The Greek word *dikaios* (righteous) means that a person is faithful and their actions justified before God. When Pilate's wife refers to Jesus as "righteous" she is labeling him as a man who feels justified in his beliefs; he is the Son of God, the Messiah, and the *King of the Jews* (Matt 26:63; 27:11). Only the Romans may appoint a king, but Jesus is behaving like a king, entering the city in a grand procession and answering to no one, not even the prefect from Rome! Pilate's wife fears this self-righteous Jesus will not back down and shrink away after his brush with the law. If left unchecked and empowered with his sense of "righteousness," Jesus will continue to grow in popularity, and he therefore poses a direct threat to Roman supremacy.

As if to bolster her advice, she frames it in terms of a dream she has about Jesus—one that causes her great suffering. People in the ancient world believe that dreams occur in a sacred space between Heaven and earth. In the transcendent world of the dreamscape, the gods (or God) often convey important messages or prophecies to Humans. Viewed as Divine gifts, these otherworldly communications are taken very seriously, and Matthew's Gospel demonstrates the way in which dreams allow God to communicate with humans. For example, an angel appears to Joseph in a dream and confirms Mary's pregnancy as emanating from the Holy Spirit, and Joseph decides not to divorce her (Matt 1:20–24). The magi who visit the Christ child are warned in a dream not to reveal his whereabouts to King Herod, who wishes to destroy the infant (Matt 2:12), and in Matt 2:13, Joseph is directed in a dream to take Mary and Jesus to Egypt in order to escape Herod. These dreams function as a means to protect Jesus; the first spares his mother's possible death by stoning, the usual punishment for adultery (Lev 20:10), while the second two dreams protect the Christ child from Herod's murderous grasp. The dream of Pilate's wife, however, is antithetical to the other dreams in Matthew and functions as a means to destroy Jesus.

Pilate seems to concur with his wife's conviction that Jesus is a threat who must be eliminated. After her message is delivered, Pilate's wife disappears from the narrative, her mission apparently accomplished, and we know the rest of the story: Jesus is ultimately condemned to death by Pilate; he is crucified, dies, and is resurrected from the dead. His official crime is placed on the cross on a sign above his head and reads, "This is Jesus, the King of the Jews" (Matt 27:37).

After Jesus' death, according to Josephus, the brutality of Pilate continues, culminating in a massacre of Samaritans and some of their leaders that is so savage, Pilate is recalled to Rome in the year 36 CE (*Antiquities* 18.85–87). We have no official Roman documents detailing what happens to Pilate or his wife after they return to Rome. According to the Roman historian Eusebius (d. 340 CE), Pilate is eventually exiled to Gaul, where he commits suicide in about 37 CE. If this is the case, can we assume that Pilate's wife goes with him into exile? And if so, what is her ultimate fate? History does not tell us, but as we shall see, Pilate's wife becomes a figure of fascination and legend.

Pilate's Wife's Enduring Lessons

We begin our exploration of Pilate's wife's enduring lessons with a "traditional" view of her. This view comes not from historical sources, for as I mention earlier, history records next to nothing about her. It does not come from what we know about Pilate or the tense situation of Roman occupation and the persecution of Christians during the time Matthew composes his Gospel. And it certainly does not come from a careful reading of Matthew.

> While he was still seated on the bench, his wife sent him a message, "Have nothing to do with that righteous man. I suffered much in a dream today because of him." (Matt 27:19, NAB)

The transformation of Pilate's wife comes from an innate desire to read her story sympathetically, to imagine that she intervenes in an effort to save Jesus' life. I mention earlier that some translations of Matt 27:19 render the word "righteous" to read "innocent." It is easy to see how readers of this alternative translation might begin to think about Pilate's wife in a very different way. If Jesus is "innocent," then Pilate's wife, by extension, is also innocent. These leaps of logic happen all the time when people read the Bible. And if the hand-wringing, indecisive image of Pilate is taken literally, we can understand why the pair are exonerated and even elevated to saints, for this is precisely what happens!

Because of an unawareness of the difficult political situation under which the Gospels are written and the unlikely veracity of the biblical version of Pilate as a wishy-washy ruler who believes that Jesus is innocent, stories and legends about Pilate's wife begin to emerge as early as the second century. Chief among the beliefs during the centuries following Jesus' death is that Pilate's wife is a secret follower of Jesus. In "The Acts of Pilate," part of the apocryphal Gospel of Nicodemus, written between the fourth and fifth century, Pilate himself proclaims his wife a practitioner of Judaism, and upon hearing that Jesus has died, Pilate and his wife are filled with grief and fast. Another interesting text written during this time period is *Paradosis Pilati*. In this book, the death of Pilate and his wife are revealed as follows: Both are apparently converts to Christianity. Pilate goes to Rome and appears before Caesar; he is summarily condemned and beheaded. An angel takes away the severed head of Pilate, and his wife, upon seeing this, dies from the sheer religious ecstasy of the moment.

Over time, Pilate's wife is rehabilitated; she is no longer the villainous wife of a brutal man, but instead, she is regarded as a saint in the Eastern and Ethiopian Orthodox Churches. She even receives a name: Saint Claudia Procula (the keeper of the gate) and she is commemorated on her feast day every October 27 (Eastern Orthodox Churches). In the Ethiopian Orthodox Church, *both* Pilate and his wife are saints who are celebrated together every June 25.

Given the very different perspectives regarding her actions in Matt 27:19, Pilate's wife's enduring lessons depends on whether you view her as a good girl, a saint who tries to rescue Jesus from the cross, or a bad girl who urges her husband to get rid of the self-righteous preacher from the Galilee. Presented with these alternative views of Pilate's wife, my students often express confusion in trying to decipher the "real story" and whether or not she plays a role in the death of Jesus at all. In light of the historical information we have about Pilate, first-century Roman politics, and the issues of translations, it is easy to see why my students might be confused. I understand their confusion and uncertainty, as do most biblical scholars, because in truth, there are things about the Bible and the world of antiquity that we simply do not know or understand.

While I have made my position clear in the matter—I am convinced that Pilate and his wife are both villains when it comes to the death of Jesus—I have not always held this position. Recall that in the introduction, I mention the importance of paying close attention to the words of the text and staying true to the author's intentions. I also freely admit that my interpretations, while well researched, are not definitive—and neither are yours, or anyone else's for that matter. Having spent a great deal of time studying the Bible and material outside its pages, I have, over the years, changed my verdict concerning Pilate's wife from "innocent" to "guilty." Assuming that my readers are probably of a mixed jury, let us explore both sides. We will begin by assuming that Pilate's wife believes in Jesus' innocence and that she urges her husband, based on a powerful dream she has about Jesus, to release him. What can we learn from *this* Pilate's wife? What are *her* enduring lessons?

The Pilate's wife who professes Jesus' innocence teaches us to be tolerant of other faiths, to trust the inner voice within, and to act. Pilate's wife travels with her husband to Jerusalem and witnesses first-hand the religious devotion of the Jews, many of whom have traveled a long distance to celebrate Passover. The Roman Empire is generally tolerant of most religions, and Pilate's wife has probably been exposed to a wide variety of religious expression, including a conclave of Jews in Rome. She is familiar with the traditional Roman gods and goddesses, such as Jupiter (the god of gods), Mars (the god of war), and Juno (goddess and special protector of women), and like most Romans, she probably also venerates certain household deities, or spirits, such as the goddess Vesta, protector of the fireplace. In addition to the official deities and household spirits, she publicly venerates the emperor as a means of proving herself a good citizen, rather than actually believing that he is a god. During this time period, it is also quite fashionable for Romans to worship foreign gods and goddesses. For example, the Egyptian goddess Isis is very popular during the first century. Excavations at Pompeii, one of the cities destroyed by the eruption of Mt. Vesuvius in 79 CE, reveal a temple to Isis, attesting to her popularity among many of the residents of that ill-fated city.

The Pilate's wife who believes in Jesus' innocence views Jesus as a human being who is not guilty of the charges brought against him, and his religious beliefs do not seem to be a factor in her decision to intervene in his trial in an attempt to dissuade her husband from crucifying him. She therefore teaches *us* to refrain from negative judgment based solely on someone's faith. In our ever-expanding global society, many of us now have the opportunity to meet and interact with those whose religious beliefs differ from our own. In the workplace, in school, and even in our own neighborhoods, now, more than at any other time in history, we are likely to encounter people whose religious beliefs are not the same as ours. If we embrace religious diversity as a learning opportunity, we will soon realize that education helps to dispel ignorance and hatred, the twin culprits that give life to every form of sanctimonious judgment, violence, and discrimination.

The Pilate's wife who proclaims Jesus' innocence does so because of a dream she has about him. There is evidence of an internal struggle, for she "suffers much" from the dream, but she trusts her "gut instinct" to act on the dream. Paying attention to her intuition, or that inner voice present in all of us, Pilate's wife takes action and sends a message to her husband on Jesus' behalf. How often do we ignore the voice within? How many times have we refused to take action because of the paralyzing fear of failure or rejection, or out of pure laziness? How many opportunities have we missed, how many chances have we let slip through our fingers, and how many times have we failed to put things right simply because we did not take action? Pilate's wife demonstrates the importance of stepping up, speaking up, and simply being proactive, even when we are uncertain of the outcome. Of all her enduring lessons, this is perhaps her most powerful.

In sum, the enduring lessons of the Pilate's wife who avows Jesus' innocence are threefold. She teaches us to practice tolerance of other religions; to pay attention to the voice of God within us; and to take action if the situation demands it, even when we are afraid. What then can be said of the other version of Pilate's wife, the nameless woman who is not a saint, but a sinner?

Pilate's wife the villain introduces us to the brutality of the Roman occupation of Judea and its equally brutal prefect, Pontius Pilate. Her story allows us to see the deadly effects of absolute power and to witness first-hand the dangerous individuals who align themselves with a system of profound evil. In Matthew, these individuals include Pilate; his wife, who acts as his advisor; the high priest Caiaphas and his gaggle of impious comrades who conspire against Jesus; and the countless soldiers, toadies, sycophants, and hit men who serve Pilate in blind obedience.

On a larger scale, the story of Pilate's wife warns us to learn from the past—to be wary of modern empires and corrupt political regimes that threaten our world. Her story also teaches us not to accept evil, or worse, participate in it as she does, but instead, to speak out against injustice and, when possible, to take action to prevent the expansion of political and economic systems that exploit, manipulate, and harm God's creation. On a smaller scale, the circle of those who plot against Jesus, who falsely accuse him, and who are ultimately responsible, either directly or indirectly, for his death serves as a stark reminder for us to be mindful when it comes to the company we keep. We must be unwavering in our refusal to compromise our values in order to "fit in," and we should refrain from exclusionary behavior that deems only some individuals worthy of inclusion.

Pilate's wife the villain who proclaims that Jesus is a "righteous man" uses the designation "righteous" against him, as a term of derision. Remember that the Greek word *dikaios* (righteous) refers to a person who is faithful and their actions justified before God. Pilate's wife does not, however, believe Jesus is justified in claiming to be the King of the Jews, the Son of God, or the Messiah (Matt 26:63–64). Only the empire has the right to appoint kings and convey lofty titles. Pilate's wife views Jesus' teachings about the Kingdom as a threat to her way of life. There is no place for Roman imperialism, class privilege, corruption, or brute force in the Kingdom for the righteousness of God will sweep away such evils as a new age of peace and harmony is ushered in. The Kingdom is liberating—the Roman Empire, oppressive. Jesus is righteous and his claims are authentic; he *is* the King of the Jews, the Son of God, and the Messiah. The claims of Jesus' enemies—Pilate and his wife, Caiaphas, and the Temple elite—are inauthentic, ephemeral, and self-serving. They have power only through vice and the promulgation of injustice. The sour fruits of their labors will wither on the vine in the blazing glory of the Kingdom.

In sum, Pilate's wife the villain teaches us about the abuse of power and the reality of evil. As Aristotle once observed, "Evil draws men together," and this is certainly the case with those associated with Jesus' arrest, trial, and crucifixion in Matthew's Gospel. Like the men who conspire against Jesus, Pilate's wife fears Jesus' teachings about the coming of the Kingdom because her world rests upon its polar opposite.

In the end, whether you view Pilate's wife as a saint or a sinner and her message regarding Jesus as one of condemnation or rescue, she will forever be remembered as the woman who is motivated to act though the power of a dream.

11

Prisca: Missionary

Spreading the Good News

Acts 18:2–3, 18–19, 24–26; Rom 16:3–5;
1 Cor 16:19; 2 Tim 4:19

There he found a Jew named Aquila, a native of Pontus, who had recently come from Italy with his wife Priscilla, because Claudius had ordered all Jews to leave Rome. Paul went to see them, and, because he was of the same trade, he stayed with them, and they worked together—by trade they were tentmakers. . . .

Now there came to Ephesus a Jew named Apollos, a native of Alexandria. He was an eloquent man, well-versed in the scriptures. He had been instructed in the Way of the Lord; and he spoke with burning enthusiasm and taught accurately the things concerning Jesus, though he knew only the baptism of John. He began to speak boldly in the synagogue; but when Priscilla and Aquila heard him, they took him aside and explained the Way of God to him more accurately. (Acts 18:2–3, 24–26)

THE EVOLUTION of Christianity from a small sect within Judaism to an independent religion that is today the dominant religion in the world is a fascinating story. At the heart of the story is a group of missionaries that includes Prisca, who work tirelessly to spread the Good News of Jesus Christ to the far reaches of the Roman Empire. The earliest Christians do not consider themselves to be "Christians" at all, but a unique sect within Judaism. These early supporters of the Jesus Movement are generally referred to as the followers of "the Way" (Acts 9:2; 18:25; 19:9, 23; 22:4; 24:14), or less often, as *Nazarenes* (Acts 24:5) rather than as "Christians." Little by little, the Way emerges as a distinct religion with its central focus rooted in the life, death, and resurrection of Jesus of Nazareth. Before we examine what the New Testament has to say about Prisca, we must first discuss the early days of Christianity with particular emphasis on the leader of the missionary movement that allows it to flourish: a man named Paul. Knowing something about the life of Paul and his role in the birth of Christianity enables us to better understand Prisca's missionary work and places her life into meaningful context.

We begin with the central question: Who is Paul? The simple answer to that question is that he is a charismatic missionary who travels around the eastern Mediterranean gathering converts to the Jesus Movement. He is the founder of several communities or churches, which will become the grassroots of the movement. More specifically, Saul, who will later change his name to Paul, is born in about 2 CE in Tarsus, a city that is today located in Turkey and was then part of the Roman Empire. This makes Paul a contemporary of Jesus, who is probably born around 6 BCE. We know very little about Saul's family, other than that he seems to have at least one sister (Acts 23:16) and appears not to have been married, or perhaps he is widowed (1 Cor 7:8). Tarsus is a "free city" in the empire, and thus, Saul is considered a free man and a Roman citizen (Acts 22:25–29).

During the years 12–15 CE, Saul studies in Jerusalem under one of the greatest Jewish teachers of his day, Gamaliel (Acts 22:3), and Saul eventually becomes a Pharisee (Acts 23:6; 26:4–5). The Pharisees, a popular Jewish sect during the Second Temple period (530 BCE–70 CE), are often somewhat demonized in the New Testament, though historically, they are actually fairly moderate. Most come from what we would call the middle class, and they espouse what is then a somewhat unique belief in the resurrection of the dead. Unlike other sects during this time period—including the Sadducees and the scribes, who are also mentioned in unflattering terms in the New Testament—the Pharisees generally do not collaborate with Rome.

The pivotal event in Saul's life comes in about 33 CE following the martyrdom of St. Stephen, who is stoned to death for boldly professing his faith in Jesus (Acts 6–7). Saul witnesses Stephen's death, and he is apparently tasked with keeping an eye on the cloaks of the stone throwers, who shed their bulky garments so that they might take better aim (Acts 7:58). Saul does not seem to be involved in the actual stoning of Stephen, but he is nonetheless in the business of persecuting the followers of the Way (Acts 8:1–3; 9:2). According to Acts, Saul receives written permission from the Sanhedrin to root out, arrest, and bring to trial those who confess a faith in Jesus as the Messiah (Acts 9:1–2). But then, something amazing happens that will forever alter Saul's life. Saul travels to Damascus, along with several others, to search the synagogues in order to apprehend followers of the Way. As he approaches the city, a burst of light engulfs him, knocking him to the ground as he hears Jesus ask him, "Saul, Saul, why do you persecute me?" (Acts 9:3–4). Saul is struck blind and must be led into Damascus by his traveling companions. Three days later, Jesus appears in a vision to a disciple named Ananias and instructs him to go to Saul and heal him of his blindness. No longer sightless, Saul is then baptized, and the man who once despised the followers of the Way becomes the most zealous missionary among them (Acts 9:4–18). This dramatic conversion as narrated in Acts is the object of much discussion among scholars, as Paul himself has a slightly different version of events (Gal 1:11–17; 1 Cor 15:8). Whatever the exact nature of his conversion experience, the result is the same; we know it is a powerful one, for it completely changes the trajectory of his life.

Saul, now *Paul* (Acts 13:9), begins to publicly proclaim the Good News in Damascus, but the local Jews reject his missionary efforts and even conspire to kill him (Acts 9:20–25). This will not be the last time Paul's life is threatened. He leaves Damascus under the cover of darkness and goes to Arabia. He remains there for three years, during which time Paul claims his Gospel is revealed to him by Jesus (Gal 1:11–12). The post-resurrection followers of Jesus are based in Jerusalem, led by James and Peter. This core group of Apostles and others consider themselves to be Jews who also accept Jesus as their Messiah. They continue to read and follow the Torah, circumcise their baby boys, and worship in their synagogues. Peter insists that converts to the Jesus Movement must first become Jews, which means, among other things, that men must submit to the Jewish rite of circumcision. Paul vociferously argues against this regulation, and he ultimately prevails. (I will have more to say about this in the Enduring Lessons section.) Gentiles are allowed to enter the fold without submitting to circumcision, and with this, Christianity becomes a religion distinct from Judaism. In a real sense, then, Paul is the founder of Christianity.

There are thirteen letters in the New Testament attributed to Paul, but most scholars agree that only seven are from his own hand; the other six are written a generation or two after Paul's death and address concerns of those later generations of Christians. The so-called authentic Pauline Epistles are, in chronological order, 1 Thessalonians, 1 Corinthians, Galatians, 2 Corinthians, Romans, Philippians, and Philemon. All of Paul's surviving letters (we can assume that he wrote many more that are lost to us) are written roughly during the years 49–63 CE, with commentators hotly debating the exact dates. In any case, all of the letters predate the Gospels, making Paul the earliest Christian writer.

With this brief introduction to Paul in mind, let us now explore what we know about Prisca. Her unique story is inexorably linked to two men: her husband, Aquila, and the Apostle Paul. The three work together as close colleagues, friends, and missionaries to help spread the Good News of Jesus Christ throughout the Roman Empire. Her name is from the Latin, *priscus*, meaning "ancient." In Acts, she is referred to not as Prisca, but as "Priscilla" the diminutive form of "Prisca." It is unclear why Luke (the purported author of Acts) chooses to use the diminutive form of Prisca's name; perhaps it is a way of acknowledging the closeness of the relationship between Prisca and Paul, reflecting the human tendency to use nicknames or pet names for those friends and relatives who occupy a special place in our inner circle. Or maybe "Priscilla" is the name by which she is known in certain Christian circles. In both Paul's letter to the Romans and in 1 Corinthians, she is called Prisca; she is also addressed as Prisca in 2 Tim 4:19. (Before we go any further, I feel the need to insert a brief editorial note to avoid confusion: In this chapter, I will refer to Prisca as *Priscilla* only when I am discussing her appearances in Acts of the Apostles; otherwise, I will use the name "Prisca," including references to her in the Enduring Lessons section.)

In all six of the references to Prisca (Acts 18:2–3, 18–19, 24–26; Rom 16:3–5; 1 Cor 16:19; 2 Tim 4:19), her name appears alongside that of her husband, Aquila, and in four instances, her name appears first. Most commentators are quick to point out that the ordering of names—even when there are only two, as in the case of Prisca and Aquila—is significant. Normally, the more prominent person is listed first, and if this is the case, then we can assume that perhaps Prisca is better known or that she comes from a more renowned or wealthier family than her husband, Aquila.

It is also important to note that Prisca is mentioned in the New Testament at three distinct periods of time. The two authentic Pauline

Epistles that mention Prisca, 1 Corinthians and Romans, are written in the middle of the first century—1 Corinthians around 53–54 CE and Romans, around 56–58 CE. The anonymous author of Luke–Acts is writing around 85 CE or later—nearly a generation after Paul and Prisca—and the unknown author of 2 Timothy comes to us from the early second century, around 125 CE, nearly *two* generations after Paul and Prisca. The frequent mention of Prisca's name in the generations *after* her death is a testimony to her importance in the evolution of Christianity.

The most information we have about her appears in Acts 18. Scholars are generally cautious about relying on Acts alone for information about Prisca. Indeed, the prevailing scholarly opinion tends to question the historicity of Acts, insisting that Acts presents a more idealized (or, as some scholars assert, a more fictionalized) version of the advent of Christianity. On the flip side, however, there is much in Acts that can be corroborated using outside sources. Since we have no way of knowing whether one thing is definitively true or not, we cannot dismiss Acts in our search for information about Prisca. I will therefore first explore what Acts has to say about her, then examine Paul's mention of her in two of his letters, before finally turning to the anonymous author of 2 Timothy and his brief mention of Prisca.

According to Acts, Priscilla and Aquila are a Jewish couple who live, at least for a time, in Rome. We know that Aquila is from Pontus, a region located in northeastern Asia Minor, along the southern shores of the Black Sea; unfortunately, we do not know anything about Priscilla's origins. Some commentators assume that Priscilla too hails from the region of Pontus and that the couple likely meets and marries there before traveling together to Rome. Plausible as it may seem, there is nothing in the text to support this assumption. In any case, Priscilla and Aquila are expelled from Rome when, in 49 CE, the emperor Claudius issues an edict banishing all Jews from the city. There is historical evidence to support the exodus of Priscilla and Aquila from Rome contained in the writings of the Roman historian Suetonius, who indicates that there is some discord among the Jews and the so-called Jewish-Christians living in the city (*The Life of Claudius* 25.4). This small detail is an exciting one and offers us a rare look at the nexus between the Jews who remain steadfastly Jewish and those Jews who depart from the Judaism of their youth and embrace a new faith in Christ. The tension between these two groups apparently causes such a fracas that the emperor expels *both* groups. We must remember that at this time, Jewish converts to the Way still consider themselves to be Jewish, so the conflict appears to be more of an internal one within Judaism. This eventually changes, but for the moment, the connection, though tenuous, remains.

Once expelled from Rome, Priscilla and Aquila relocate to the Greek city of Corinth, where they are living when Paul arrives in the city. It appears that Priscilla and Aquila are already believers in Christ before Paul's arrival in Corinth; that is, Paul does not convert the couple. We do not know how long the couple lives in Corinth before they meet up with Paul, but they are there long enough to establish a house church. House churches are a staple for the followers of the Way. Early Christians gather in the house of (usually) a wealthy woman where they pray, celebrate a meal together, and discuss Jesus. Paul stays with Priscilla and Aquila and works alongside the couple in their shared trade as tentmakers. Tentmaking and the repairing of tents is an important trade in the Roman Empire. It is the sort of occupation that one can set up almost anywhere, and thus it is the perfect profession for missionaries on the move, like Paul, Priscilla, and Aquila.

With the constant influx of Roman soldiers traveling from post to post, itinerant merchants, and other wayfaring citizens, tents and the skillful hands that know how to make and repair them are in high demand, undoubtedly keeping Priscilla, Aquila, and Paul quite busy. Their work together has many benefits, besides the obvious utility of making an honest living. Spending their days together plying their trade affords the three the opportunity to deepen their friendship, to discuss their faith, and to perhaps strategize their future missionary journeys. Having a tentmaking shop has another, very important benefit: such an establishment provides an excellent venue for gaining converts to the Way. If you have ever wondered why Paul chooses to go to a city like Corinth in hopes of gaining converts to the Jesus Movement, wonder no more. Corinth is a city that is bursting at the seams with people from all over the empire. It is a port city, brimming with sailors, soldiers, and merchants hawking their wares; bars and brothels are found on nearly every street corner. Amid the clamor and rush of people as they travel in and out of the city are the locals, who settle down and call Corinth home. Those who live in the city likely belong to one of the pagan cults dedicated to a variety of gods and goddesses. In addition to the old pagan cults, now added to the mix is a sudden influx of Jews expelled from Rome and followers of the new religious movement that will blossom into Christianity.

While we might view Corinth as the last place in the world to set up a Christian house church, Paul does not see it that way. Like someone who can look at an old, dilapidated house and envision painted shutters, lace curtains in the windows, and a white picket fence, Paul views Corinth as an orchard with low-hanging fruit, fully primed for the picking. In other words, he sees potential converts all around him in this city. Priscilla and

Aquila see this potential too. With thousands of people passing through the city on a daily basis, there is a constant demand for new tents and repair of old tents. This gives the missionary trio a chance to talk with their customers and to perhaps have more than one meeting with them. A typical scenario might go something like this: A Roman soldier needs to have his tent repaired. He asks around to find out where the tentmakers' shop is located. He finds the shop and upon entering it, barters with the proprietor for a good price. Once a price is agreed upon, the soldier is invited to share a drink or a morsel of food and the inevitable chin-wag that goes along with Mediterranean hospitality. This is the way business is still conducted in much of the Middle East. I have often been invited to sit and talk over a cup of tea or coffee with a business owner after I have purchased something in their shop, and though this might seem strange to Americans and others in the West, it is nonetheless considered a more "civilized" way to conduct business.

Returning to our scenario, after the tent is repaired, the soldier returns to the shop. He comments on the repair, and perhaps another conversation ensues. We can imagine that Paul, Priscilla, and Aquila might seize such opportunities and guide the conversation from the practical—buying or repairing a tent—to the spiritual. Perhaps Paul, Priscilla, or Aquila might begin by simply asking the question Have you heard about Jesus, the Messiah?

If the customer shows an interest in learning more, then he or she would likely be invited to the local house church to meet other followers of the Way. It is largely assumed that Priscilla and Aquila are in charge of several house churches during their long missionary careers. One church is perhaps in their prior place of residence, Rome; another, in Corinth; then a third in Ephesus; and finally, a fourth house church is established when the pair return to Rome, roughly a decade after their expulsion.

Paul stays with Priscilla and Aquila in Corinth "for a considerable time" working with them in their shared trade and continuing their missionary work (Acts 18:18). Eventually, the three set sail to Ephesus, where they part company; Priscilla and Aquila remain in Ephesus and set up another house church and presumably, another tent shop, and Paul travels from city to city, preaching the Good News of Jesus Christ (Acts 18:19–23).

While in Ephesus, Priscilla and Aquila meet a fellow Jew and follower of the Way named Apollos, from Alexandria, Egypt (Acts 18:24–26). Apollos is described as "an eloquent man, well-versed in the scriptures" (Acts 18:24). Evidently an ardent convert to the Jesus movement, he nonetheless makes a few public blunders, and Priscilla and Aquila, not wishing to humiliate him in front of others, meet privately with him and correct his misconceptions regarding the Way.

> He had been instructed in the Way of the Lord; and he spoke with burning enthusiasm and taught accurately the things concerning Jesus, though he knew only the baptism of John. He began to speak boldly in the synagogue; but when Priscilla and Aquila heard him, they took him aside and explained the Way of God to him more accurately. (Acts 18:25–26)

Priscilla's interaction with Apollos helps us to learn more about her. Most obvious is the kindness she shows to Apollos when he preaches inaccuracies in the synagogue. When I read the story of Apollos in Acts 18, I am often reminded of the adage "A little knowledge can be a dangerous thing." Apollos has received instruction, but his education regarding Jesus and the Way seems quite limited and therefore incomplete. This does not, however, stop him from speaking "boldly in the synagogue" (Acts 18:26). Priscilla and Aquila demonstrate through their actions the way in which Christians ought to treat one another: with kindness, respect, and love.

Priscilla comes to Apollos as a teacher who possesses superior knowledge; she corrects his inaccuracies and fills in the gaps left by his previous instructor. It is important to point out here that the notion of a wise woman teaching a man in this way is virtually unheard of in the Bible. Added to her already impressive credentials (tentmaker, missionary, and church leader) is teacher. Apollos, fortified with a more solid education, thanks to Priscilla and Aquila, moves on to Corinth, Priscilla's and Aquila's old stomping grounds, where he continues to boldly proclaim the Good News (Acts 18: 27–28).

Two important letters support Prisca's central role in the missionary efforts of Paul and help to make the information in Acts more credible. We begin with Paul's First Letter to the Corinthians in search of Prisca. (Recall that it is only in Acts that she is referred to as Priscilla; I will now refer to her as Prisca.) Writing from the city of Ephesus where he lives and works with Prisca and Aquila, Paul sends a letter to the Christian community in Corinth to address some rather serious issues, including factionalism (1 Corinthians 3), sexual immorality (1 Cor 7:1–17, 25–28), and the lure of pagan cults (1 Corinthians 8). In short, the Corinthian Christians are struggling with their new faith and they write to Paul in Ephesus for guidance. Paul responds to them, using what is at times some very harsh words. But we are most concerned with Paul's mention of Prisca, and for that, we must turn to the final chapter of his letter.

In the closing of 1 Corinthians, Paul writes, "The churches of Asia send greetings. Aquila and Prisca, together with the church in their house, greet you warmly in the Lord" (1 Cor 16:19). This brief mention of Prisca, one of two times in which her name comes *after* her husband's, corroborates the fact that the couple has a house church in Ephesus, something we generally assume from Acts. Notable is the manner in which Paul links his greetings with Prisca and Aquila and members of their house church; this brief mention of Prisca provides for us a powerful link to Paul and her central role as co-missionary, along with Aquila. Perhaps Paul singles out Aquila and Prisca in his letter to the Corinthians because of their ties to that city. Before moving to Ephesus with Paul, the couple has a house church in Corinth, a fact that is also supported in Acts (Acts 18:1–3). Their friends and fellow followers of the Way back in Corinth probably appreciate a brief update on the pair. Additionally, Paul's mention of Prisca and Aquila in what is, to some extent, a letter of reprimand addressing some of the Corinthians' distinctly un-Christian-like behavior may be Paul's way of softening the blow, so to speak, with some friendly greetings. Paul's mention of Prisca and Aquila also helps to fortify his own position, which basically adjures the Corinthians to discontinue their disreputable conduct. Paul presents the beloved pair as his allies in hopes that a united front might be more effective in healing the fractured Corinthian community.

In his final letter, written around 56–58 CE to the Christian community in Rome, Paul again sends greetings on behalf of Prisca and Aquila in his closing.

> Greet Prisca and Aquila, who work with me in Christ Jesus, and who risked their necks for my life, to whom not only I give thanks, but also all the churches of the Gentiles. Greet also the church in their house. (Rom 16:3–5)

Most scholars feel that Paul's letter to the Romans contains the fullest expression of Paul's theology. Written while he is in Greece, most likely in the city of Corinth, Paul plans to visit Rome, and the letter is a way to introduce himself to the Christian community there. Paul mentions that Prisca and Aquila (in this instance, Prisca's name precedes her husband's name) "risked their necks" for his life (Rom 16:4). Some scholars feel that Paul is alluding to a riot that breaks out in Ephesus after Paul and his companions preach there. Apparently, some of the locals who make their living by casting and selling statues of the fertility goddess Artemis worry that Paul has ruined their business with all of his talk about Jesus (Acts 19). The riot eventually subsides, but Paul and his traveling companions, Gaius and

Aristarchus, narrowly escape the crowd's wrath. Paul himself mentions his fight with the "wild animals at Ephesus" (1 Cor 15:32), which may or may not refer to this riot. Whatever the actual circumstances, Prisca and Aquila are somehow instrumental in rescuing Paul—perhaps through negotiations with certain officials or using their connections with notables in the city to protect Paul—though their exact role is unclear. Paul offers thanks to them and specifically mentions their house church in Ephesus.

Prisca's final mention is again in the form of a greeting, found in 2 Timothy, one of three so-called Pastoral Epistles along with 1 Timothy and Titus. Though there is always some debate among scholars concerning authorship, most assume that 2 Timothy is a *pseudepigraphical* text, that is, a text that is written in the name of another—in this case, Paul—by an anonymous author, which was a common practice in antiquity. The Pastoral Epistles can best be described as mini guide books for pastors shepherding Christian congregations during the early second century, long after Paul's death (in about 67 CE). Unfortunately, as Christianity grows, the role of women within the Church slowly diminishes and the Pastoral Epistles reflect some of these changes. For example, in 1 Tim 2:11–12, women are no longer leaders in house churches but instead are instructed to remain silent: "Let a woman learn in silence with full submission. I permit no woman to teach or to have authority over a man; she is to keep silent." This is a far cry from the autonomy and equality women enjoy in the early days of Christianity, when the followers of the Way preserve in their communities the inclusive nature of Jesus' ministry.

In 2 Tim 4:19, we find mention of Prisca: "Greet Prisca and Aquila, and the household of Onesiphorus." Once again, her name comes before her husband's name. What is most striking about the greeting in 2 Timothy is that Prisca is still remembered by the Christian community decades after her death. Her missionary work and association with Paul are held in such high esteem that her name evokes reverence and respect among a whole new generation of Christians, many of whom unfortunately resonate with that ancient, shrill voice that commands women to learn in silence and submission (1 Tim 2:11–12). In light of the reduced role women play in the Christian Church of the second century, it is remarkable that Prisca is singled out by the author at all. Significantly, she is also linked with "the household of Onesiphorus" (2 Tim 4:19). Onesiphorus is Paul's friend from Ephesus who travels to Rome and assists Paul after the Apostle is arrested and imprisoned there (2 Tim 1:16–18). Like Onesiphorus, Prisca is a trusted and cherished friend who, along with her husband, is a central figure in the life and mission of Paul. An educated businesswoman, loyal helpmate to her husband, compassionate, worldly, and faithful, Prisca stands in the company of those early Christian pioneers who in spirit and love help to spread the Good News of Jesus Christ to the ends of the earth.

Prisca's Enduring Lessons

Prisca's life provides for us a window into the world of the post-resurrection Christian community, and her actions, as a member of the Christian missionary movement, enable us to understand how the religion that would become Christianity spread throughout the Roman Empire. As I mention in the introduction, one of the most obvious and practical reasons why Christianity is able to gain a large number of converts in a relatively short period of time has to do with Roman infrastructure. A network of roads, constructed with great precision by Roman engineers, provides Christian missionaries with the means to move freely and expediently to and from cities within the empire. Their initial efforts result in a series of small house churches, many in the homes of wealthy women. Soon, there are house churches in nearly every major city within the empire, and within decades, they expand beyond the confines of their rafters and are replaced by the first primitive churches. Eventually, a hierarchy is established, and in less than a few hundred years, the Church is off and running.

Prisca lives during this exciting and perilous time in history, and she is both a witness to and active participant in the birth of the Church. As thrilling as all of this seems to us, we must remember that while many eagerly embrace Christianity, there are countless more who oppose it. There are many years of widespread abuse and martyrdom in the few hundred years it takes for Christianity to gain a firm footing and become the official religion of the Roman Empire. Still, the movement inaugurated by Jesus receives its lifeblood through the missionary movement that carries his message of salvation, mercy, and eternal life from Jerusalem all the way to Rome. Beyond offering us a brief look back to those fractious and exhilarating days of the earliest Christians, her story also imparts to us two significant enduring lessons: the importance of teamwork; and the meaning of partnership in marriage.

I have read many books and commentaries about Paul and I have even taken my students to visit some of the places associated with Paul's missionary work, including Rome, Corinth, and Ephesus, places where we know that Prisca, with the help of Aquila and Paul, set up house churches. I have always thought of Paul as the founder of Christianity as we know it today because without Paul, and other missionaries like him, Christianity might have remained just another sect within Judaism. I must confess that I have harbored a somewhat glorified vision of Paul as a trailblazer whose powerful conversion experience galvanizes him into action and turns him into perhaps the greatest missionary who ever lived. Today, I realize that Paul is an extraordinary individual, but he does not convert the masses on his own; he has help. In fact, he has a lot of help, including Prisca. In addition to the popular husband-and-wife missionary team Prisca and Aquila, whose names survive and have become part of the Christian historical narrative, there are hundreds, if not thousands of other early Christian missionaries, the unsung heroes and heroines whose names are known only to God.

Prisca's missionary work is commendable; she works alongside her husband and sometimes with Paul, traveling from place to place, teaching and proclaiming Jesus as Lord. We admire her talents as a craftswoman, businesswoman, teacher, and wife; but it is helpful, I think to view her not only in terms of her efforts as part of a famous missionary team, but also as someone who represents those countless other missionaries, both male and female, who work to make Christianity a reality. The teamwork and camaraderie that characterize these early Christian missionaries remind us of those who know Jesus and who labor beside him, healing the sick, preaching, and proclaiming the Good News of the Kingdom of God. In the years following Jesus' death, as the missionary movement begins, the followers of the Way are mindful of the example Jesus sets for them: they are to love one another, treat others with respect and compassion, and pray often. This all sounds quite lovely, and in our imaginations, we might envision Prisca, Aquila, and Paul as Spirit-filled comrades who travel together around the Roman Empire, joyfully gathering converts to the Jesus Movement.

Historically, we know that it is not uncommon for Christian missionaries to travel in small teams; husband-and-wife missionaries like Prisca and Aquila are also fairly common.

Anyone who has ever been part of a team, however, knows that there are inherent challenges. Differences of opinion, conflicting strategies, and personality clashes, just to name a few, can make teamwork an unpleasant experience. I have already stated that Acts, a text that prominently features Prisca, presents a somewhat idealized version of early Christian community life. In real life, however, whenever there is a group of individuals living and working together, there are inevitable problems and conflicts— in families, in religious orders, and even in college dormitories. The wing of the Jesus Movement comprised of missionaries, like Prisca and Aquila, is no exception. At its best, the group might consist of faithful individuals who are mindful of Jesus' example to treat others with loving kindness; at its worst, there is surely dissention, misinformation, and squabbling in the ranks. The story of Apollos, a recent convert to the Way, is a case in point (Acts 18:24–26). Recall that Apollos, who is a bit of a loose cannon, has only partial knowledge about Jesus, limited to the baptism of John. Despite this, he speaks with great authority in the synagogue at Ephesus, and Prisca and Aquila must take him aside and tutor him properly. We can imagine that this sort of thing happens often and must be a source of great consternation to Paul and his missionary team.

In addition to the internal problems that likely face Prisca's missionary work, there are external issues that threaten to divide Paul's missionary teams. People with big personalities, strong opinions, and deeply held beliefs often attract admirers and adversaries in equal number, and Paul certainly has his share of fans and foes. Up-and-coming religious movements, like Christianity, sometimes branch out in a variety of directions, often with competing beliefs, resulting in diverse "brands" of Christianity. It is clear that not everyone who embraces Christianity sees things Paul's way. For example, in the opening of this chapter, I briefly mention that in the early days of Christianity, there is a difference of opinion between some of the original Apostles based in Jerusalem and Paul regarding circumcision—specifically, whether circumcision should be a prerequisite for Gentile converts to Christianity. Although this issue is resolved at a council meeting between Paul and the Jerusalem Apostles (Acts 15; Galatians 2), there are some who reject the council's decision to dispense with the circumcision requirement. These detractors are usually referred to as "Judaizers": a group of Jewish Christians who believe that circumcision and the observance of Mosaic Law should be obligatory requirements for Gentile converts. Many scholars suspect that the Judaizers come from Jerusalem, though, truth to tell, we do not know exactly who they are or where they are from. What we *do* know is that they undermine Paul and his missionaries, causing a great deal of trouble within the fledgling churches founded by Paul. Prisca and Aquila are clearly aligned with Paul's brand of Christianity, and so it is likely that they, too, must deal with the infiltrating Judaizers.

All in all, it is not often easy to be a member of a team. We must often exercise a good deal of patience and, to put it bluntly, learn when to speak up and when to shut up! Prisca's patience in instructing Apollos, her willingness to uproot her family and travel from place to place, and her courage in facing outside troublemakers teaches us that a team working together for the greater good outweighs any potential difficulties. As a woman working closely with two men, she demonstrates the inclusive nature of the early Christian movement, which mirrors Jesus' egalitarian treatment of women. Whether our "team" happens to be our family, coworkers, neighbors, friends, or any other group with whom we are associated, Prisca reminds us that we must learn the art of give-and-take, lessons that can be difficult but imperative for the success of the team's collective mission.

Prisca is not only a member of a team of missionaries, she is also a wife. Her relationship with Aquila gives us a chance to reflect upon the meaning of true partnership in marriage, which brings us to her second most-enduring lesson. In the West today, where more than half of all marriages end in divorce, more than ever, we need to understand what it means to be an equal partner within the context of marriage. As a wife, Prisca faces challenges that are not unlike those of many modern wives. And as a businesswoman who works alongside her husband in their tentmaking trade, she must find a balance between work, her obligations as a spouse, and the additional challenges of her missionary work. We do not know if Prisca and Aquila have children together, but since most first-century married Jewish couples want and are expected to have children, it seems likely that she does. If Prisca is indeed a mother, then the added responsibilities of children means that she must have a very busy and full life. Many modern women who attempt to juggle the demands of family and work will resonate with Prisca's full-plate life. If you, too, have a full-plate life, you may find yourself wondering how Prisca is able to accomplish so much, especially in light of what we might consider the primitive circumstances of the first century, devoid of the technology and other modern conveniences that we today take for granted. Of course, not all technology is good all of the time. For instance, I am always amazed to see married couples having dinner together in a restaurant but, instead of talking or engaging with one another, they are reading or writing text messages to someone else!

As I read Prisca's story, I see a woman who is completely dedicated to God, her husband, and her missionary work. Unlike most women during the first century, who rarely, if ever, travel more than a few miles from their place of birth, Prisca moves often—from Rome, to Corinth, to Ephesus, and then back to Rome. Moving from place to place would likely preclude the possibility of help from her immediate or extended family, which means that Prisca and Aquila must rely heavily on each other for support. Earlier, I note that Prisca's name is always mentioned in conjunction with her husband's name, indicating that they are always together. The two work together and travel together; they preach and teach the Good News to potential converts together. They work together with Paul and, together, they operate a house church for the local followers of the Way. If you reread the last three sentences, you will find the key to Prisca's success in managing a life that seems, at least for most of us, to be quite unmanageable. The key, just in case you missed it, is togetherness. Their marriage is an alliance, and it is successful because both Prisca and Aquila share common interests and goals. They do not have to worry about how they will handle the many responsibilities and challenges that they must face every day because they will face whatever comes together. Togetherness in marriage means more than simply spending time with one another; togetherness represents solidarity, a secure base forged by the assurance of love, loyalty, respect, devotion, and friendship that unites two people in an unspoken and unshakable bond. In the patriarchal world of biblical antiquity, where many women are little more than slaves to their husbands, Prisca and Aquila's partnership is quite unique. Perhaps their marriage reflects shifting attitudes regarding the nature of marriage for the followers of the Way. If Jesus' fair and equal treatment of women is replicated in early Christian communities, it makes sense that his egalitarian view is extended to Christian marriage.

Prisca and Aquila have each other, but they also enjoy the support of their church community, their friend Paul, and, of course, God. Unfortunately, many young couples today lack this sort of essential support, and some marriages are doomed before they are even able to take root. In the fast-paced, technological world of the twenty-first century, many of us are overworked, overscheduled, and just plain exhausted. Most of the married couples I know use their weekends not for leisure time or family time but to catch up on all of the things they are unable to do during the busy workweek.

Prisca's story nudges us to look up from our iPhones and return to one another in the spirit of togetherness. Now, more than ever, her story presents couples with another model, a better model, for married life. Prisca is empowered by the unfailing solidarity of her husband and her community of faith; she reminds married couples to share their interests with one another, to offer support, affirmation, and kindness to each other. Prisca, the powerful missionary and steadfast spouse, speaks to us as bravely today as she undoubtedly speaks to her converts over two thousand years ago, urging us ever forward in faith, hope, and love.

12

The Woman at the Well: Missionary

A Conversation with Jesus

John 4:4–30; 39–42

But he had to go through Samaria. So he came to a Samaritan city called Sychar, near the plot of ground that Jacob had given to his son Joseph. Jacob's well was there, and Jesus, tired out by his journey, was sitting by the well. It was about noon.

A Samaritan woman came to draw water, and Jesus said to her, "Give me a drink." (His disciples had gone to the city to buy food.) The Samaritan woman said to him, "How is it that you, a Jew, ask a drink of me, a woman of Samaria?" (Jews do not share things in common with Samaritans.) Jesus answered her, "If you knew the gift of God, and who it is that is saying to you, 'Give me a drink,' you would have asked him, and he would have given you living water." The woman said to him, "Sir, you have no bucket, and the well is deep. Where do you get that living water? Are you greater than our ancestor Jacob, who gave us the well, and with his sons and his flocks drank from it?" Jesus said to her, "Everyone who drinks of this water will be thirsty again, but those who drink of the water that I will give them will never be thirsty. The water that I will give will become in them a spring of water gushing up to eternal life." The woman said to him, "Sir, give me this water, so that I may never be thirsty or have to keep coming here to draw water."

Jesus said to her, "Go, call your husband, and come back." The woman answered him, "I have no husband." Jesus said to her, "You are right in saying, 'I have no husband'; for you have had five husbands, and the one you have now is not your husband. What you have said is true!" The woman said to him, "Sir, I see that you are a prophet. Our ancestors worshipped on this mountain, but you say that the place where people must worship is in Jerusalem." Jesus said to her, "Woman, believe me, the hour is coming when you will worship the Father neither on this mountain nor in Jerusalem. You worship what you do not know; we worship what we know, for salvation is from the Jews. But the hour is coming, and is now here, when the true worshippers will worship the Father in spirit and truth, for the Father seeks such as these to worship him. God is spirit, and those who worship him must worship in spirit and truth." The woman said to him, "I know that [the] Messiah is coming" (who is called Christ). "When he comes, he will proclaim all things to us." Jesus said to her, "I am he, the one who is speaking to you."

Just then his disciples came. They were astonished that he was speaking with a woman, but no one said, "What do you want?" or, "Why are you speaking with her?" Then the woman left her water-jar and went back to the city. She said to the people, "Come and see a man who told me everything I have ever done! He cannot be the Messiah, can he?" They left the city and were on their way to him. . . .

Many Samaritans from that city believed in him because of the woman's testimony, "He told me everything I have ever done." So when the Samaritans came to him, they asked him to stay with them; and he stayed there for two days. And many more believed because of his word. They said to the woman, "It is no longer because of what you said that we believe, for we have heard for ourselves, and we know that this is truly the Savior of the world." (John 4:4–30, 39–42)

SOME OF the most memorable and meaningful conversations I have ever had have been with complete strangers. I travel often, mostly to Europe and the Middle East, and the conversations I remember most usually take place in the back of the plane in the middle of the night as we fly across the Atlantic. There, I meet a variety of passengers: the sleepless folk, like me, who simply cannot fall asleep on a plane; those with bad backs or anxious minds who cannot sit strapped into their seats for hours on end; and the blessed but weary flight attendants, taking a break from their chores as the majority of their passengers, contorted uncomfortably in their seats, bellies full of airplane food and wine, snore into the ears of their neighbors. During these chance encounters, I meet men and women from all over the world with various occupations and interests: business-men, poets, lawyers, actors, professional gamblers, clerics, chefs, garden-ers, sailors, and many more. I do not know if it is the circumstances or the hour, but some of the back-of-the-plane-conversations I have shared with people, most of whom have lives completely different from my own, have been interesting, amusing, and in one case, life changing. Perhaps this is why the story of Jesus and the woman at the well is one of my most cherished biblical tales.

When Jesus has a chance meeting with the woman at the well—com-monly referred to as "the Samaritan woman"—he, too, is on a journey, and what transpires between them changes her life forever. Passing through the somewhat hostile territory of Samaria, he pauses in the city of Sychar (called Shechem in some translations of the Bible) in the heat of the day to rest and refresh himself. Sending off his disciples to buy food, Jesus is left alone and he settles himself by the coolness of Jacob's well, an ancient site connected to the Patriarchs Jacob and his son Joseph. The site today is a small tourist attraction located in the city of Nablus on the West Bank. It is here that he encounters a local woman who has come to the well to draw water (John 4:7). Astute readers of the Bible will immedi-ately think of other chance encounters between men and women at wells: Rebekah and Abraham's servant, the latter of whom is sent on an errand to procure a wife for Abraham's son, Isaac (Genesis 24); Jacob and Rachel (Gen 29:1–12); and Moses and Zipporah (Exod 2:15–21). These previ-ous chance encounters are often referred to as "wooing-scenes" because the meetings result in marriage. Though some commentators attempt to connect these "well scenes" with the story of the Samaritan woman and thus infer some sort of romantic liaison between Jesus and the woman, a careful reading of the text does not support this notion; the well merely provides the setting for the conversation between the Samaritan woman and Jesus.

When Jesus first meets the Samaritan woman, John provides for us an important, but often-overlooked detail: the hour of the day is about noon (John 4:6). Before the conversation between Jesus and the woman even begins, this small detail furnishes us with some provisional information about the unnamed Samaritan woman. One of the many chores expected of women during biblical times is to provide water for the family (and animals, if they have any). Wells are usually located within walking distance of the town, and most women come to the well early in the morning, or more rarely, in the evening. That the Samaritan woman comes to the well at midday suggests that she is not your average first-century housewife. What is she doing in the early morning hours, when most decent women are up, standing in line at the well in order to procure water for their families? Sleeping in perhaps? She certainly does not seem to be a conscientious wife and mother. Later, we will learn that she has had five "husbands" and currently has a lover who is not her husband at all (John 4:17–18). Today, many people shrug at a sexual and marital history such as hers, but in the patriarchal times in which she lives, her situation is nothing short of scandalous. Gossip moves with astonishing speed during biblical antiquity, spreading through the cities, towns, and villages like a YouTube clip gone viral. Perhaps her late arrival at the well is avoidance behavior; the other women of the city, aware of her sullied reputation, are likely to shun her.

As she approaches the well alone, she meets a strange man. Any upright woman would leave such a scene immediately, but she remains. Unaccompanied by her father, brother, husband, or other male family member, she saunters up to the well and to Jesus. As noted in previous chapters, men and women, even of the same family, generally do not speak with each other in public, yet Jesus, ignoring this social convention, speaks directly to her: "Give me a drink" (John 4:7), which seems more like a command then a request. The woman's response indicates that she is also in the habit of ignoring social boundaries between men and women: "'How is it that you, a Jew, ask a drink of me, a woman of Samaria?' (Jews do not share things in common with Samaritans.)" (John 4:9). The woman's question and John's parenthetical notation indicate that there are boundaries beyond gender being crossed here.

First-century Jews and Samaritans are a little like the Hatfields and the McCoys in that they generally despise each other and avoid any kind of communication at all. Jews consider Samaritans ritually unclean, and Jesus' request for a drink from the cup of a Samaritan woman is therefore unthinkable. The animosity between these two groups can be traced as far back as 920 BCE when Israel splits in two, with the nation of Judah to the south, with its capital, Jerusalem, and Israel to the north, with its capital,

Samaria. The flames of hatred are further fanned by the fall of the north-ern kingdom to the Assyrians in 721 BCE. While a good portion of the populace is taken into exile to Assyria, those who are left behind begin to intermarry with the local Canaanites and people from many other nations. According to 2 Kgs 17:24–41, the king of Assyria imports to Samaria foreigners from a variety of nations, who bring along with them what the Israelites consider their disreputable gods and odious religious practices. An attempt is made to purge these other religions, but it fails miserably, and Israel's beloved Yhwh becomes one of a pantheon of deities.

> They also worshipped the LORD and appointed from among them-selves all sorts of people as priests of the high places, who sacrificed for them in the shrines of the high places. So they worshipped the LORD, but they also served their own gods, after the manner of the nations from among whom they had been carried away. To this day they continue to practice their former customs. They do not worship the LORD and they do not follow the statutes or the ordinances or the law or the commandment that the LORD commanded the children of Jacob, whom he named Israel. (2 Kgs 17:32–34)

All of this, of course, is abhorrent to the Jews in Judah. To make matters more complicated, the Samaritans reject the centralized worship in the Jerusalem Temple and instead recognize the city of Shechem (Sychar) as their holy city, installing a temple on nearby Mt. Gerizim that is later de-stroyed by the Jewish leader John Hyrcanus sometime around 128 BCE. The memory of their temple still lingers in the hearts of the Samaritans of Jesus' day and they continue to worship on the holy mountain where it once stood. As a religious group, there are a number of practicing Samaritans today. Estimates vary, but there may be roughly 500–1,000 Samaritans, most of whom live in Israel/Palestine and still worship on Mt. Gerizim. Much more can be said of this irreparable rift in relations between the Jews and the Samaritans, but for our purposes, understanding a bit of the history behind this split and the sense of loathing between the two groups is important for understanding much of our present story.

Scholars are eager to point out that when the Samaritan woman calls Jesus a Jew (John 4:9), it is the only time in the Gospels that he is ever referred to as such. John's Gospel is sometimes accused of being anti-Se-mitic, mainly because of the way in which John characterizes Jesus' ene-mies using the catchall term "the Jews" when referring to them. This is an unfair accusation as John's use of the term "the Jews" refers only to the small but treacherous group of fellow Jews who are bent on destroying

Jesus. Jesus responds to the woman's question "How is it that you, a Jew, ask a drink of me, a woman of Samaria?" (John 4:9) with a deeply theological retort: "If you knew the gift of God, and who it is that is saying to you, 'Give me a drink,' you would have asked him, and he would have given you living water" (John 4:10). The woman, thinking on a concrete level, misunderstands Jesus' offer of true life in the spirit. She assumes that Jesus is stating his preference for flowing water, such as from a stream or fountain, rather than the still water one finds in a well, and she asks him how he proposes to find this flowing water when he doesn't even have a bucket (John 4:11). Jesus clarifies and tells her,

> "Everyone who drinks of this water will be thirsty again, but those who drink of the water that I will give them will never be thirsty. The water that I will give will become in them a spring of water gushing up to eternal life." (John 4:13–14)

Unfortunately, the woman again misunderstands. Jesus is offering her the gift of eternal life in the spirit, but the woman thinks he is offering her a personal water supply that mitigates her frequent trips to the well, an idea she very much likes (John 4:15).

Sensing that the woman is still missing the point, Jesus decides to try another approach, instructing the woman to go home and return with her husband. When woman replies that she does not have a husband, Jesus tells her, "You are right in saying, 'I have no husband'; for you have had five husbands, and the one you have now is not your husband. What you have said is true!" (John 4:17–18). With this statement, a slow dawning begins and the woman affirms Jesus as a prophet (John 4:19). Some commentators offer long-winded statements regarding the woman's numerous husbands and her current lover, to whom she is not married. Since Jews are allowed to marry only three times, some assume that the same is true of Samaritans, which would mean that the Samaritan woman is, at the very least, considered a sinner. Other scholars, including this one, feel that Jesus' mention of the woman's rather exceptional marital history is not meant as a means of judgment; after all, Jesus is regularly in the company of all sorts of people, including sinners. The reason why Jesus mentions the multiple husbands is his attempt to move her to another level of understanding.

The woman, thinking that Jesus is a prophet, mentions a bone of contention between Jews and Samaritans, namely, the disagreement concerning the central place of worship—Jerusalem for Jews and Mt. Gerizim for Samaritans (John 4:19–20). Jesus is moving her along, but she is still thinking concretely. Dismissing her divergence from the path along which he is attempting to lead her, Jesus minimizes her comment concerning centralized worship and skillfully guides her to a place of spiritual enlightenment. Addressing her only as "Woman"—a polite form of address at this time, as I've noted—Jesus tells her,

> "Woman, believe me, the hour is coming when you will worship the Father neither on this mountain nor in Jerusalem. You worship what you do not know; we worship what we know, for salvation is from the Jews. But the hour is coming, and is now here, when the true worshippers will worship the Father in spirit and truth, for the Father seeks such as these to worship him. God is spirit, and those who worship him must worship in spirit and truth." (John 4:21–24)

Quibbling over which place is the better to worship is swept aside as Jesus proclaims that from the roots of Judaism, something new and marvelous is sprouting. The Kingdom is coming, and is indeed upon us, ushering in a new world-order in which "true worshippers" will worship God the Father in "spirit and truth" (John 4:23). The old ways that divide worshippers into temples—us versus them—will not flourish in the Kingdom. I have referred to the Kingdom many times in this book, as it is central to the teachings of Jesus. For Jesus, the Kingdom is closely tied to his apocalyptic view of the end of days, which he believes will usher in a new, harmonious, transformed world that will replace the evil and corrupt present age. God is not described in anthropomorphic terms like the stone and wood-carved deities of Israel's neighbors but as "spirit" (John 4:24), and believers come to him in the same way, in truth and in spirit.

The woman understands this, for though Samaritans accept only their version of the Torah as their authoritative religious text (rejecting other texts in the Hebrew Bible, including the prophetic literature), they nonetheless expect a Messiah (whom they call *Taheb*, "the one who returns") and therefore comprehend theological concepts such as "spirit" and "truth." The Samaritan woman tells Jesus, "I know that [the] Messiah is coming. . . . When he comes, he will proclaim all things to us" (John 4:25). At last, we have the woman moving from misunderstanding to comprehension. Knowing that she has made this leap, Jesus reveals his true identity: "I am he, the one who is speaking to you" (John 4:26). Jesus' messianic self-designation carries a significant, additional weight as he refers to himself: "I am." The term "I am," first used here, is a common feature in John's Gospel. Most scholars suggest that Jesus' use of this term infers his divinity, often connecting it to Exod 3:14, a verse in which God reveals his Divine name to Moses: "God said to Moses, 'I AM WHO I AM.'"

Interrupting this dramatic scene, the disciples return from their food run, dismayed to find Jesus talking to the woman, but possessed enough of their senses to keep their mouths shut (John 4:27). As if annoyed at their intrusion, the woman hurries away, leaving behind her water jar. This seemingly small detail—the woman's abandoned water jar—is important for two reasons. First, the water jar remains at the well, a concrete symbol of the woman's past misunderstanding. She comes to the well to draw water, and through her conversation with a complete stranger, she receives "living water" and life in the spirit. Second, the woman is so moved by her encounter with Jesus that she rushes off to the city to tell others. She becomes, in a very real sense, a missionary; now filled with living water, she will not be encumbered by the burden of an empty vessel as she hastens to spread the Good News to her neighbors.

Upon entering the city, the woman urges her countrymen and women to "come and see a man who told me everything I have ever done! He cannot be the Messiah, can he?" (John 4:29). Despite her dubious reputation, her testimony is apparently convincing, as people begin to flock to Jesus. The Samaritans invite Jesus to stay with them for two days, during which time they come to recognize him as the "Savior of the world" (John 4:42). John makes it clear, however, that while the Samaritan woman's proclamation is the impetus behind what appears to be a mass conversion of the people in the city of Sychar, their declaration of Jesus as "Savior of the world" results from their own personal encounter with him. It would appear that Jesus makes good use of his time during his two-day sojourn in what most would consider hostile territory.

The story of the Samaritan woman reveals to us a Jesus who looks beyond such stereotypes of gender and religion to focus on the person. If Jesus is represented in the story as a charismatic and competent teacher, then it is only because he chooses a student who is able and willing to move beyond the concrete to the sublime. His pupil is a social outcast, much as Jesus is in a city that despises Jews, and their relationship is an unlikely one, crossing the social boundaries of their day that dictate scores of rigid social and religious taboos. Jesus nonetheless chooses her and she, in a sense, chooses him, for she might just as easily walk away from the strange man at the well. Perhaps something inside her urges her to remain, to look beyond their differences for a chance to learn something more, about herself, about the man, Jesus, and about God. In the spirit of a disciple, she learns her lessons and then, in the spirit of ministry, she reaches out to her neighbors to share what she has learned with them. Thus it is that a woman with a checkered past, considered the least among her people, becomes a missionary to them, leading them to the ever-flowing waters of truth and spirit.

The Samaritan Woman's Enduring Lessons

I began this chapter with a musing of sorts on chance encounters and the ways in which random meetings can be a rich source of information. There are many people who subscribe to the notion that there is no such thing as a chance encounter, insisting instead that there is a Mind Behind it All who weaves with great care the tapestry of our lives. In each person's complex design are strands, representing others who come into their lives at precise moments: friends, neighbors, colleagues, the person who stands behind us at the market or even a fellow passenger on a plane late at night. I cannot say for certain whether or not this is true, but I remain open to the idea.

In any case, I am particularly fond of a saying relayed to me by a colleague many years ago: "When the student is ready, the teacher will come." I think of this saying often when I read the story of the Samaritan woman, for she was truly a student who was ready to receive her teacher.

Jesus' conversation with the Samaritan woman is the longest conversation Jesus has with anyone in the Gospels. For that reason alone, we ought to pay close attention to it. Their meeting is an extraordinary tale that challenges the prevailing social norms of the day relating to gender, ethnicity, and religion. These are important and enduring lessons, but as a lifelong educator, I view these lessons in the context of learning. Mindful that Jesus is a skillful rabbi, or teacher, who challenges his students, or disciples, to consider alternative perspectives and to look at others in a different light, we will examine the Samaritan women's enduring lessons under the umbrella of education.

If you are reading this book, you are probably the sort of person who is interested in learning. More than likely, you are someone who also has an interest in religion and the Bible. Such interests place you miles ahead of most of my students, most of whom enroll in one of my classes not because they necessarily want to, but because of a university requirement that stipulates they take a requisite number of religious studies courses. Of course, this is not always the case; some students are majoring in religious studies and others take religious studies courses simply because they are interested in the topic. None of this really matters to me, for I welcome each and every one of them. I know that once they begin to read the Bible or explore other world religions, they will learn a great deal and most will come to appreciate the history and valuable lessons of the discipline.

When I read the story of the Samaritan woman, I think of my students, many of whom have never taken a religious studies class before. Like the woman at the well, it often takes patience and time to move some students from one level of thinking to another. Getting them to think biblically and theologically, rather than concretely and scientifically, is often a painstaking process. This is complicated by the fact that, for the most part, I deal with what sociologists and theologians refer to as an "un-churched generation." This means that most—but certainly not all—of my students have had very little formal religious education taught by professionals in the field: individuals with degrees in religious education, religious studies, biblical studies, or theology. Many attend church, temple, meeting hall, or mosque only sporadically, and some have abandoned the practice completely by the time they come to sit before me in my college classroom. The reasons for the decline in religious practice and, consequently, the reading of the Bible in America and Western Europe are varied and complex and beyond the focus of this chapter. (I discuss this issue in my book *What the Bible Really Tells Us: The Essential Guide to Biblical Literacy*, 2011.) That I mention it at all here, however, is germane, for Jesus' encounter with the Samaritan woman can best be described as a series of lessons. The lessons she learns, imparted to us by the Fourth Evangelist, have endured for over two thousand years and serve as a model of Christian behavior toward others.

Jesus begins to teach these valuable lessons with his first words to the Samaritan woman: "Give me a drink" (John 4:7). His words seem harmless enough: a thirsty traveler asks a woman who is about to draw water from a well for a cup. Ancient readers, however, are shocked that Jesus speaks to a Samaritan woman, for this violates several religious and social rules mentioned earlier, namely, that men and women do not speak to each in public, and Jews and Samaritans are sworn enemies. But Jesus is not like most Jewish men of his day. Indeed, throughout the Gospels, Jesus is portrayed as someone who treats women fairly, with the respect and dignity they deserve. Most of the women profiled in this book attest to this fact.

If Jesus speaks to the woman, despite her gender, the lesson of equality is obvious. But the woman is also a Samaritan, and thus we learn another important lesson: we should not discriminate against others based on their ethnic background. When I teach the story of the Samaritan woman, I usually pause after the woman responds to Jesus' request for a drink, "How is it that you, a Jew, ask a drink of me, a woman of Samaria?" (John 4:9) and have my students turn to Luke 10:25–37, and together we read the Parable of the Good Samaritan (I mention this parable briefly in chapter 1). I do this as a way to further emphasize Jesus' acceptance of others, like the Samaritan woman, regardless of their ethnicity. Unique to the Gospel of Luke, the Parable of the Good Samaritan is one of the best known of Jesus' parables, and you are probably already familiar with it. But even if you are, consider taking a few moments to read it again, as I will simply summarize it here.

The parable is designed to give an answer to a question posed by a lawyer in a crowd of people gathered around Jesus. The question is this: "Who is my neighbor?" (Luke 10:29). The tale begins when a man, presumably a Jew, is robbed, beaten, and left for dead on the side of the road (Luke 10:30). Two temple officials, a priest and then a Levite, pass by the injured man and do nothing (Luke 10:31–32). But when a Samaritan traveler notices the man on the side of the road, he tends to his wounds, takes him to an inn, and pays the innkeeper to care for the wounded man until he (the Samaritan) returns for him (Luke 10:33–35). When Jesus finishes telling the story, he turns to the lawyer and, presumably, the crowd, and asks, "Which of these three, do you think, was a neighbor to the man who fell into the hands of the robbers?" (Luke 10:36), to which the lawyer responds, "The one who showed him mercy" (Luke 10:37). Jesus instructs the lawyer, "Go and do likewise" (Luke 10:37), thus providing a response to the lawyer's question "Who is my neighbor?" If you missed the point, the answer is *everyone*.

In the divisive world of ancient Israel—where Jews and Samaritans are sworn enemies—this is a radical message. We can almost hear the gasps of shock, the hissing, and the foot stamping rising from the incredulous crowd as Jesus tells the story. Of course, parables are one of Jesus' primary methods of teaching, precisely because of the shock value parables provide. That Jesus makes the kindhearted Samaritan the hero in the story is what contributes to its surprising twist. Today, most people do not know the crucial backstory—that Jews and Samaritans despise one another—and they totally miss the powerful punch of a lesson this parable provides.

Jesus' rejection of the Jews' blatant discrimination against Samaritans, as illustrated in the Parable of the Good Samaritan, is taken to an even higher level in the story of the woman at the well, for not only is she a detestable Samaritan, she is also a woman. The preliminary lessons of gender equality and acceptance of others are, in academic terms, prerequisites for the course. Having imparted these first two lessons to the woman and, ostensibly, to the reader, Jesus turns his attention to the other lessons of the day.

Fortunately for Jesus, his pupil, like most people during biblical antiquity, demonstrates a working knowledge of her own religion. We know, for example, that the Samaritan woman recognizes the sacred site of Mt. Gerizim, the place where a Samaritan temple once stood, as the central place of worship and that she obviously believes in God, prophets, and the coming of the Messiah (John 4:19–20, 25). These are all basic tenets of the Samaritan faith, of which scholars, by and large, know very little. Because the Samaritan woman possesses such knowledge, Jesus' task as her teacher is much easier in that he is not starting with a blank slate. He knows that the woman is capable of thinking theologically, and he structures his lessons accordingly, bringing her along, step by step.

Today, teachers cannot assume that their students possess what we once took for granted as common knowledge as recently as fifty years ago when most people understood key biblical stories and central figures, such as Moses, David, and Jesus. In the past, most people were taught basic theological truths and religious ideas in school and in their place of worship; all of this was reinforced in the home. Modern teachers of religion or biblical studies, however, know that this is no longer the case. We therefore must spend a significant amount of time engaged in remedial work before actually teaching the objectives of the course. And this is also true for a variety of other disciplines. Imagine, for example, the challenges an art professor might face when presenting the great religious works of Italian Renaissance art, or an English professor's frustration in teaching Dante's epic poem, the *Divine Comedy*, both of which center on biblical characters and themes, to a group of students who know nothing about the Bible.

Religious and biblical illiteracy is one thing—we cannot expect students to know something that has never been taught to them—but resistance to learning is an entirely different matter. Although I rarely find my students to be resistant to learning, there are, occasionally, a few who feel threatened when presented with new information that may conflict with what they have been taught in the past. I do not think this is a problem in any other academic discipline; for example, if a math professor presents a new method for solving an equation, I doubt that many students would feel threatened. But when it comes to matters of religion, especially if it involves the Bible, I have witnessed people who clamp tight their minds, refusing to entertain the slightest possibility that there may be other ways of looking at things or that what they have been taught in the past is, in a word, wrong. Judaism and Christianity have rich histories of scholarship; lively discussions and debates are encouraged. In the New Testament, Jesus is featured as a powerful teacher who challenges his disciples and others to stretch their minds and hearts. He encourages questions and calls us to envision the Kingdom, a new world based on kindness, goodness, hope, and love. Imagine if those earliest followers of Jesus had walked away, slamming shut the doors of their minds and refusing to consider the possibility that they might learn something from the wise rabbi from the Galilee. I feel a great sense of gratitude to those who did not walk away but instead listened, changed, and then passed on Jesus' teachings to future generations.

At the start of each new semester, or when I speak to groups publicly, I try to stress two things at the outset: first, I am a teacher, not a preacher. I am not interested in converting people, evangelizing, or offering a sermon. Second, when I speak about biblical topics, my interpretations of certain stories and events in the Bible are based on years of academic study and research. Nonetheless, I remain open to other interpretations and welcome them, even as I may disagree. I ask my students or audience to approach whatever topic we might consider with the same openness.

The Samaritan woman models this sort of openness. Jesus capitalizes on what she already knows, corrects her misperceptions, and moves her to envision a new life in truth and in spirit. When she misunderstands his allusion to "living waters," thinking, indeed, hoping that there might be an alternative water supply that she can use instead of lugging her heavy water container to the location of the present well, Jesus realizes that he needs to take another tack, one that is more personal. When he reveals intimate knowledge of her complicated marital history, she recognizes Jesus as one who has been given the gift of prophecy. Jesus, like any good teacher, knows that a shift has occurred; he has brought her to a higher level of thinking. He will not allow her to slide backward, dismissing her off-topic comment regarding centralized worship for Jews versus Samaritans, and instead opens wide the doors of the Kingdom (John 4:20–24).

When Jesus speaks to her about worshipping God in spirit and truth, the Samaritan woman connects this sort of worship with the coming of the Messiah, at which point Jesus reveals his true identity (John 4:23–26). The woman believes Jesus' claim and dashes off to tell her neighbors. She is an unlikely missionary, but her testimony is convincing, and the people of the city set out to find the rabbi from the Galilee (John 4:30). We can't help but puzzle over the Samaritan woman's apparent success in her first missionary efforts. Why do the people of the city believe a woman who is generally scorned, snubbed, and viewed as an outcast? We can imagine that the woman's conversation with Jesus has, in some discernable way, transformed her. Her neighbors recognize a change, maybe in much the same way that the Israelites recognize Moses' transformation after his encounter with God on Mt. Sinai (Exod 34:29). Is her countenance glowing in the way that Moses' face shines as he descends the holy mountain? Probably not, but the Samaritan woman is somehow different. Her neighbors see it, and they want answers. Perhaps her transformation offers us a glimpse of what life is like in the Kingdom, where gender, ethnicity, race, religion, and all the other petty contrivances we humans construct as barriers no longer divide us. To worship in truth and spirit releases us from the fallacy of such barriers and brings us into a new life.

13

Concluding Thoughts

I HAVE ALWAYS been a voracious reader. When I was a child, I would devour book after book, sometimes reading two or three books on a variety of topics at the same time (though not simultaneously!). Over the years, I learned to think deeply about what I was reading, and though most of my books belonged to the local public library, whenever I was lucky enough to actually own the book, I would make notations in the margins as I read. When I finished reading a particular book, I would review my notes, or at the very least, sit back and reflect upon what I had read before jumping into a new book. If the book was a novel, I would think about the characters, the plot, and what I liked most (or least) about the book. If I read a nonfiction book, I would think about what I had learned and make connections to other books I had read on the subject. For example, during the summer between my exit from elementary school and my entrance into junior high school, I recall reading two books about birds. One book was filled with illustrations, while the other was more like a dictionary of birds. In thinking about both books, I realized that I was able to visually recognize many local birds, but I could also recall certain facts about them, such as the size and shapes of their nests and whether or not the birds were migratory.

I retained this practice of note-taking and reflection in adulthood, and I try to instill this practice in my university classroom, where I call it "critical reading." As we conclude our exploration of some of the most fascinating women of the New Testament, let us pause and put our critical reading skills to the test. We began our journey with a brief exploration of the New Testament as a whole. Generally speaking, we can say that the New Testament is a collection of sacred writings that is central to Christian religious thought and faith. In order to read, understand, and fully appreciate the New Testament, however, we must be mindful of the historical time frame and geographical compass that serve as the backdrop for these ancient texts. Accordingly, we traveled back in time to the world of the ancient Near East. Our focus, of course, was on women: the way in which they lived, worked, cared for their families, and worshipped their God. The pioneering efforts of archaeologists, biblical scholars, and historians have helped us to imagine, at least to some degree, what life was like for the average woman living in Roman-occupied Judea during the first few centuries of the Common Era, the period of time when Jesus walked the earth and the first rumblings of a new religion, Christianity, could be heard in the far reaches of the empire.

Patriarchy was the norm, and women were considered to be inferior to men in most areas of life. Strict social and religious rules, all instituted by men, governed much of women's behavior. From this tightly regulated, corseted society in which women have little or no power to determine their own destiny, a paradox arises. If women are viewed as second-class citizens who lack political, religious, and individual freedom, we might logically expect an absence of women's stories in the New Testament, but this is not the case. As this book attests, the stories about women abound, in both the Hebrew Bible and New Testament, leading us to question why it is that a society so steeped in patriarchy bothers to include stories about women at all. This question has captivated scholars for decades, resulting in a cavalcade of articles, papers, and tomes that attempt to wrestle this paradox into a plausible theory. Among the most popular theories is the notion that the stories about women are, in a sense, metaphorical; that is, women, who are viewed as weak and marginalized individuals, represent the underdog status of ancient Israel. At first glance, Israel appears to be a tiny strip of land nestled along the eastern shores of the Mediterranean; a closer look, however, reveals the fact that we are talking about some prime real estate. In antiquity, Israel is part of a larger trade route that is much coveted by the various nations that rise to power on the world stage. Consequently, Israel endures centuries of foreign occupation—from the Assyrians to the Babylonians, Persians, Greeks, and, during New Testament times, the Romans—who threaten to erode Jewish life and culture. And while some erosion does occur, by and large, Israel manages to survive them all.

The same can be said of women. One would think that the inflexible world of patriarchy should naturally lead to the oppression of women, but time and time again, we find women who circumvent the system, emerging as leaders (Mary Magdalene, chapter 5), powerful missionaries (Prisca, chapter 11), and philanthropists (Tabitha, chapter 6). Some even behave as ruthlessly as their male counterparts (Herodias, chapter 9). In the same way, ancient Israel is resourceful and resilient, often outwitting the designs of the power-hungry foreign oppressors.

This theory—that the stories about women are metaphorical representations of Israel as a nation—is an impressive one, but I think something else might account for the variety of stories about women in the New Testament. We need only look to the ministry of Jesus for the answer. Jesus values women, not only as persons equal in the eyes of God, but also as comrades, friends, and helpers. Jesus' practice of inclusivity represents a radical change from the status quo, a fact that is often lost on modern audiences who often impose contemporary notions of equality of the sexes on the Gospels. In my college classroom, it takes weeks before my students are able to momentarily divest themselves of their modern social consciousness so that they may read the New Testament objectively. This is not an easy task, but when they are able to do this, there is a dawning sense of just how unconventional the Jesus Movement really was. Many students report that for the first time, they see Jesus' life and ministry not only as an invitation to the reader to envision a new and different relationship with God, but as a radical social movement, unrivaled in their short lifetimes.

Jesus' egalitarian treatment of women becomes an inherent feature of the early Christian movement initiated by Paul. Women become the backbone of the followers of the Way, leading church services in their homes and working alongside men to evangelize the masses. Jesus and Paul's progressive treatment of women is a critical factor to keep in mind as we weave together the various strands of life lessons passed on to us through each woman's individual story.

The two parts of this book (part I, "Sisters, Sinners, and Supporters"; and part II, "Mothers, Murderers, and Missionaries") helped to loosely categorize the type of woman in each story. These, of course, are not the only categories of women in the New Testament. For example, in the story of Herodias (chapter 9), we also meet her daughter, Salome, who appears to collude with her mother in a plan that results in the beheading of John the Baptist. And the tale of the woman with the twelve-year hemorrhage (chapter 4) is part of a diptych featuring the dying daughter of Jairus. Salome and Jairus's unnamed daughter could be thus classified under a new category, Daughters. Additionally, a particular woman may fit under more than just one category. Using my categories in part II, Herodias fits under two categories: Mothers and Murderers.

The categories of women and their stories help us to recognize the fact that in the New Testament, there are certain "type tales" that feature women. This is also the case in the Hebrew Bible, where we find categories of women as victims, virgins, prophetesses, and much more. One of the most popular categories in the Hebrew Bible is that of "woman as trickster." The trickster character is both admired and respected in the ancient world for her (or his, as men can be tricksters too!) skillful use of manipulation to bring about God's plan. Modern readers often bristle at the idea of manipulation of any kind, but in the Bible, tricksters can use just about any means on God's behalf. Perhaps the most popular female trickster in the Hebrew Bible is the matriarch Rebekah. During her tumultuous pregnancy with twin sons, Rebekah receives a stunning birth oracle from God designating Jacob, the *second-born* twin, as the one who will follow his father Isaac in the line of powerful patriarchs that begins with Abraham.

"Two nations are in your womb,
and two peoples born of you
shall be divided;
the one shall be stronger than the
other;
the elder shall serve the
younger." (Gen 25:23)

For Rebekah, the fulfillment of this Divine oracle will become the driving force behind her future actions. We can almost hear her life's mantra: "Jacob must prevail. Jacob must prevail. Jacob must prevail!" Not surprisingly, when she learns of Isaac's plan to pass the torch of leadership to her firstborn son, Esau, Rebekah swings into action and arranges one of the Bible's most popular hoodwinking stories. While Esau is off hunting, Rebekah disguises Jacob in a makeshift Esau costume and presents him to the blind and dying Isaac for a final blessing meant for Esau (Gen 27:28–29). Jacob is blessed, and Rebekah succeeds in subverting the primacy of her firstborn son in order to fulfill the command of the oracle. Unlike the Hebrew Bible, however, there are few female tricksters in the New Testament. In the Gospels and Acts, most women are presented in a straightforward narrative style; in the various epistles, written by Paul and others, women are most often mentioned in the context of a greeting, or, to use a more modern term, a "shout-out."

When we're thinking about the way women are presented in the Gospels, a wheel analogy is quite helpful. Most women can be imagined as the spokes in a wheel, connected in one way or another to the hub, Jesus. Not surprisingly, there are very few "stand-alone" stories about women in the New Testament. In the Gospels, women are nearly always mentioned in the context of their association with Jesus; beyond the Gospels, they appear in stories that feature powerful men, most often Peter or Paul. Let us briefly review these connections insofar as this book is concerned.

Recall that some women are members of Jesus' family, including his mother, Mary (chapter 8); her kinswoman, Elizabeth, who is perhaps Mary's cousin (chapter 7); Jesus' unnamed aunt who appears at the foot of the cross in John's Gospel (John 19:25–27) and is mentioned briefly in chapter 8; and the group that includes at least two women, probably Jesus' stepsiblings (chapter 8), who accompany Mary to retrieve Jesus from a potentially dangerous situation (Mark 3:21). Other women are part of Jesus' inner circle of friends, disciples, and supporters, including Martha and Mary of Bethany (chapter 1) and Mary Magdalene (chapter 5). I find it interesting that many people imagine Jesus as a somewhat solitary figure, ringed at a respectable distance by the Twelve Apostles. But a more careful reading of the Gospels reveals a constellation of friends and family who love and care about Jesus. This latter image of Jesus surrounded by friends and loved ones represents a more authentic portrait of the cultural and social norms of first-century Judea. The emphasis on family and friends is still very much part of Middle Eastern culture today.

Some of the females associated with Jesus are the recipients of miracles, such as the woman with the twelve-year hemorrhage (chapter 4). Though she has been considered ritually unclean and rendered a social pariah for over a decade, her deep faith wins out over her fear of being recognized and punished for being ritually unclean in a heaving crowd where she might contaminate others. In one of the most moving moments in the Gospels, the bleeding woman is healed when she touches Jesus' garment. Other miracle stories include the resurrection of the dead daughter of Jairus (chapter 4) and the healing of Mary Magdalene, whom Jesus cures of an apparent seizure disorder (chapter 5).

There are also stories that feature women who are connected to Jesus' role as teacher. In one of the stories associated with Martha and her sister Mary (chapter 1), we find Mary assuming the sitting position of a student while Martha rushes around the house, consumed with chores. Jesus affirms the choice of his friend and student, Mary, and chides her sister: "Martha, Martha, you are worried and distracted by many things; there is need of only one thing. Mary has chosen the better part, which will not be taken away from her" (Luke 10:41–42). The woman caught in the act of committing adultery (chapter 3) offers us a concrete lesson in the dangers of judging others, while Jesus' conversation with the woman at the well (chapter 12) is a meditation of sorts on the spiritual life.

So far, all of the spokes in the wheel reflect a positive connection to Jesus, but not all of the women in Jesus' life are positive. Herodias (chapter 9) arranges the murder of John the Baptist, and according to Matthew's Gospel, when Jesus learns of John's death, he withdraws and grieves alone (Matt 14:13). Matthew's presentation of John's murder also foreshadows Jesus' own execution. While Herodias's actions have a somewhat indirect effect on Jesus, this is not the case with the unnamed wife of Pontius Pilate (chapter 10). In my opinion, Pilate's wife is a villainess who urges her husband to dispatch without delay the danger-ous preacher from the Galilee. Jesus' teaching about the coming of the Kingdom is antithetical to everything Pilate's wife holds dear, for there is no place for corrupt rulers, Roman imperialism, greed, and untethered power in the Kingdom of God.

Thus far, all of the women discussed appear in the Gospels during Jesus' lifetime. Two women, Tabitha (chapter 6) and Prisca (chapter 11), however, offer us a window into the world of the earliest Christians. The final resurrection story mentioned in this book (the first involves Jesus' resuscitation of Lazarus in chapter 1; the second is the resurrection of Jairus's daughter in chapter 4) involves the Apostle Peter. A respected and much-loved benefactor, Tabitha is the only woman in the New Testament with the designation *disciple* (Acts 9:36). Her sudden death sends a tidal wave of grief through her small community. Tabitha's ministry as a fol-lower of the Way appears to center on the welfare of local widows, often an impoverished group in antiquity. Peter continues the work of Jesus as he restores Tabitha to life and returns her to her charitable work. Prisca, also known as "Priscilla" in Acts of the Apostles, is part of a missionary pair, and together with her husband Aquila, she travels around the Roman Empire, proclaiming the Good News of Jesus Christ and netting converts. Prisca is a close friend and associate of the Apostle Paul; she is also a busi-nesswoman, teacher, and leader of several house churches.

Two other women in Acts are also connected to Paul: the sisters Ber-nice and Drusilla (chapter 2). For reasons that are not entirely clear, Luke mentions that Bernice and Drusilla are present during Paul's imprisonment and trial at Caesarea. The sisters seem to agree that Paul is innocent, and Luke presents them as royal women who approve of the new "Christian" religion. Both sisters also have a somewhat shady past, at least according to the historian Josephus, but Luke does not mention this. Bernice and Drusilla turn our attention to the title of this book, *Good Girls, Bad Girls of the New Testament,* as we ask, What makes a good girl good and a bad girl bad? Bernice and Drusilla are in the shadow-lands of a definitive answer to this central question. Their behavior in Acts is somewhat laudable; but outside the pages of the Bible, their reputations are to a degree sullied by questionable marriages and, in the case of Bernice, rumors of incest with her brother and an illicit love affair with a soon-to-be Roman emperor, Titus.

The answer to the basic question regarding the designation of good girl versus bad girl in the New Testament can be summed up quite simply: It depends on your point of view and on who is telling the story. This is clearly the case with Bernice and Drusilla, where the stark contrast between Luke's version and Josephus's version is obvious, but what about the other women presented in this book?

Let us first examine the good girls. The sisters Martha and Mary (chapter 1) are quintessential good girls by almost any standard. As Jesus' beloved friends and disciples, they are part of Jesus' inner circle, the core group of individuals I mention frequently in this volume. This is the group of roughly twenty to thirty men and women that consists of the Twelve Apostles, a small but powerful cluster of women, certain members of Jesus' family, and others who join the group after Jesus heals them, either physically or spiritually. This inner circle is crucial to the success of Jesus' mission on a variety of levels. Practically speaking, the group travels and works alongside Jesus, teaching, healing, and spreading the Good News of the Kingdom of God. On a deeper level, Jesus' inner circle is a wellspring of friendship and goodwill. They support and encourage one another; they pray together and stand shoulder to shoulder against Jesus' foes. I suggest that in the future, when you read the Gospels, notice who is with Jesus in any given story. We often neglect these small details, but if you shift your focus ever so slightly, this inner circle will begin to emerge and you will gain a fuller understanding of Jesus and those near and dear to him. This core group serves as a model for generations of later Christians.

Jesus' mother, Mary (chapter 8), is also part of his inner circle, and she too is an undisputed "good girl." A woman of great courage and *chutzpah*, she shares her son's belief in the coming of the Kingdom and continues his work after his death. Mary Magdalene (chapter 5) is another member of the close-knit group, and though history erroneously tarnishes her image, for centuries portraying her as a rehabilitated prostitute, we now know that this image is a false one. In the Gospels, Mary is not considered a sinner of any kind; her bad reputation does not occur until centuries later when Pope Gregory the Great delivers a public sermon confusing her with two other completely unrelated biblical figures: Mary the sister of Martha, and an unnamed female sinner from Luke's Gospel (7:37–50).

Though not part of Jesus' entourage, the woman with the twelve-year issue of blood (chapter 4) is deemed a sinner not by confused popes or later commentators but by the religious purity laws of the first century. Her deep faith is inspiring and admirable, particularly in light of her prolonged suffering. In the same way, the elderly and barren Elizabeth (chapter 7) is also considered a sinner from whom God withholds the gift of a child. When she becomes pregnant with John the Baptist, she is redeemed from her suffering. Today, we would not view either woman as sinful, and both would top the list of good girls.

The Samaritan woman (chapter 12), with her checkered sexual history, is another example of someone who is thought of as a sinner during biblical antiquity. Following a highly theological conversation with Jesus, she experiences a conversion of sorts and shares the Good News with the locals. She is presented as a positive character, despite the fact that she has had five husbands and is currently living with a man to whom she is not married. Though Jesus comments on this, he does not chastise her. This is not the first time, however, that Jesus encounters a woman who has committed adultery. The woman in John 8 (chapter 3) who is caught in the very act of extramarital relations is brought to Jesus for judgment. Jesus does not condemn her either, but he does advise her to not commit further sins (John 8:11). Should we include these two women on our list of undisputed good girls? Here, the cases are not as clear-cut. We can point to the fact that Jesus refrains from judging either woman, and for most of us, that is enough to place them in the category of good girls rather than bad girls, but once again, it is all a matter of perspective.

There are two women associated with the post-Easter community who are, without question, good girls: the loving benefactor Tabitha (chapter 6); and the relentless missionary Prisca (chapter 11). Each works in different ways to live and share the Gospel message. Moreover, Tabitha's work with the poor widows of Joppa and Prisca's evangelizing efforts demonstrate women's varied roles in the early Church.

As already mentioned, Herodias (chapter 9) and Pilate's wife (chapter 10) are on the naughty list. It is important to note that the bad-girl stories are included in the Bible because they are instructive, teaching us how *not* to behave. They are, in a sense, cautionary tales. Of course, I have often argued that perhaps the question regarding who is bad and who is good is really the wrong question to ask. The differences in time, culture, and societal shifts in perspectives, especially regarding the status of women, make this question a difficult one. Perhaps a better question is What am I supposed to learn from this story? To that end, I have included Enduring Lessons after each woman's story and have urged you, the faithful reader, to ponder your own enduring lessons, as each story can evoke different reactions in different people.

Finally, in the introduction, I discussed the notion of reading the New Testament along with this book. It is my sincere hope that this book inspires you to pick up the Bible and read it critically—both the Hebrew Bible and New Testament—not only to increase your knowledge, but also to nourish your spirit.

Resources

Achtemeir, Paul J. *HarperCollins Bible Dictionary*. San Francisco: HarperSanFrancisco, 1996.

Albright, William Foxwell. *Archaeology and the Religion of Israel*. Fifth edition. Garden City, NJ: Doubleday, 1968.

Bartman, Elizabeth. *Portraits of Livia: Imaging the Imperial Woman in Augustan Rome*. Cambridge: Cambridge University Press, 1998.

Barrett, Antony A. *Livia: First Lady of Imperial Rome*. Cambridge, MA: Yale University Press, 2002.

Barrett, C. K. *The New Testament Background: Writings from Ancient Greece and the Roman Empire That Illuminate Christian Origins*. New York: HarperSanFrancisco, 1989.

Berlin, Adele, and Marc Zvi Brettler. *The Jewish Study Bible*. New York: Oxford University Press, 2004.

de Boer, Esther. *Mary Magdalene: Beyond the Myth*. Harrisburg, PA: Trinity Press International, 1992.

Brown, Raymond E. "The Gospel According to John: XIII–XI." *Anchor Bible Series*, volume 29A. New York: Doubleday, 1970.

Brown, Raymond E., Joseph A. Fitzmyer, and Roland E. Murphy, eds. *The Jerome Biblical Commentary*. Englewood Cliffs, NJ: Prentice-Hall, 1999.

Brown, Raymond E., Karl P. Donfried, Joseph A. Fitzmyer, and John Reumann, eds. *Mary in the New Testament: A Collaborative Assessment by Protestant and Roman Catholic Scholars*. Philadelphia, PA: Fortress Press, 1978.

Carter, Warren. *Pontius Pilate: Portraits of a Roman Governor*. Edited by Barbara Green. Collegeville, MN: Liturgical Press, 2003.

Collins, Raymond F. "Divorce in the New Testament." *Good News Studies* 38. Edited by Robert J. Karris, O.F.M. Collegeville, MN: Liturgical Press, 1992.

———. *Sexual Ethics and the New Testament: Behavior and Belief*. Companions to the New Testament. New York: Crossroad Publishing, 2000.

Coogan, Michael David, ed. *The New Oxford Annotated Bible with the Apocryphal/Deuterocanonical Books*. Third edition. New York: Oxford University Press, 2001.

Corley, Kathleen E. *Women & the Historical Jesus: Feminist Myths of Christian Origins*. Santa Rosa, CA: Polebridge Press, 2002.

———. *Private Women, Public Meals: Social Conflict in the Synoptic Tradition*. Peabody, MA: Hendrickson, 1993

Deen, Edith. *All the Women of the Bible*. New York: HarperCollins, 1988.

Demers, Patricia. *Women as Interpreters of the Bible*. New York: Paulist Press, 1992.

Ehrman, Bart D. *Lost Christianities*. New York: Oxford University Press, 2003.

———. *A Brief Introduction to the New Testament*. New York: Oxford University Press, 2008.

Elliott, J. K., ed. *The Apocryphal Jesus: Legends of the Early Church*. New York: Oxford University Press, 1996.

Evans, Craig A. *Ancient Texts for New Testament Studies: A Guide to the Background Literature*. Peabody, MA: Hendrickson Publishers, 2005.

Finkelstein, Israel, and Neil Asher Silberman. *The Bible Unearthed: Archaeology's New Vision of Ancient Israel and the Origin of Its Sacred Texts*. New York: Simon & Schuster, 2002.

Freedman, David Noel, ed. *Anchor Bible Dictionary*. New York: Doubleday, 1992.

Garbini, Giovanni. *History and Ideology in Ancient Israel*. Translated by John Bowden. New York: Crossroad, 1988.

Gaventa, Beverly Roberts. *Mary: Glimpses of the Mother of Jesus*. Columbia: University of South Carolina Press, 1995.

Getty-Sullivan, Mary Ann. *Women in the New Testament*. Collegeville, MN: Liturgical Press, 2001.

Gibson, Shimon. *The Final Days of Jesus: The Archaeological Evidence*. New York: HarperOne, 2009.

Gillman, Florence Morgan. *Herodias: At Home in That Fox's Den*. Edited by Barbara Green, O.P. Collegeville, MN: Liturgical Press, 2003.

Ginzberg, Louis. *The Legends of the Jews*. Baltimore, MD: Johns Hopkins University Press, 1998.

Godolpin, F. R. B., ed. *Great Classical Myths*. New York: Random House, 1964.

Gollwitzer, Helmut. *Song of Love: A Biblical Understanding of Sex*. Philadelphia, PA: Fortress Press, 1979.

Guhl, E., and W. Knoner. *The Romans: Their Life and Customs*. Middlesex, UK: Senate, 1994.

Harrelson, Walter. *The New Interpreter's Study Bible: New Revised Standard Version with the Apocrypha*. Nashville, TN: Abingdon Press, 2003.

Harris, Stephen L. *The New Testament: A Student's Introduction*. Second edition. Mountain View, CA: Mayfield, 1995.

———. *Understanding the Bible*. Sixth edition. Boston: McGraw-Hill, 2003.

Haskins, Susan. *Mary Magdalen: Myth and Metaphor*. London: HarperCollins, 1993.

Hone, William. *The Lost Books of the Bible.* Avenel, NJ: Gramercy Books, 1979.

Ilan, Tal. *Jewish Women in Greco-Roman Palestine in Texts and Studies in Ancient Judaism.* Edited by Martin Hengel and Peter Schäfer. Volume 4. Tübingen, Germany: Mohr Siebeck, 1995.

Josephus, Flavius. *The Complete Works of Josephus.* Translated by W. Whiston. Grand Rapids, MI: Kregel, 1981.

Kaiser, Walter C. Jr., and Duane Garrett, eds. *NIV Archaeological Study Bible: An Illustrated Walk Through Biblical History and Culture.* Grand Rapids, MI: Zondervan, 2006.

Karris, Robert J., ed. *The Collegeville Bible Commentary: The New Testament.* Collegeville, MN: Liturgical Press, 1988.

Keck, Leander E. *Paul and His Letters.* Philadelphia, PA: Fortress Press, 1988.

Kee, Howard Clark. *The Beginnings of Christianity: An Introduction to the New Testament.* New York: T & T Clark International, 2005.

Keener, Craig. *Paul, Women and Wives: Marriage and Women's Ministry in the Letters of Paul.* Peabody, MA: Hendrickson, 1992.

Kokkinos, Nikos. *The Herodian Dynasty: Origins, Role in Society and Eclipse.* London: Spink & Son, 2010.

Kurz, William S. *Reading Luke–Acts: Dynamics of Biblical Narrative.* Louisville, KY: Westminster John Knox, 1993.

Kysar, Robert. *John.* Augsburg Commentary on the New Testament. Minneapolis, MN: Augsburg, 1986.

Mason, Steve. *Josephus and the New Testament.* Peabody, MA: Hendrickson, 1992.

Macurdy, Grace H. *Vassal Queens and Some Contemporary Women in the Roman Empire.* Baltimore, MD: Johns Hopkins University Press, 1937.

McHugh, John. *The Mother of Jesus in the New Testament.* New York: Doubleday, 1975.

Metzger, Bruce M., and Roland Murphy, eds. *The New Oxford Annotated Bible: with Apocryphal/Deuterocanonical Books.* New York: Oxford University Press, 1994.

Meyers, Carol, Toni Craven, and Ross S. Kraemer, eds. *Women in Scripture: A Dictionary of Named and Unnamed Women in the Hebrew Bible, the Apocryphal/ Deuteroncanonical Books, and the New Testament.* New York: Houghton Mifflin, 2000.

Newsom, Carol H. *Luke.* Louisville, KY: Westminster John Knox, 1995.

Newsom, Carol A., and Sharon H. Ringe, eds. *The Women's Bible Commentary.* Louisville, KY: Westminster John Knox, 1992.

Osiek, Carolyn, and David L. Balch. *Families in the New Testament World: Households and House Churches.* Louisville, KY: Westminster John Knox Press, 1997.

Perkins, Pheme. *Reading the New Testament: An Introduction.* Second edition. New York: Paulist Press, 1988.

———. *Ministering in the Pauline Churches.* New York: Paulist Press, 1982.

Pregeant, Russell. *Engaging the New Testament: Interdisciplinary Introduction.* Minneapolis, MN: Fortress Press, 1995.

Perowne, Stewart. *Herod the Great: His Life and Times*. New York: Dorset Press, 1991.

Puskas, Charles B. Jr. *The Letters of Paul: An Introduction*. Collegeville, MN: Liturgical Press, 1979.

Reid, Barbara E. *Women in the Gospel of Luke: Choosing the Better Part?* Collegeville, MN: Liturgical Press, 1996.

Reinhartz, Adele. *Why Ask My Name? Anonymity and Identity in Biblical Narrative*. New York: Oxford University Press, 1998.

Ricci, Carla. *Mary Magdalene and Many Others: Women Who Followed Jesus*. Translated by Paul Burns. Minneapolis, MN: Fortress Press, 1994.

Robinson, James M. *The Nag Hammadi Library: The Definitive Translation of the Gnostic Scriptures Complete in One Volume*. New York: HarperCollins, 1990.

de Satagé, John. *Mary and the Christian Gospel*. London: SPCK, 1976.

Schaberg, Jane. *The Resurrection of Mary Magdalene: Legends, Apocrypha, and the Christian Testament*. New York: Continuum, 2002.

Seim, Turid Karlsen. *The Double Message: Patterns of Gender in Luke–Acts*. Nashville, TN: Abingdon Press, 1994.

Senior, Donald, ed. *The Catholic Study Bible*. New York: Oxford University Press, 2006.

Smelik, Klaas A. D. *Writings from Ancient Israel: A Handbook of Historical and Religious Documents*. Louisville, KY: Westminster John Knox, 1991.

Soards, Marion L. *The Apostle Paul: An Introduction to His Writings and Teaching*. New York: Paulist Press, 1987.

Stambaugh, John E., and David L. Balch. *The New Testament in Its Social Environment*. From *Library of Early Christianity*, edited by Wayne A. Meeks. Philadelphia, PA: Westminster John Knox Press, 1986.

Strong, James. *New Strong's Expanded Exhaustive Concordance of the Bible*. Nashville, TN: Thomas Nelson, 2010.

Thurston, Bonnie. *Women in the New Testament: Questions and Commentary*. New York: Crossroad Publishing Company, 1998.

Vardaman, Jerry. "A New Inscription Which Mentions Pilate as 'Prefect.'" *Journal of Biblical Literature* 81 (1962): 70–71.

de Voragine, Jacobus. *The Golden Legend: Readings on Lives of the Saints*. Translated by William Granger Ryan. Princeton, NJ: Princeton University Press, 2012.

Wilson, A. N. *Paul: The Mind of the Apostle*. New York: W. W. Norton, 1997.

Wray, T. J. *Good Girls, Bad Girls: The Enduring Lessons of Twelve Women of the Old Testament*. Lanham, MD: Rowman & Littlefield, 2008.

———. *What the Bible Really Tells Us: The Essential Guide to Biblical Literacy*. Lanham, MD: Rowman & Littlefield, 2011.

Wray, T. J., and Gregory Mobley. *The Birth of Satan: Tracing the Devil's Biblical Roots*. New York: Palgrave Macmillan, 2005.

Wright, N. T. *Romans and the Theology of Paul*. Pauline Theology. Volume 3. Minneapolis, MN: Fortress Press, 1995.

Wroe, Ann. *Pontius Pilate*. New York: Random House, 2003.

Electronic Resources

Bible History online (maps): www.bible-history.com/maps/.
Eusebius, *Historia Ecclesiae* 2:7. www.ccel.org/ccel/schaff/npnf201.toc.html.
Hurley, Donna. "Livia (Wife of Augustus)." De Imperatoribus Romanis: An Online Encyclopedia of Roman Emperors. www.luc.edu/roman-emperors/livia.htm.
Ilan, Tal. "Berenice." Jewish Women: A Comprehensive Historical Encyclopedia. Jewish Women's Archive. http://jwa.org/encyclopedia/article/berenice.
Juvenal. *Satire 6*. Translated by G. G. Ramsay. "The Ways of Women." www.tertullian.org/fathers/juvenal_satires_06.htm#20.
Kirby, Peter. "Suetonius." Early Christian Writings. www.earlychristianwritings.com/suetonius.html.
Kirby, Peter. "Historical Jesus Theories." Early Christian Writings. www.earlychristianwritings.com/text/1clement-hoole.html.
Macrobii, *Saturnalia* 2. http://penelope.uchicago.edu/Thayer/L/Roman/Texts/Macrobius/Saturnalia/2*.html.

Index

Abraham, 113, 18–19, 197, 212
adulterous woman: accusers, tables turned on, 3, 57; in Gospel of John, 51, 52–53, 55–58, 59, 61; Jesus, not condemning, 51, 58–59, 60–61, 62, 216; lesson of judging others, 59–61, 213–14; as unnamed, 3
Aeneas, 67, 99
Ahab, 155–56
anointing stories, 20, 24–25
Antiquities of the Jews (Josephus): Bernice and Drusilla, 32, 35, 37, 38–39, 40; Herodias, 148; Pontius Pilate, 163, 174; Roman censorship, 5
anti-Semitism, 171, 199
apocalyptic thought, 83–84, 138, 169, 201
apocryphal writings, 26, 154, 175
Apollos, 179, 185–86, 191
apostles of John the Baptist, 152
Aquila: Apollos, instructing, 179, 191; expulsion from Jerusalem, 183; house churches, establishing, 184, 185, 187, 188, 189, 192, 214; missionary work, 4, 12, 182, 184–88, 190, 192–93

Aretas, 147
Arimathea, Joseph of, 83, 84, 85–86, 87
Aristobulus, 34, 145
Augustus, 34, 128, 164, 170
Azizus of Emesa, 37, 38

Barabbas, 172
barrenness: barren woman motif, 113; of Elizabeth, 9, 112, 115, 116, 122, 157, 216; of Sarah, 9, 118–19
Bernice: Agrippa II, sister of, 33, 34, 35–36; Drusilla, jealously toward, 38, 41, 44, 47–48, 214; Herodias, niece of, 4, 34; history as unkind, 3; incest rumors, 35–36, 37, 41, 44, 45, 215; nazirite vow, 36, 114; Paul and, 31, 32, 36, 41, 44, 46, 48
Bethany: as a base of operations, 18, 23–24, 167, 168; Lazarus, house located in, 23, 28, 98; Martha and Mary, hometown of, 3, 18, 21, 23, 29, 167; Simon the leper and, 18–19, 24
biblical literacy, 43, 45, 70, 78–79, 91–92, 204, 206
Brown, Dan, 2, 78, 90

Caiaphas, 83, 169, 170, 177, 178
circumcision, 35, 37, 39, 117, 128,
181, 191
Claudia Procula, St. *See* Pilate's wife
Claudius, 179, 183
conversion: Apollos as convert, 185–
86, 191; circumcision and, 35, 37,
39, 181, 191; Corinthian converts,
184; of Gentiles, 102; of Jews to
the Way, 183; mass conversion of
Sychar, 202; Paul and missionary
work, 96, 180, 184, 185, 191; of
Paul to Jesus Movement, 42, 96,
181, 190; of Pontius Pilate and
his wife, 175; Prisca and Aquila as
missionaries, 192, 193, 214; Roman
infrastructure aiding in conversion
efforts, 189; of Samaritan woman,
216
critical reading, 209

daughter of Jairus: Jesus, raising from
the dead, 67, 69, 97, 100, 213,
214; pairing story, as part of, 5, 67;
Tabitha, similarities with, 100; as
unnamed, 2, 211
The Da Vinci Code (Brown), 2, 78
demonic possession, 72–73, 79, 81
dikaios, 173, 178
divorce, 11, 38, 48, 55, 147, 148–49,
153
dreams: of Joseph, 32, 129, 130, 131,
173; of Pilate's wife, 161, 165, 172,
173, 174, 176–77, 178
Drusilla: Bernice as jealous of, 38, 41,
44, 47–48, 214; Felix and, 31, 37–
39, 40–41, 44, 46; Herodias, niece
of, 4, 34; Josephus, in writings of,
32, 34, 37–38, 40, 43, 215

egalitarian utopia, 12
Ein Karem, 127–28
Elephantine documents, 148
Elijah, 97, 99, 114–15, 147, 148, 155
Elisha, 94, 97, 99, 100, 114
Elizabeth: barrenness, 9, 112, 115,
116, 122, 157, 216; as faithful, 3,

119–20; John the Baptist, mother
of, 3–4, 9, 112, 115, 117–18, 122,
157, 216; Mary of Nazareth and,
111, 112, 116–17, 127–28, 129,
131, 137, 140, 213; Zechariah and,
111, 113–14, 118, 127
emperor worship, 10–11, 170–71, 176
Esau, 212
Eusebius, 174
Eutychus, resurrection of, 98

Felix, Antonius, 31, 37–39, 40–41, 44,
46
Festus, Porcius, 31, 41
Florus, Gessius, 36, 44, 48
forgiveness, 24, 27–28, 59, 61–62,
158

Gabriel: annunciation of Jesus, 99,
116, 127, 137; Mary of Nazareth,
questioning of, 127, 129, 131;
Zechariah, appearing to, 99,
113–14, 115–16, 117, 127
Gaius, 153
Gentiles: circumcision waived for, 39,
181, 191; inclusion of, 99, 102;
Paul, converting, 96; preaching to,
4, 91, 187
Gerizim, Mt., 199, 200, 206
Gnostic texts, 89–90
The Golden Legend (de Voragine), 91
Good Samaritan parable, 27, 204–5
Gospel of Philip, 89–90
gossip, 34, 42, 43–44, 47, 158, 198
Gregory I, Pope, 45–46, 79–80, 92–93,
215
grief: complicated grief, 121;
crucifixion causing, 103; John the
Baptist, grieving for death of, 157;
Kingdom of God, lack of grief in,
138; Martha and Mary, grieving for
brother, 22, 28; Mary Magdalene
and, 86, 88, 107; of Pilate and his
wife, 175; Tabitha, mourning for,
100, 103–4, 214
grudges, 143, 149–50, 153, 155,
157–58, 159

Hagar, 118–19, 120
Hannah, hymn of, 118, 128, 137
Heaven, 18, 83, 96, 105, 115
hemorrhaging woman. *See* woman
   with twelve-year hemorrhage
Herod Agrippa I, 32, 33, 34, 35, 37,
   38, 48, 153
Herod Agrippa II, 31, 33, 34, 35–36,
   41, 44
Herod Antipas: building project, 81;
   Herodias, relationship with, 4, 12,
   143, 146–47, 148, 149, 152, 153;
   Herod the Great, son of, 11, 146;
   John the Baptist, ordering execution
   of, 32, 143, 149, 151, 152, 155;
   Salome, dancing before, 143, 150
Herod Archelaus, 11, 32, 38
Herodians, 11
Herodias: as a bad girl, 216; Bernice
   and Drusilla, aunt of, 4, 34; female
   killers, compared to, 154–56;
   Herod Antipas, relationship with,
   4, 143, 146–47, 148, 149, 152,
   153; Herodian dynasty, as part of,
   145–46, 158, 159; John the Baptist
   and, 12, 143–44, 148, 149, 150–51,
   153, 155, 156, 158, 211; Salome,
   mother of, 5, 143, 146, 150–52,
   157, 211
Herod II, 145–46, 147
Herod of Chalcis, 34, 35
Herod the Great: division of territories
   upon death, 11, 146; Herodian
   dynasty ancestor, 3, 11, 47, 114;
   Herodium, possible burial in, 33,
   145; infant Jesus, attempting to kill,
   32, 130–31, 140, 145, 173; King of
   the Jews, title given to, 172; murder
   of family members, 11, 34
Holofernes, 154
house churches: of Prisca, 184, 185,
   187, 188, 189, 192, 214; as typical
   in early Christianity, 101; women
   as leaders of, 3, 12, 96, 189, 211

Infancy Gospel of James, 125, 131–34
Isaac, 118, 119, 197, 212

Ishmael, 119
Isis, 10, 176

Jacob, 195, 197, 212
Jael, 154–55, 156
Jairus, 5, 67, 69. *See also* daughter of
   Jairus
James, 80, 81, 82, 133, 134, 139, 181
Jeremiah, 56, 113
Jesus Christ: adulterous woman
   and, 51, 52–59, 59–62, 216;
   annunciation, 99, 115–16, 127,
   137, 139–40; crucifixion, 85, 86,
   87, 103, 126, 134, 135, 137, 140;
   daughter of Jairus, raising from the
   dead, 67, 69, 97, 100, 213, 214;
   demons, exorcising, 79; economic
   status, 81, 86, 131; Elizabeth,
   recognizing Jesus as Lord, 111,
   116, 118; female followers, 81, 82–
   83, 86, 135, 211, 213, 215; Good
   Samaritan parable, 27, 204–5; on
   grudge-holding, 157–58; Herod
   Antipas and, 32, 146–47, 147–48,
   152–53; in infancy narratives,
   112, 128–29, 130–31; Jerusalem,
   traveling to, 165–68; John the
   Baptist and, 116, 147–48, 150, 157,
   214; Kingdom of God as focus, 81,
   84, 138, 166, 169, 206–7; Lazarus
   and, 18, 21–24, 26, 94, 98, 135,
   167, 214; marriage speculations,
   1–2, 78, 88–90; Martha and,
   18–22, 23–24, 28–29, 94, 213; in
   miracle stories, 106; Pilate's wife,
   dream of Jesus, 161, 165, 172,
   173, 174, 176–77, 178; Pontius
   Pilate and, 46, 147, 150, 152–53,
   170, 171–72, 174; resurrection,
   77, 84–88, 107; Samaritan woman
   at well, 195–96, 197–203, 204,
   206, 207, 216; Saul, appearing
   to, 181; suffering, transforming
   understanding of, 71–72; Temple,
   left behind in, 126, 132–33, 166;
   wife of Pilate, dreaming of, 161,
   165, 172, 173, 174, 176–77, 178;

woman with hemorrhage and, 3, 63, 67–69, 73, 74. *See also* Mary Magdalene; Mary of Bethany
Jesus Movement: Apollos as follower, 185; Corinthian converts, 184; Gentile members, 96, 102, 181; Kingdom of God as central to, 83; Mary Magdalene, role in, 12, 91; as a middle-class movement, 86; missionaries, 190; select members, 25; as unconventional, 211; as the Way, 96, 180
Jesus Wife fragment, 1–2, 90
Jewish marriage customs, 129–30
Jezebel, 154, 155–56
Joachim, 125, 132
Job, 21, 71
John: adulterous woman, 3, 51, 52–53, 55–59, 59–61, 216; Bethany, importance of, 18; Jerusalem, Jesus in, 166; Lazarus, 21–24, 26, 28–29, 98; Mary Magdalene, Jesus appearing to, 3, 77, 87–88, 107; Mary of Bethany, wiping of Jesus' feet with hair, 20; Mary of Nazareth at foot of the cross, 126, 135, 136, 139; Passion Narrative, 57, 167; Samaritan woman at well, 4, 195–96, 198, 199–202, 204, 207; Synoptic Gospels, Gospel of John differing from, 8; wealthy background, 81, 82
John the Baptist: beheading, 144, 147, 150–52, 155, 157, 211; Elizabeth, son of, 3–4, 9, 112, 115, 117–18, 122, 157, 216; Gabriel, announcing birth, 99, 127; Herodias as enemy, 4, 5, 12, 34, 143, 145, 151–52, 153, 159, 214; imprisonment, 32; marriage of Herodias, denouncing, 147, 148, 149, 152, 153, 156, 158; as a nazirite, 36, 114. *See also* Salome
Joseph: angelic dream encounters, 32, 129, 130, 131, 173; Jesus left at Temple, 132, 166; Mary of Nazareth and, 125, 126, 128,

129–30, 140; occupation, 81; as a widower, 134
Josephus, Titus Flavius: *Antiquities of the Jews*, 5, 32, 35, 37, 38–39, 40, 148; Bernice, 32, 34, 35, 36, 44, 47–48, 214, 215; Drusilla, 34, 37–38, 40, 214, 215; Herodias, 146, 147, 148–49, 152, 153, 159; Magdala, describing, 80; Miriamne, 145; Pontius Pilate, 163–64, 165, 170, 174; rumors, perpetrating, 43; Salome, dance of, 150; *Wars of the Jews*, 5, 32, 40
Judaizers, 39–40, 191
Judas Iscariot, 24, 93–94, 167, 169
judgment: anger, judgment for experiencing, 157; at end of days, 31, 40, 41, 43; eternal judgment, 105; examination of conscience before judging, 61; Jesus, refraining from, 52, 59–60, 62, 200, 216; lack of, between Mary, Martha and Jesus, 26; Pilate's wife, not judging faith of others, 176; rumors and hearsay, based on, 48–49
Judith, 154, 155, 156
Juvenal, 35, 36, 44

King, Karen, 1, 90
Kingdom of God: in apocalyptic thought, 83–84, 138, 169; as imminent, 41, 85, 201; Jesus focusing on, 81, 84, 138, 166, 169, 206–7; Mary of Nazareth as Kingdom person, 139, 140, 141, 215; Pilate's wife, fearing, 178, 214

Lazarus: death of, 21, 28, 29, 105; as friend of Jesus, 18, 25, 26, 135, 167; raised from dead, 18, 23–24, 94, 98, 214; tomb of, 22–23
Leviticus on purity laws, 65–66
Livia, 164, 172
Luke: Acts of the Apostles, as author, 7, 32, 96, 97; adulterous woman, 52, 55; anger over teachings of Jesus, 135; Bernice and Drusilla,

33, 40–42, 45–46, 48, 214, 215;
Good Samaritan parable, 18, 27–28,
204–5; Herod Antipas, 146–47,
148, 152–53; infancy narrative,
111, 112–18, 126–29, 130, 131,
137; Jerusalem, Jesus' visits to, 166;
Jesus left at Temple, 132; Joseph of
Arimathea, collecting body of Jesus,
85–86; Martha and Mary, 17, 18–
24, 25, 26–28, 53; Mary Magdalene,
80–81; Mary of Nazareth and
annunciation, 139–40; ministry of
Jesus, financing, 81, 82–83; nameless
sinner, 24–25, 45, 79, 215; pairing
stories, 67; Peter, healing of lame
man, 106; Pontius Pilate, 46, 164;
Priscilla, 182; siblings of Jesus,
possible, 133; Tabitha, 96, 98–99,
101, 102; widow of Nain, Jesus
raising son from dead, 98; woman
with hemorrhage, 64

magi, 112, 130, 173
Magnificat, 117, 118, 123–24, 128,
137–38, 139
Marcus, Julius Alexander, 34–35
Mark: anointing story, 24; crucifixion
of Jesus and aftermath, 82–83,
84–86; daughter of Jairus, Jesus
raising from the dead, 97; Gospel
as apocalyptic, 84; Herodias, 146,
147–48, 149–51, 152, 156, 159;
Jerusalem, Jesus in, 166, 167,
168; Jesus as son of Mary, 133;
as oldest Gospel, 7; siblings of
Jesus, possible, 134; woman with
hemorrhage, 63, 64, 67–69
Martha: Bethany as hometown, 3, 18,
23, 29, 167; as a good girl, 42, 215;
as hostess, 24, 26–27, 213; Jesus
and, 21, 28–29, 94, 213; Mary of
Bethany, request for help from,
17, 19–20, 25–26; tomb opening,
objection to, 22, 23, 29
Mary Magdalene: angelic encounter at
tomb, 84, 86, 87–88; at crucifixion,
3, 85, 86, 87, 135; friendship

with Jesus, 88, 91, 93–94, 213;
in Gnostic texts, 89–90; healing
through Jesus, 79, 81, 213; as a
leader, 211; Magdala as hometown,
80, 82, 125; marriage to Jesus,
speculations, 1–2, 78, 88–90;
ministry of Jesus, financing, 3,
12, 81, 82–83; Pope Gregory I,
confusing with sinner, 45–46,
79–80, 92–93, 215; prostitution,
associated with, 45, 79, 91, 92,
93, 94, 215; resurrected Jesus,
encountering, 3, 77, 85, 87, 88, 107
Mary of Bethany: Bethany as
hometown, 3, 18, 23, 29, 167;
confrontation with Jesus, 22, 28;
as friend of Jesus, 94, 213; as a
good girl, 42, 215; hair, wiping feet
of Jesus with, 20, 24; mourning
of Lazarus, 21; Pope Gregory I,
conflating, 45, 79, 215; as student
of Jesus, 17, 19–20, 26, 27, 53,
213; unnamed sinner, confused
with, 24–25
Mary of Nazareth: annunciation of
Jesus, 115–16, 127, 137, 139–40;
as courageous, 3, 125, 136, 139,
140–41; at crucifixion, 58, 126,
135–36, 140; Elizabeth and, 111,
112, 116–17, 127–28, 129, 131,
137, 140, 213; Gabriel, questioning,
127, 129, 131; in Infancy Gospel
of James, 125, 131–32; in infancy
narratives, 126–31; Joseph and,
125, 126, 128, 129–30, 140; as
Kingdom person, 139, 140, 141,
215; *Magnificat* and, 117, 118,
123–24, 128, 137–38, 139; as a
widow, 133–34, 135
Matthew: anointing story, 24; divorce,
Jesus questioned on, 55; dreams
featured in Gospel, 173; Gospel as
particularly treasured, 7; Herodias,
146, 147–48, 149–50, 151, 152,
159; infancy narrative, 32, 112,
126, 129–31, 145; Jerusalem, Jesus
traveling to, 165–68; Jesus and

the moneychangers, 169; John the Baptist, Jesus mourning for, 214; Magadan, Jesus boating to, 80; massacre of the infants, 32; Passover drama, 169–70; Pilate's wife, 161, 162, 165, 167, 172–74, 177, 178; siblings of Jesus, possible, 133, 134; speck in neighbor's eye, 60; tomb of Jesus, two Marys keeping vigil, 86–87; woman with hemorrhage, 64, 68
mikva'ot, 169
miracle stories, 69, 106, 213
Miriamne, 34, 38, 48, 145
Moses, 201, 207
Mount of Olives, 51, 137, 167, 169

Naboth, 155–56
Nag Hammadi documents, 84, 89
Nazarenes, 12, 96, 180
nazirite vow, 36, 114
Netzer, Ehud, 33
Nicodemus, 87, 175

Onesiphorus, 188

pairing stories, 5, 67, 99, 115–16
Palm Sunday, 166
Passover: in Bethany, 23; crucifixions during, 168, 171; Elijah as hoped-for presence, 115; in Jerusalem, 10, 131, 165, 166–67, 172, 176; *mikva'ot* use, 169; Sanhedrin trial, 170
Pastoral Epistles, 188
patriarchy, 11–12, 25, 46, 93, 210
Paul: Acts, image of Paul in, 97; Bernice and Drusilla, 31, 36, 40, 41, 44, 45, 46, 48, 214; conversion experience, 42, 96, 181, 190; earliest Christian writer, 6–7; Eutychus, raising from dead, 98; founder of Christianity, 11, 182, 189, 211; Gentiles, outreach to, 102; imprisonment, 31, 33, 39, 40, 41; letters, 182; missionary outreach, 96, 180, 184, 185,

191; Prisca, friendship with, 179, 186–88, 192, 193; tent-making work, 179, 184
Peter: Aeneas, healing, 99; apostolic leadership, 96; Bethsaida as hometown, 80; circumcision of converts, favoring, 181; lame beggar, healing, 106; Tabitha, raising from the dead, 3, 95, 100–101, 102, 104, 214; tomb of Jesus, inspecting, 86, 87; wealthy background, 81, 82
Pharisees: adulterous woman and, 51, 54, 55, 59; divorce, questioning, 55; Nicodemus the Pharisee, 87; Paul as a Pharisee, 96, 180; Simon the Leper as a Pharisee, 18; Simon the Pharisee, 24; tracking of Jesus, 53
Phasaelis, 147
Philo, 34, 170
Pilate's wife: as a bad girl, 175, 216; as Claudia Procula, St., 162–63, 175; dream of Jesus, 161, 165, 172, 173, 174, 176–77, 178; as follower of Jesus, 4, 175; Kingdom of God, fearing, 214; as political counselor, 164; procession of Jesus, awareness of, 168
pillared houses, 65
Polemo, 35, 44
Pontius Pilate: brutality of, 164, 170, 174, 177; Caiaphas and, 83, 169; as indecisive and weak, 172, 174; interrogation of Jesus, 152–53; in Jerusalem, 165, 168; Jesus and, 46, 147, 150, 152–53, 170, 171–72, 174; Josephus, reporting on, 163–64; as a saint, 175; Sanhedrin and, 57
Prisca: Apollos, instructing, 179, 185–86, 191; as a church leader, 20; house churches, establishing, 12, 184, 185, 187, 188, 189, 192, 214; Jerusalem, expulsion from, 183; missionary work, 4, 180, 182, 184–89, 189–193, 211, 216
Priscilla. *See* Prisca

pseudepigraphical texts, 188
pseudo menses, 66

Rebekah, 113, 197, 212
resurrection stories, 94, 97–98, 99, 100, 105, 106, 214
ritual impurity, 65–67, 68, 69, 73, 198, 213
Roman occupation of Judea, 9–11, 177, 210

Salome, daughter, 5, 143, 146, 150–52, 157, 211. *See also* Herodias
Samaritan woman at well, 4, 195–96, 197–98, 199–203, 204–8, 216
Samuel, 36, 114, 118
Sanhedrin, 57, 83, 170, 181
Sarah, 9, 113, 118–19, 119–20
Satan, 72–73, 166
Shechem. *See* Sychar
sheol, 105–6
shiva, 21
Shunammite woman, 2, 94, 98, 99, 100
siblings of Jesus, possible, 133, 134, 213
Simeon, 128–29
Simon the leper, 18–19, 24
Simon the magician, 37–38, 40
sin: of adulterous woman, 51, 52, 57–59, 61, 62; maladies, sin resulting in, 3, 72, 73, 115, 216; Mary Magdalene, false association with sin, 45, 79–80, 92, 215; nameless sinner in Gospel of Luke, 24–25, 45, 79, 215; Samaritan woman as sinner, 200
Sisera, 155
Stephen, St., 97, 181
Suetonius, 36, 42, 183
Sychar, 195, 197, 199, 202
Synoptic Gospels, 7–8, 11, 55, 64, 87, 126, 133, 135, 147, 166

Tabitha: Dorcas, alternate name, 2, 95, 98–99, 162; as a good girl, 216; pairing story, part of, 67; Peter raising from the dead, 3,

95, 100–101, 102, 104, 214; as a philanthropist, 211; *sheol*, lingering in, 105–6; widows grieving for, 99–101, 102, 103–4
The Golden Legend (de Voragine), 91
theodicy, 71
Titus, Flavius Josephus, 5, 36, 37, 44, 48, 215
trickster, woman as, 212
twelve, importance of number, 4–5, 67

uncleanliness. *See* ritual impurity

Vesuvius, eruption of, 38–39, 176
visitation stories, 18
de Voragine, Jacobus, 91

Wars of the Jews (Josephus), 5, 32, 40
the Way: Apollos, associated with, 179, 185–86, 191; Christians, followers not known as, 96, 180; converts, 38, 39, 183; Drusilla, tacit approval of movement, 46; Felix and, 40–41; house churches, importance of, 184; kindness in actions, 102, 190; marriage, attitudes towards, 193; Paul, persecution of followers, 96, 181; Prisca and Aquila as adherents, 187, 192; Tabitha, role of, 101, 214; women members, 188, 211
widow of Nain, 98, 115
widow of Zarephath, 97, 98, 99
wife of Pilate. *See* Pilate's wife
woman at well. *See* Samaritan woman at well
woman with twelve-year hemorrhage: Jesus, healed by, 3, 63, 67, 68–69, 73, 74; ritual impurity, 65, 67–68, 71, 213; suffering and, 67, 70, 71, 74–75, 216
wooing scenes, 197

Zechariah: Elizabeth, husband of, 111, 112–14, 118, 127; Gabriel appearing to, 99, 113–14, 115–16, 117, 127

About the Author

Dr. T. J. Wray is associate professor of religious studies at Salve Regina University in Newport, Rhode Island, and author of several books, including *The Birth of Satan: Tracing the Devil's Biblical Roots*; *Good Girls, Bad Girls: The Enduring Lessons of Twelve Women of the Old Testament*; and *What the Bible Really Tells Us: The Essential Guide to Biblical Literacy*. She lives in Rhode Island.